WRITING ACROSS DIFFERENCE

WRITING ACROSS DIFFERENCE

Theory and Intervention

EDITED BY
JAMES RUSHING DANIEL,
KATIE MALCOLM, AND CANDICE RAI

UTAH STATE UNIVERSITY PRESS
Logan

Published by Utah State University Press
An imprint of University Press of Colorado
245 Century Circle, Suite 202
Louisville, Colorado 80027

 The University Press of Colorado is a proud member of
the Association of University Presses.

The University Press of Colorado is a cooperative publishing enterprise supported, in part, by Adams State University, Colorado State University, Fort Lewis College, Metropolitan State University of Denver, Regis University, University of Alaska, University of Colorado, University of Northern Colorado, University of Wyoming, Utah State University, and Western Colorado University.

∞ This paper meets the requirements of the ANSI/NISO Z39.48–1992 (Permanence of Paper)

ISBN: 978-1-64642-172-5 (paperback)
ISBN: 978-1-64642-173-2 (ebook)
https://doi.org/10.7330/9781646421732

Library of Congress Cataloging-in-Publication Data

Names: Daniel, James Rushing, editor. | Malcolm, Katie, editor. | Rai, Candice,
    1976– editor.
Title: Writing across difference : theory and intervention / edited by James Rushing
    Daniel, Katie Malcolm, Candice Rai.
Description: Logan : Utah State University Press, [2021] | Includes bibliographical refer-
    ences and index.
Identifiers: LCCN 2021035797 (print) | LCCN 2021035798 (ebook) |
    ISBN 9781646421725 (paperback) | ISBN 9781646421732 (ebook)
Subjects: LCSH: English language—Rhetoric—Study and teaching (Higher)—Social
    aspects—United States. | English language—Composition and exercises—Study
    and teaching (Higher)—Social aspects—United States. | Individual differences. |
    Interdisciplinary approach in education—United States. | Discrimination in higher
    education—United States.
Classification: LCC PE1405.U6 W726 2021 (print) | LCC PE1405.U6 (ebook) | DDC
    808/.042071—dc23
LC record available at https://lccn.loc.gov/2021035797
LC ebook record available at https://lccn.loc.gov/2021035798

Cover: "Wrought, Knit, Labors, Legacies," Alexandria, Virginia, by Olalekan Jeyifous; photograph by Ron Cogswell

CONTENTS

    Rhetoric Classroom
    Shui-yin Sharon Yam   153

    **PART III: INSTITUTIONAL, COMMUNITY, AND PUBLIC
    TRANSFORMATIONS**

9. Designing across Difference: Intersectional, Interdependent
    Approaches to Sustaining Communities
    Laura Gonzales and Ann Shivers-McNair   175

10. Antiracist Translingual Praxis in Writing Ecologies
    Sumyat Thu, Katie Malcolm, Candice Rai, and Anis Bawarshi   195

11. Confronting Superdiversity Again: A Multidimensional Approach to
    Teaching and Researching Writing at a Global University
    *Jonathan Benda, Cherice Escobar Jones, Mya Poe,
    and Alison Y. L. Stephens*   218

    Index   239
    About the Authors   247

ACKNOWLEDGMENTS

We would like to begin by expressing our gratitude to the authors of this collection for their important and incisive contributions to conversations on difference, which we see as a crucial but underexplored subject in composition.

This book is itself the product of scholars working across institutional, professional, and personal differences. Our work began in 2016 as a cross-disciplinary research cluster, Writing across Difference, funded by the University of Washington's Simpson Center for the Humanities. We are grateful for this support. This collaborative project, co-led by Megan Callow and Anis Bawarshi, sought to understand how power, difference, and inequality function in communication and to develop antiracist pedagogy, cross-campus collaboration, and research aimed at transforming our learning environments and university. The cluster gathered graduate students, writing and teaching experts, and professors from various departments and centers including the departments of English, Human Centered Design & Engineering, and Genome Sciences as well as UW's Odegaard Writing & Research Center and Center for Teaching & Learning. We acknowledge and thank these core founding members, many of whom have contributed to this collection and all of whom were a part of the inception of this book, including Anis Bawarshi, Megan Callow, James Rushing Daniel, Carrie Matthews, Katie Malcolm, Candice Rai, Katherine Xue, and Mark Zachry.

Last, we wish to express solidarity with those engaged in the struggle for racial justice and with the victims of racial violence. The events of 2020 have been devastating—with the killings of George Floyd, Ahmaud Arbery, Breonna Taylor, and so many others, police violence against peaceful protestors, and the dehumanization of essential workers. With the proliferation of Black Lives Matter protests across the nation and the world, calls for defunding the police, and increased resistance to the racist rhetoric of the GOP and authoritarian leaders worldwide, there are also reasons to remain hopeful and vigilant. We hope this collection can help to further disciplinary conversations and practices to continue to advance equity and racial justice in the field.

WRITING ACROSS DIFFERENCE

INTRODUCTION
Centering Difference in Composition Studies

James Rushing Daniel, Katie Malcolm, and Candice Rai

Communicating equitably and ethically across the differences that divide and unite groups is arguably the central work of composition studies. To this core work, we might add the labor of understanding and responding to the unjust structures of racial capitalism, settler colonialism, and other frameworks that unevenly shape literacy education and the terrains of communication. From explorations of decoloniality (King, Guebele, and Anderson 2015; Ruiz and Sánchez 2016), translingualism (Bou Ayash 2019; Canagarajah 2013; Horner, NeCamp, and Donahue 2011), multimodality (Alexander and Rhodes 2014; Gonzales 2018), feminisms (Enoch and Jack 2019; Glenn 2018; Jarratt and Worsham 1998; Ratcliffe 2005; Royster and Kirsch 2012), gender and sexuality (Alexander 2008; Pritchard 2016; Waite 2017), disability (Cedillo 2018; Dolmage 2016; Kerschbaum 2014; Yergeau 2018), and race/antiracism (Cushman 2016; Inoue 2015; Richardson and Gilyard 2001; Royster 1996; Ruiz 2016; Villanueva 1993), the field has been animated by an attempt to understand how various axes of difference function to distance and distinguish, enrich and empower, and, frequently, marginalize and exclude. The field is also shaped by an activist energy aimed at transforming these axes toward more socially just classrooms and institutions. In attending to these issues, compositionists have long considered how writing practice and instruction can help negotiate division to create more equitable, inclusive, and diverse classrooms, though few in the field have engaged difference directly or acknowledged the extent to which composition relies upon and centers the concept. Instead, writing scholars have generally favored interrogating difference within the context of various subdisciplines. Scholars of translingualism, for instance, have discussed difference in their critique of monolingual frameworks and their concomitant promotion of pluralistic, nonnormative linguistic models (Bou Ayash 2019; Canagarajah 2013; Lu and Horner 2016; Malcolm 2017; Trimbur 2016). From a distinct, though

https://doi.org/10.7330/9781646421732.c000

not unrelated, perspective, composition scholars working in the areas of race and antiracism have critiqued the presumptive Whiteness[1] of the writing classroom and have sought to center the language practices, perspectives, and experiences of students of color (Baker-Bell 2020; Gilyard 1991; Kynard 2014; Martinez 2020; Perryman-Clark, Kirkland, and Jackson 2014; Smitherman 1986; Smitherman and Villanueva 2003). Both these areas of inquiry are intensely invested in difference, yet few who take up these and similar critiques have named the concept as a specific core disciplinary concern.

Redressing this lack of attention, *Writing across Difference* gathers scholars who engage with difference in the field. Difference, in our view, is indispensable for understanding how communication takes place among individuals; for focalizing meaningful separations among groups that result from social, political, institutional, or linguistic forces; and for thinking programmatically about how racism, inequality, and colonial logics might be better theorized and combatted in classrooms, institutions, and broader public life. Accordingly, we believe a deeper and more comprehensive understanding of difference can illuminate how divisions among individuals or groups emerge; how they are maintained through rhetorics, practices, and policy; how they are variously occluded or made to "matter" (Barad 2007, Pitts-Taylor 2016); and how they can be bridged and negotiated in writing programs and instruction.

We believe this work is particularly necessary today as the fractures among individuals, identities, and communities deepen. One particularly critical site of division is the global economy—recent years have seen deepening economic inequality (Milanovic 2018; Piketty 2014), the explosion of student debt and its destabilizing effects (Zaloom 2019), and declining working conditions (Hyman 2018). In the United States, far-right groups are also growing (Neiwert 2017) and hate crimes are increasing (Faupel et al., *Washington Post*, August 13, 2019). The recent killings of George Floyd, Breonna Taylor, Rayshard Brooks, and many other Black people by police demonstrate not only the depth of long-standing racial divisions and White supremacy prevalent in our society but also the horrifying lengths to which those in power will go to protect the asymmetries that benefit them. Adding to this, the devastating global shifts of the Anthropocene, including climate change, pollution, and unregulated resource exploitation, increasingly threaten not only human life in ways that deepen inequities by affecting the most disadvantaged and marginalized populations around the world (Wallace-Wells 2019) but also multispecies life, given widespread scientific data that suggest we are on the brink of global ecological collapse and mass extinction.

Despite these troubling trends and forces, the growing collective will and civic-mindedness emerging to address many of these crises of difference bring hope. In recent years, activists across the globe have marched against exclusion, inequality, antidemocratic norms, and climate change with the Women's March, climate strikes (Gambino, *Guardian*, September 7, 2019), and, most notably, the global Black Lives Matter protests of 2020 (Savage 2020). As Keeanga-Yamahtta Taylor (*New York Times*, June 8, 2020) writes of the latter, "For once in their lives, many of the participants can be seen, heard, and felt in public. People are pulled from the margins into a powerful force that can no longer be ignored, beaten, or easily discarded." For Taylor, these protests raise the crucial question of how the country must change in order to deal with its history and maintenance of division. In her view, it is not simply a matter of addressing racial difference but, crucially, of confronting the extensive, intersectional forms of inequality that afflict the nation "beyond the racism and brutality of the police." As she writes, "We must also discuss the conditions of economic inequality that, when they intersect with racial and gender discrimination, disadvantage African-Americans while also making them vulnerable to police violence." Effectively, while various forms of difference appear to be increasing, so too are coalitional and intersectional efforts to confront them. Building on a long tradition of scholarship in public and community-based activism and writing, scholars in composition studies are also notably devoting increasing attention to foregrounding socially just collective action (Alexander, Jarratt, and Welch 2018; Blair and Nickoson 2019; Grabill 2007; Lee and Kahn 2020); community-based approaches and interventions (Guerra 2016; Handley 2016; Gonzales 2018; Kells 2016); developing ethical dispositions for listening and cooperating across radical difference (Blankenship 2019; Diab 2016; Duffy 2019; Glenn and Ratcliffe 2011; Ratcliffe 2005; Stenberg 2015); and cultivating capacities for intervening in public writing and rhetorics (Ackerman and Coogan 2013; Farmer 2013; Rai 2016; Reiff and Bawarshi 2016).

We acknowledge that increased attention to issues of difference—not only with regard to how differences divide, exclude, and perpetuate inequities but also concerning how they enrich and open possibilities for new ideas, ways of being, and collaborating—is crucial for addressing deepening inequity, division, and precarity. We also recognize that difference is a troublesome construct. While it serves as a productive framework for isolating the kinds of divisions balkanizing the contemporary world, difference is always an act of judgment and an assignment of deviation that participates in the reification or institutionalization of division. As Stephanie Kerschbaum (2014) argues, naming difference holds the potential to "fix individual writers or groups of writers in time and space" (6). Because difference implies a normative center, a site from which something differs, naming an axis of difference risks normalizing privileged identity markers and endorsing subordination. We additionally acknowledge that attention to difference can also risk the co-optation of minorities to serve institutional needs. As Roderick Ferguson (2012) argues, while minority difference was once effectively banished from the academy, contemporary institutions now seek to domesticate difference, "trying to redirect originally insurgent formations and deliver them to the normative ideals and protocols of state, capital, and academy" (8). For Ferguson, difference is ultimately vulnerable to institutionalization and repurposing that would rob it of its radical capacities.

With respect to the conflicted aspects of the concept, chapters within this collection draw upon theories of intersectionality to challenge notions of difference that render various categories of discrimination, exclusion, and marginalization as discrete, static, or monolithic. Coined by legal scholar and Black feminist Kimberlé Crenshaw in her groundbreaking 1989 essay "Demarginalizing the Intersection of Race and Sex," *intersectionality* is a qualitative and analytic praxis for understanding and transforming the various ways different forms of oppression (based on categories such as race, class, gender, ability, sexuality, faith) interlock to compound the discrimination and material harm experienced by particular individuals and communities. Crenshaw critiques White feminism's erasure of Black women's experiences in its treatment of all forms of gender discrimination as homogenous; she contends that one cannot understand the discrimination Black women face through the axis of gender or of race alone but only through an analysis of lived experiences that reveal how gender and race (or possibly other categories of marginalization) collide to doubly or triply discriminate. The theories of intersectionality, which have been taken up by scholars in various fields, including writing and rhetorical studies (Bliss 2016; Chávez and Griffin 2012; Nash 2016) and in this collection by Laura Gonzales and Ann Shivers-McNair; Stephanie L. Kerschbaum; and Sumyat Thu, Katie Malcolm, Candice Rai, and Anis Bawarshi, help us resist and challenge conceptions of difference as essentializing and equivalent or as additive and discrete. Intersectionality, as we understand it, must focus on how structures of exclusion, inequity, and discrimination multiply the burdens and negative impacts for certain individuals and communities. Hence, when we imagine what it means to write across difference, we consider how intersectional forms of discrimination interlock to unevenly shape the mechanisms of access, mobility, exclusion, erasure, and reward associated with various language and literate practices, cultures, and identities.

One noteworthy critique and limitation of this book is that even as this volume strives to theorize the possibility of encounters across various forms of difference and to decenter dominant forms of identity and language it nevertheless operates through a form of institutionalized and raced academic discourse that has long functioned to protect rather than eliminate differences. This, of course, is a contradiction endemic not just to this collection but also to academic discourse more broadly. Even as scholars in the humanities are increasingly engaging in institutional critique (Newfield 2018; paperson 2017; Kezar, DePaola, and Scott 2019), our discourse remains largely constrained by publication conventions, disciplinary and standardized language norms, and the instrumental function academic publications serve with respect to career advancement. While this volume is mostly rendered using conventional academic English, we nevertheless recognize and celebrate those scholars in the field who enact critiques of difference through language, employing nonstandard forms, code-meshing, and multimodality to question disciplinary conventions, scholars like Vershawn Ashanti Young (2007), Iris D. Ruiz (2016), and Jonathan Alexander (2017). In this collection's approach to translingualism, narrative, and challenging disciplinary, academic, and cultural norms, we seek to affirm the extensive value of this work and we hope this collection sparks conversation on these questions and inspires future scholarship that adopts a wider range of linguistic repertoires, forms, and genres.

FRAMES OF DIFFERENCE IN COMPOSITION STUDIES

This volume emerges from numerous prominent conversations in composition studies that explore difference. Most centrally, we build on recent work by Juan C. Guerra (2016), whose concept of "writing across difference" (146) in *Language, Culture, Identity and Citizenship in College Classrooms and Communities* orients our collection and inspires our title. Guerra critiques discourses that standardize identity, calling upon teachers of language to approach identity, and identity difference in particular, as social, rhetorical, and mercurial enterprises: "We, as educators in composition and literacy studies, must delve into the intricacies of what it means to live in social spaces where nothing—not our languages, cultures, identities, or citizenship status—ever stands still" (2). Guerra advocates the teaching of insurgent language practices, "multilingual (code-switching) and translingual (code-meshing)" (28) and teaching students to conceptualize identity and difference as emergent and dynamic rather than static and locked in normative categories. Our collection embraces this dynamic understanding of language and identity as performances in motion—always constrained, situated within social and material contexts, and subject to asymmetrical power—but nevertheless shifting, transforming, and nimble. We also subscribe to the position of Thu, Malcolm, Rai, and Bawarshi, who argue in this volume that such an embrace of linguistic diversity and fluidity—hallmarks of translingualism—must be paired with antiracist analysis that explicitly calls attention to and seeks to transform the unevenly sedimented structures of power and privilege, and of White supremacist and settler-colonial logics, that underscore and become associated with certain language practices, identities, and bodies.

We are additionally inspired by the work of Kerschbaum (2014), whose research on disability has deeply informed composition's engagement with difference. In *Toward a New Rhetoric of Difference*, Kerschbaum interrogates how discourses constructing difference as fixed and essential destabilize productive encounters with identity (6). Against such essentialist models, she proposes "marking difference" (7) as a tactic for acknowledging the performativity and rhetoricity of identity differences. Marking difference, she contends, "can reveal a way to simultaneously attend to the myriad resources available for working through our own and our students' classroom identities . . . and to the specific and situated classroom encounters in which and our students bring differences alive" (7). Essays in this collection particularly resonate with her rejection of binary difference, a rejection notably shared by other disability scholars in the field (Dolmage 2016; Jung 2007; Wilson and Lewiecki-Wilson 2001), and with her contention that unruly perspectives and idiosyncratic subjectivities are often discounted through articulations of equivalence.

We additionally strive to answer Asao Inoue's call for rigorous self-examination and greater attention to difference made in his 2019 CCCC chair's address, "How Do We Language So People Stop Killing Each Other, or What Do We Do about White Language Supremacy?" As Inoue contends, contemporary "languaging" fundamentally involves racial and racist judgement grounded in the perception of difference. He connects the racist conditions that dehumanize minorities to the practices of "White language supremacy" (355) that pervade the contemporary scene of language including, notably, the composition classroom. Inoue accordingly calls upon composition teachers to interrogate their "White racial *habitus*" (358) and to examine their "White fragility" (361) as they consider their personal biases. In conceptualizing this collection, we have similarly strived to engage in rigorous self-examination regarding the often implicit role of Whiteness in theorizing difference and similarly advocate for others in the field to consider the normativity entailed in naming difference.

The call for a disposition of listening and empathy across radical difference is an additional thread in composition scholarship that this collection explores. Radical listening is commonly imagined as an ethical imperative for negotiating collective life in the face of radical, incommensurable ideological, political, cultural, species, and other forms of difference—whether explicitly for participating in democratic publics (Farmer 2013; Fleming 2009; Jackson 2007; Weisser 2002) or for engaging across radical difference with an interest in increasing the chances of understanding, cooperation, and more equitable social transformation. John Duffy, for example, has recently critiqued the "intolerant and irrational, venomous and violent, divisive and dishonest" (2019, 5) nature of contemporary US discourse, calling for greater attention to the study of ethics in order to prepare students for the work of intimate connection, to give them opportunities "to 'talk to strangers' and perhaps begin to repair the broken state of our public arguments" (12). *Writing across Difference* accordingly figures difference as a modality of forging alliances and connections in a sociopolitical context of increasing divergence.

Responding to these and other disciplinary interventions, the following chapters represent an array of approaches to difference through the lenses of antiracism, decoloniality, interdisciplinarity, trans work (approaches in composition to translingualism, transmodality, transdisciplinarity that theorize the fluidity, resources, challenges, and politics underscoring new communicative practices in our increasingly interconnected digital and global contexts), and numerous other perspectives. Together, they provide a range of theoretical, methodological, and pedagogical resources for understanding the role difference plays in the field of composition and for addressing difference more conscientiously in the classroom. While each broadly examines difference as it relates to writing pedagogy, educational policy, or writing program administration, the problems these chapters raise, the methods they utilize, and the solutions they offer are as variegated as the field itself.

The chapters in part 1, "Personal, Embodied, and Theoretical Engagements," offer conceptual investigations and interventions on difference, working in the areas of autoethnography, narrative, and critical and cultural theory to analyze division, exclusion, and inequity as they relate to the teaching of writing. In "An Embodied History of Language Ideologies," Guerra explores the concept of language ideologies through narratives of his own embodied engagements with language—both in his personal life and in his teaching career of nearly five decades. Guerra speaks poignantly of his experience as a monolingual Spanish-heritage speaker forced to unlearn Spanish and of his subsequent work as an academic seeking to address the language and cultural needs of underrepresented students. Conceptualizing translingualism and multiculturalism as pluralistic alternatives to monolingualism, Guerra calls on teachers of writing to respond more proactively to the restrictive ideologies that govern the contemporary scene of language. In " 'Gathering Dust in the Dark': Inequality and the Limits of Composition," James Rushing Daniel questions disciplinary claims regarding the capacity of the composition classroom to materially empower students and enable social mobility. Illuminating the increasingly unbridgeable class divides of twenty-first century neoliberalism, Daniel contends that rather than striving to promote students' social mobility in the short term, scholars should instead shift their attention to service learning in order to engage students in the necessary long-term work of combating economic inequality. In "*Desconocimiento*: A Process of Epistemological Unknowing through Rhetorical *Nepantla*," Iris D. Ruiz draws on her identity as a Chicana/ Indigena/India/Mexicana/Latinx academic as she questions dominant constructions of race, identity, and disciplinarity. Employing Gloria Anzaldúa's concept of *nepantla*, a term denoting marginal, liminal, or otherwise uprooted subjectivity, Ruiz conducts a decolonial critique of composition studies, analyzing the field's Western and imperialist tendencies and calling for a disciplinary culture that embraces difference and Indigenous knowledge. In the section's final chapter, "Exploring Discomfort Using Markers of Difference: Constructing Antiracist and Anti-ableist Teaching Practices," Stephanie Kerschbaum builds upon her concept of "marking difference" (2014, 6) to theorize the teaching persona and its relationship to difference between students. As she argues, antiracist and anti-ableist pedagogy necessitates that teachers reconcile their identities and teaching methods with the histories, interrelationships, and presences of racism, sexism, ableism, and classism that permeate higher education environments throughout the United States. She specifically calls upon teachers of writing to reflect on their experiences of pedagogical discomfort to discover how these narratives can reveal underlying assumptions and practices that foreclose possibilities for engagement and learning.

The chapters in part 2, "Classroom and Curricular Praxis," consider practical, classroom-based approaches to many of the issues of difference theorized in the first section. Examining such diverse pedagogical contexts and issues as disability, disciplinary language and conventions, and political difference, these chapters strive to demonstrate how attention to difference can productively inform the composition classroom. In part 2's opening chapter, Nadya Pittendrigh's "Whole-Self Rhetoric: Teaching the Justice Situation in the Composition Classroom" poses restorative justice as an alternative to forensic rhetoric, a model of rhetoric the author contends problematically saturates not only the justice system but also argumentation pedagogy and the composition classroom. As she argues, restorative justice is a species of "whole-self rhetoric," a rhetorical stance that, unlike courtroom rhetoric, promotes the bridging of difference and foregrounding civic engagement and vulnerability. Megan Callow and Katherine Xue's "Rewriting the Biology of Difference: How a Writing-Centered, Case-Based Curricular Approach Can Reform Undergraduate Science" challenges dominant narratives in science and technology studies (STS) that defend a biological basis for difference, elaborating how undergraduate science education, through critical, investigative, and narrative-based assignments, can introduce students to the epistemic construction of difference—among groups, scientific categories and fields—and, accordingly, promote more sophisticated writing and better science. In the following chapter, "Disability Identity and Institutional Rhetorics of Difference," Neil F. Simpkins analyzes disability in the context of higher education through the framework of difference. In a qualitative study, he analyzes how three rhetorical forms—diagnosis, bureaucratic institutional structures of accessibility, and interpersonal encounters with classmates—function to shape the experience of disability identity for college students. As Simpkins argues, analyses of these forms demonstrate how difference works rhetorically to shape identity categories as well as impact how or if disabled students access classroom spaces. Part 2 concludes with "Interrogating the 'Deep Story': Storytelling and Narratives in the Rhetoric Classroom"[2] by Shui-yin Sharon Yam, a chapter contending that inviting students to interrogate and share their worldviews through personal narratives could promote mutual inquiry across difference. Drawing upon a series of assignments and activities developed from the model of invitational rhetoric, Yam analyzes students' writing and reflections to demonstrate how mutual listening and inquiry function as an effective means to cultivate self-reflexivity and ethical relations with others who do not share the same positionality.

The collection's third and final section, "Institutional, Community, and Public Transformations," examines how consideration of difference in a variety of contexts beyond the writing classroom, both within and beyond the university, can attend to the politics of exclusion and to the work of creating inclusive, antiracist communities in various institutional settings. In the section's opening chapter, "Designing across Difference: Intersectional, Interdependent Approaches to Sustaining Communities," Laura Gonzales and Ann Shivers-McNair defend a multiperspectival approach to difference, arguing that three conceptual topoi—intersectionality, interdependency, and community sustainment—are vital in supporting an informed engagement with the concept. Employing these topoi, Gonzales and Shivers-McNair develop a set of interventions in research, teaching, and community building that strive to redress contemporary manifestations of difference. In the following chapter, "Antiracist Translingual Praxis in Writing Ecologies," Sumyat Thu, Katie Malcolm, Candice Rai, and Anis Bawarshi forward a translingual writing praxis grounded in an antiracist critique of structural inequity, which they argue requires ongoing activist work by writing instructors and writing program administrators to transform the structures of privilege and inequity embedded within writing program ecologies. The authors anchor this conversation within stories about the efforts their own writing program has made to realize an antiracist translingual praxis. The book concludes with "Confronting Superdiversity Again: A Multidimensional Approach to Teaching and Researching Writing at a Global University," in which Jonathan Benda, Cherice Escobar Jones, Mya Poe, and Alison Y. L. Stephens employ the term "superdiversity," a concept that acknowledges complex forms of diversity related to national origin, mobility, race, and economic privilege, to analyze difference across multiple educational sites at Northeastern University (NU). As they contend, superdiversity both illuminates and obscures the movement of multilingual writers through the writing program at NU. Through this analysis, they argue that writing programs must focus on the intersections of privilege and language emerging in multilingual classrooms.

While the chapters gathered here represent a broad array of approaches and orientations, they nevertheless collectively suggest a set of personal, curricular, and programmatic strategies teachers and administrators of composition can adopt to address and navigate difference in teaching, research, writing programs, and community-engaged collaborations. First, these chapters exhort compositionists to undertake a rigorous and pluralistic accounting of difference in ways that highlight personal biases and divisions between individuals, particularly those in the classroom, in preparation for developing opportunities for equity, connection, and encounter. They encourage scholars to investigate, theorize, and historicize difference in order to understand how it operates, how it appears, how it is occluded, and how it is represented and misrepresented in language, pedagogy, institutions, and publics. Per Kerschbaum, this work must entail an ongoing, meticulous *self*-interrogation in which teachers of writing must evaluate how their teaching, grading practices, writing, and research methods create or deepen difference. For Guerra, we must concomitantly seek to understand the complexities of identity and language, how translingualism "behaves in the world," and how to address the needs of minority students who, because their languages and identities do not conform to accepted norms, "often find themselves in worlds not designed for them" (chapter 1).

Second, these chapters encourage compositionists to create spaces of encounter so that students can engage with one another, and with writing, in ways that evade the social, cultural, and institutional logics of difference. As scholars in this collection argue, teachers and administrators of writing must position students to interrogate and resist the racist, sexist, ablest, classist, homophobic, transphobic, and otherwise discriminatory views that pervade our society and our spaces of higher education. Pittendrigh advocates implementing the methods of restorative justice in the composition classroom in place of traditional modes of persuasion, a method that positions students as collaborators engaged in discovery and self-exploration rather than adversaries engaged in rhetorical warfare. Yam similarly encourages the interrogation of *deep stories*, affectively entangled narratives that often link identities to political orientations, in order to "help eradicate toxic and dehumanizing rhetoric across political difference and positionality" (155).

Third, writing across difference also entails working to transform our institutions and communities such that inequitable differences are not structurally reproduced. As scholars in this collection contend, difference must be addressed through the application of solidaristic and antiracist values to institutions and writing program ecologies. Gonzales and Shivers-McNair advocate for creating "space for all our expertises, vocabularies, and practices to intersect across institutional and disciplinary boundaries in ways that highlight our interdependence" (185). Thu, Malcolm, Rai, and Bawarshi similarly advocate identifying and eliminating various forms of monolingual racism in our institutions by (re)orienting writing ecologies toward the intersectional values of antiracism. As they argue, such programmatic work should be guided by the view that "antiracist translingual praxis is an ecological phenomenon" (210)—work that requires an ongoing commitment to reflection and action in all our institutional spaces.

Cumulatively, we see this collection as a practical and methodological intervention at a time when social, political, economic, and personal divisions are deepening. We specifically understand it as aligning with the expansive and coalitional goals of the protests that, as of this writing, continue to erupt across the country and the world. While composition alone cannot hope to address the issue of difference on an expansive enough scale to appreciably redress global society's deepening divides, the scholars gathered here defend the value of transforming our classrooms, institutions, and teaching selves in ways that support solidarity and social justice in an immensely divisive time. As the contributors to this volume contend, writing and writing instruction can resist the contemporary proliferation of hatred, violence, and inequality; critique and transform the world in ways that bend toward social justice; connect dislocated interlocutors and build community; and illuminate what forms such connection might take and what implications they might hold.

NOTES

1. For a discussion of our rationale for capitalizing the term, see chapter 10.
2. This article first appeared in *Composition Forum*, volume 40, fall 2018.

REFERENCES

Ackerman, John, and David Coogan, eds. 2013. *The Public Work of Rhetoric: Citizen-Scholars and Civic Engagement.* Columbia: University of South Carolina Press.

Alexander, Jonathan. 2008. *Literacy, Sexuality, Pedagogy: Theory and Practice for Composition Studies.* Logan: Utah State University Press.

Alexander, Jonathan. 2017. *Creep: A Life, A Theory, An Apology.* Goleta, CA: Punctum Books.

Alexander, Jonathan, Susan C. Jarratt, and Nancy Welch, eds. 2018. *Unruly Rhetorics: Protest, Persuasion, and Publics.* Pittsburgh: University of Pittsburgh Press.

Alexander, Jonathan, and Jacqueline Rhodes. 2014. *On Multimodality: New Media in Composition Studies.* Champaign, IL: NCTE.

Baker-Bell, April. 2020. *Linguistic Justice: Black Language, Literacy, Identity, and Pedagogy.* New York: Routledge.

Barad, Karen. 2007. *Meeting the Universe Halfway: Quantum Physics and the Entanglement of Matter and Meaning.* Durham, NC: Duke University Press.

Blair, Kristine L., and Lee Nickoson, eds. 2019. *Composing Feminist Interventions: Activism, Engagement, Praxis.* Perspective on Writing. Fort Collins, CO: WAC Clearinghouse.

Blankenship, Lisa. 2019. *Changing the Subject: A Theory of Rhetorical Empathy.* Logan: Utah State University Press.

Bliss, James. 2016. "Black Feminism Out of Place." *Signs: Journal of Women in Culture and Society* 41 (4): 727–49.

Bou Ayash, Nancy. 2019. *Toward Translingual Realities in Composition: (Re)Working Local Language Representations and Practices.* Logan: Utah State University Press.

Canagarajah, Suresh. 2013. *Translingual Practice: Global Englishes and Cosmopolitan Relations.* Abingdon: Routledge.

Chávez, Karma, and Cindy Griffin, eds. 2012. *Standing in the Intersection: Feminist Voices, Feminist Practices in Communication Studies.* Albany: SUNY Press.

Cedillo, Christina V. 2018. "What Does It Mean to Move?: Race, Disability, and Critical Embodiment Pedagogy." *Composition Forum* 39. https://files.eric.ed.gov/fulltext/EJ1188979.pdf.

Crenshaw, Kimberlé. 1989. "Demarginalizing the Intersection of Race and Sex: A Black Feminist Critique of Antidiscrimination Doctrine, Feminist Theory and Antiracist Politics." *University of Chicago Legal Forum 1989 (1)*: 139–67.

Cushman, Ellen. 2016. "Translingual and Decolonial Approaches to Meaning Making." *College English* 78 (3): 234–42.

Diab, Rasha. 2016. *Shades of Sulh: The Rhetorics of Arab-Islamic Reconciliation.* Pittsburgh: University of Pittsburgh Press.

Dolmage, Timothy Jay. 2016. *Academic Ableism: Disability and Higher Education.* Ann Arbor: University of Michigan Press.

Duffy, John. 2019. *Provocations of Virtue: Rhetoric, Ethics, and the Teaching of Writing.* Logan: Utah State University Press.

Enoch, Jessica, and Jordynn Jack, eds. 2019. *Retellings: Opportunities for Feminist Research in Rhetoric and Composition Studies.* Anderson, SC: Parlor.

Farmer, Frank. 2013. *After the Public Turn: Composition, Counterpublics, and the Citizen Bricoleur.* Logan: Utah State University Press.

Ferguson, Roderick. 2012. *The Reorder of Things: The University and Its Pedagogies of Minority Difference.* Minneapolis: University of Minnesota Press.

Fleming, David. 2009. *City of Rhetoric: Revitalizing Public Space in Metropolitan America.* Albany: SUNY Press.

Gilyard, Keith. 1991. *Voices of the Self: A Study of Language Competence.* Detroit, MI: Wayne State University Press.

Glenn, Cheryl. 2018. *Rhetorical Feminism and This Thing Called Hope.* Carbondale: Southern Illinois University Press.

Glenn, Cheryl, and Krista Ratcliffe, eds. 2011. *Silence and Listening as Rhetorical Acts.* Carbondale: Southern Illinois University Press.

Gonzales, Laura. 2018. *Sites of Translations: What Multilinguals Can Teach Us about Digital Writing and Rhetoric.* Ann Arbor: University of Michigan Press.

Grabill, Jeff. 2007. *Writing Community Change: Designing Technologies for Citizen Action.* New York: Hampton.

Guerra, Juan C. 2016. *Language, Culture, Identity, and Citizenship in College Classrooms and Communities.* New York: Routledge.

Horner, Bruce, Samantha NeCamp, and Christiane Donahue. 2011. "Toward a Multilingual Writing Scholarship: From English Only to a Translingual Norm." *College Composition and Communication* 63 (2): 269–300.

Hyman, Louis. 2018. *Temp: How American Work, American Business, and the American Dream Became Temporary.* New York: Viking.

Inoue, Asao B. 2015. *Antiracist Writing Assessment Ecologies: Teaching and Assessing Writing for a Socially Just Future.* Anderson, SC: Parlor.

Inoue, Asao B. 2019. "2019 CCCC Chair's Address: How Do We Language So People Stop Killing Each Other, or What Do We Do about White Language Supremacy?" *College Composition and Communication* 71 (2): 352–69.

Jackson, Brian. 2007. "Cultivating Paieweyan Pedagogy: Rhetoric Education in English and Communication Studies." *Rhetoric Society Quarterly* 37 (2): 181–201.

Jarratt, Susan C., and Lynn Worsham, eds. 1998. *Feminism and Composition Studies: In Other Words.* New York: MLA.

Jung, Julie. 2007. "Textual Mainstreaming and Rhetorics of Accommodation." *Rhetoric Review* 26 (2): 160–78.

Kells, Michelle Hall. 2016. "The Rhetorical Imagination of Writing Across Communities: *Nomos* and Community Writing as Gift-Giving Economy." *Reflections* 16 (1): 149–66.

Kerschbaum, Stephanie L. 2014. *Toward a New Rhetoric of Difference.* Champaign, IL: NCTE.

Kezar, Adrianna, Tom DePaola, and Daniel T. Scott. 2019. *The Gig Academy: Mapping Labor in the Neoliberal University.* Baltimore: Johns Hopkins University Press.

King, Lisa, Rose Guebele, and Joyce Rain Anderson, eds. 2015. *Survivance, Sovereignty, and Story: Teaching American Indian Rhetorics.* Logan: Utah State University Press.

Kynard, Carmen. 2014. *Vernacular Insurrections: Race, Black Protest, and the New Century in Composition-Literacies Studies.* Albany: SUNY Press.

Lee, JongHwa, and Seth Kahn, eds. 2020. *Activism and Rhetoric: Theories and Contexts for Political Engagement.* New York: Routledge.

Lu, Min-Zhan, and Bruce Horner. 2016. "Translingual Literacy, Language Difference, and Matters of Agency." *College English* 75 (6): 582–607.

Malcolm, Katie. 2017. "Disrupting Monolingual Ideologies in a Community College: A Translingual Studio Approach." In *Crossing Divides: Exploring Translingual Writing Pedagogies and Programs,* edited by Bruce Horner and Laura Tetreault, 101–18. Logan: Utah State University Press.

Mao, LuMing, and Morris Young, eds. 2008. *Representations: Doing Asian American Rhetoric.* Logan: Utah State University Press.

Martinez, Aja Y. 2020. *Counterstory: The Rhetoric and Writing of Critical Race Theory.* Champaign, IL: NCTE.

Milanovic, Branko. 2018. *Global Inequality: A New Approach for the Age of Globalization.* Cambridge: Belknap.

Nash, Jennifer. 2016. "Feminist Originalism: Intersectionality and the Politics of Reading." *Feminist Theory* 17 (1): 3–20.

Neiwert, David. 2017. *Alt-America: The Rise of the Radical Right in the Age of Trump.* London: Verso.

Newfield, Christopher. 2018. *The Great Mistake: How We Wrecked Public Universities and How We Can Fix Them.* Baltimore: Johns Hopkins University Press.

paperson, la. 2017. *A Third University is Possible.* Minneapolis: University of Minnesota Press.

Perryman-Clark, Staci, David E. Kirkland, and Austin Jackson, eds. 2014. *Students' Right to Their Own Language: A Critical Sourcebook.* Boston: Bedford/St. Martin's.

Piketty, Thomas. 2014. *Capital in the Twenty-First Century.* Translated by Arthur Goldhammer. Cambridge: Belknap.

Pitts-Taylor, Victoria. 2016. *The Brain's Body: Neuroscience and Corporeal Politics.* Durham, NC: Duke University Press.

Pritchard, Eric Darnell. 2016. *Fashioning Lives: Black Queers and the Politics of Literacy.* Carbondale: Southern Illinois University Press.

Rai, Candice. 2016. *Democracy's Lot: Rhetoric, Publics, and the Places of Invention.* Tuscaloosa: University of Alabama Press.

Ratcliffe, Krista. 2005. *Rhetorical Listening: Identification, Gender, Whiteness.* Carbondale: Southern Illinois University Press.

Reiff, Mary Jo, and Anis Bawarshi. 2016. *Genre and the Performance of Publics.* Logan: Utah State University Press.

Richardson, Elaine B., and Keith Gilyard. 2001. "Students' Right to Possibility: Basic Writing and African American Rhetoric." *Insurrections: Approaches to Resistance in Composition Studies,* edited by Andrea Greenbaum, 37–51. Albany: SUNY Press.

Royster, Jacqueline Jones. 1996. "When the First Voice You Hear Is Not Your Own." *College Composition and Communication* 47 (1): 29–40.

Royster, Jacqueline Jones, and Gesa E. Kirsch. 2012. *Feminist Rhetorical Practices: New Horizons for Rhetoric, Composition, and Literacy Studies.* Carbondale: Southern Illinois University Press.

Ruiz, Iris D. 2016. *Reclaiming Composition for Chicano/as and Other Ethnic Minorities: A Critical History and Pedagogy.* London: Palgrave Macmillan.

Ruiz, Iris D., and Raúl Sánchez, eds. 2016. *Decolonizing Rhetoric and Composition Studies: New Latinx Keywords for Theory and Pedagogy.* London: Palgrave Macmillan.

Savage, Luke. 2020. "Black Lives Matter Is More Popular Than Donald Trump." *Jacobin*, June 11. https://jacobinmag.com/2020/06/black-lives-matter-blm-polling-donald-trump.

Smitherman, Geneva. 1986. *Talkin and Testifyin: The Language of Black America.* Detroit: Wayne State University Press.

Smitherman, Geneva, and Victor Villanueva, eds. 2003. *Language Diversity in the Classroom: From Intention to Practice.* Carbondale: Southern Illinois University Press.

Stenberg, Shari J. 2015. *Repurposing Composition: Feminist Interventions for a Neoliberal Age.* Logan: Utah State University Press.

Stengers, Isabelle. 2015. *In Catastrophic Times: Resisting the Coming Barbarism.* Translated by Andrew Goffey. London: Open Humanities Press.

Trimbur, John. 2016. "Translingualism and Close Reading." *College English* 78 (3): 219–27.

Villanueva, Victor. 1993. *Bootstraps: From an American Academic of Color.* Champaign, IL: NCTE.

Waite, Stacey. 2017. *Teaching Queer: Radical Possibilities for Writing and Knowing.* Pittsburgh: University of Pittsburgh Press.

Wallace-Wells, David. 2019. *The Uninhabitable Earth: Life After Global Warming.* New York: Tim Duggan Books.

Weisser, Christian R. 2002. *Moving beyond Academic Discourse: Composition Studies and the Public Sphere.* Carbondale: Southern Illinois University Press.

Wilson, James C., and Cynthia Lewiecki-Wilson, eds. 2001. *Embodied Rhetorics: Disability in Language and Culture.* Carbondale: Southern Illinois University Press.

Yergeau, Melanie. 2018. *Authoring Autism: On Rhetoric and Neurological Queerness.* Durham, NC: Duke University Press.

Young, Vershawn Ashanti. 2007. *Your Average Nigga: Performing Race, Literacy, and Masculinity.* Detroit, MI: Wayne State University Press.

Zaloom, Caitlin. 2019. *Indebted: How Families Make College Work at Any Cost.* Princeton: Princeton University Press.

PART I

Personal, Embodied, and Theoretical Engagements

1

AN EMBODIED HISTORY OF LANGUAGE IDEOLOGIES

Juan C. Guerra

In *Living a Feminist Life*, Sara Ahmed (2017) introduces us to a new way of thinking about the specialized concepts we develop and use in the academy "to describe something that is difficult, that resists being fully comprehended in the present" (12). "Theory itself," she observes, "is often assumed to be abstract: something is more theoretical the more abstract it is, the more it is abstracted from everyday life. [But to] abstract," she points out, "is to drag away, detach, pull away, or divert" (10). In coming to "appreciate that theory can do more the closer it gets to the skin," Ahmed reminds us, "feminism begins with sensation" (21) and is grounded in "a body that fidgets and moves around" (22; see also Christian 1987). To more accurately capture this feminist sensibility, Ahmed refers to concepts that she uses to think through difficult feminist ideas as "sweaty." Sweaty concepts, she argues, are "generated by the practical experience of coming up against a world, or the practical experience of trying to transform a world." Yes, "a concept is worldly," she admits, "but it is also a reorientation to a world, a way of turning things around, a different slant on the same thing. More specifically," she concludes, "a sweaty concept is one that comes out of a description of a body that is not at home in the world" (13).

In this essay, I want to drag translingualism, a concept Bruce Horner, Min-Zhan Lu, Jacqueline Jones Royster, and John Trimbur (2011) introduced to the field of composition studies, down from its lofty heights and bring it—along with its companion language ideologies, monolingualism and multilingualism—closer to the ground where we can make them and ourselves sweat. In the process, I want to show how two other concepts—ideology and the postmonolingual condition, which Yasemin Yildiz describes as "a field of tension in which the monolingual paradigm continues to assert itself and multilingual practices persist or reemerge" (2012, 5)—inform our understanding of how translingualism

https://doi.org/10.7330/9781646421732.c001

behaves in the world as it contends with other language ideologies and why it is important for us to make a big deal about it. To do this, I call on the embodied sensibility expressed in *Toward Translingual Realities in Composition: (Re)Working Local Language Representations and Practices* (2019), where Nancy Bou Ayash reminds us that "*language representations and the embodied literate practices they directly influence have a complex trajectory permeated by change and refinement in response to particular contextual affordances and meaningful, conscious reflection on practice*" (180; italics in original). Although I discuss the personal, professional, and pedagogical aspects of my relationship to language ideologies, especially translingualism, separately and sequentially so that I can show how they behave on their own, I make an effort to entangle them as I move along, especially toward the end, so that you can see how in different phases of my life I inter- and intra-acted (Barad 2007) with ideological language practices that have been around a long time but were only recently explicated in relation to one another.

In what follows, I examine elements of my life by deconstructing monolingualism, multilingualism, and translingualism in the ways Ahmed suggests, that is, by exploring the three concepts' entangled histories through my own lived experience as a child and young man. I also interrogate these concepts in the course of talking about my forty-seven-year career as an activist educator-scholar compelled to understand the phenomenon each describes. As I move toward closure, I bring the *personal* and *professional* together to describe how the ever-shifting *pedagogical* landscapes that I have encountered over the last several decades, as well as those that continue to emerge in the present, inform my efforts to make sense of the theories and practices these three language ideologies represent.

THE ENTANGLEMENT OF LANGUAGE, CULTURE, AND IDENTITY

It's the fall of 1956—two years after the Supreme Court ruling in *Brown v. Board of Education* supposedly led to the desegregation of public schools—and I'm sitting in a first-grade classroom on my first day at a local public elementary school in Harlingen, a small rural town in south Texas. All around me, thirty-five other little Mexican and Mexican American children are also waiting impatiently to see what we're going to do next. Our mothers, who dropped us off, are now gone, many of them to small, comfortable, but sometimes slightly dilapidated homes in the *barrio* directly across the street from the school, others like my mother to apartments in a housing project called *Los Vecinos* Homes located across a different street. Mrs. Rosales, our first-grade teacher and of Mexican heritage like us, is standing behind her desk with two grocery bags full of colorful items. Because of a state law that will remain in place in Texas until 1986, Mrs. Rosales—who is clearly bilingual—is not permitted to speak to us in Spanish, and we in turn are prohibited from speaking anything but English on school grounds. It's a conundrum, a catch-22, because most of us don't know a single word of English.

"Okay, children," Mrs. Rosales begins, "I'm going to show you several things you're already familiar with. I'm going to say the English word for each, and I want you all to repeat it after me." "*Qué dice?*" a boy next to me asks. I shrug my shoulders and return my attention to Mrs. Rosales, wondering why she's not speaking to us in Spanish. She's holding up a small round object high in the air so we can all see it. "Apple. Repeat the word, children. Apple." Once we figure out what she wants us to do, in a crescendo of voices we all say, "Ah-ple!" "No, children, apple. A—pple." "Ah-ple!" we repeat in unison. And so it goes as my classmates and I begin a lifelong journey during which a series of "language ideology brokers" will try to get us to learn English as they either impede or foster our "abilities to move with ease and confidence within and across language and semiotic resources in literate situations" (Bou Ayash 2019, 77).

According to Yildiz (2012), the monolingual paradigm firmly in place in that first-grade classroom emerged in late eighteenth-century Europe as "a key structuring principle that organizes the entire range of modern social life, from the construction of individuals and their proper subjectivities to the formation of disciplines and institutions, as well as of imagined collectives such as cultures and nations" (2). As a force, the monolingual paradigm has not only obscured multilingual practices across history but has also "led to active processes of monolingualization, which have produced more monolingual subjects, more monolingual communities, and more monolingual institutions, without, however, fully eliminating multilingualism. [Not surprisingly,] schooling has been one of the primary means of such a social engineering of monolingual populations" (2–3). As the next two vignettes illustrate, the postmonolingual condition begins as an external imposition, but in time, those of us it is intended to domesticate, to reeducate, learn to impose it on ourselves. More often than we would like, the overt and insidious violence implicated in English-only policies, along with its legacy and ties to colonization and notions of citizenship predicated on white, male, heteronormative norms, is reinforced by threats of violence, especially when we resist it.

I'm nine years old, playing hide and seek with some of my friends in the housing project where my family and I live. "*Bueno, pues, orale, escondanse,* and I'll go looking for you, okay?" the kid who is "it" tells us. We all scamper off excitedly and hide behind bushes, parked cars, and garbage cans, anything large enough to camouflage our bodies. I hide behind a large bush and hunch down quietly as I wait for the kid who's "it" to come looking for us. As I wait there, I find myself looking at and listening to the world around me as a small bird lands on an electrical line directly in front of me. "Hm," I think to myself, "I wonder what kind of bird that is." And just as I'm thinking these words, I suddenly realize that for the first time in my life—three years after my introduction to English in my first-grade classroom—I'm processing a thought in my head in monolingual English. And just like that, my world is transformed as I take a step into what will become a lifetime of making choices about which language I should use and on what occasion. What I don't know in that moment is that over the next few years, I will also pay closer attention to the way Anglo actors on television and Anglo children in my classes speak English so I can mimic them to rid myself of an accent, one that has become a burden for me because even my friends in *Los Vecinos* have started making fun of it. In time, English will come to dominate both my lived and imagined experience.

Some years later as an eleventh grader in the town's integrated public high school, a couple of my friends from the housing project and I are walking from one class to another lost in our private conversation. Even though I've been attending the high school for more than a year, I have not befriended any of the Anglo kids in my classes. When I sit in a classroom and look around, I see my friends sprinkled among Anglo kids who live in middle-class homes in Anglo neighborhoods literally on the other side of the railroad tracks. And even though I'm fair skinned and can pass for one of them, other telltale signs—my name, the accent I still have when I speak, the clothes I wear, the way my body moves—signal to the Anglo kids that I'm different from them. Outside of class my friends and I travel in our own circles, finding in each other's company a sense of belonging that we appreciate to the point where we sometimes forget we're in school and start code switching. "Are you boys speaking Spanish?" an Anglo teacher asks when she overhears several words she does not recognize. "No, ma'am, we weren't spicking Spanish, we were spicking English." "I'm sorry, boys, but I know I heard you speaking Spanish. Please, come with me to the principal's office." As we follow her down the hall, we look at each other, roll our eyes, and silently acknowledge that we've been caught violating the school's monolingual English policy.

As soon as we walk into his office, the principal asks us to close the door behind us. "So, I understand you've been speaking Spanish on school grounds." "No, sir, we weren't spicking Spanish. We were spicking English." "Are you saying that Mrs. Johnson misheard you?" "Yes, sir," Ramiro responds, "because like Juan said, we were spicking English, not Spanish." As we stand there, we are fully aware that the principal has three options: he can send us to detention hall, give us a mimeographed letter written in English to take home to our parents telling them they need to remind us not to speak Spanish in school, or spank us with a paddle he keeps in his office for just this kind of infraction. We squirm slightly, worried that he's going to pick the third option. But we luck out. He decides to send us to after-school detention where we will sit with other kids who have committed infractions that day and do our homework.

According to Teun A. van Dijk (1998), ideologies are "shared framework(s) of social beliefs that organize and coordinate the social interpretations and practices of groups and their members" (8). The vignettes I just shared make clear that the ideologies—language oriented and otherwise—that governed our lives while I was growing up in south Texas were in constant tension with one another. At home, we were expected to speak monolingual Spanish to demonstrate respect for our parents, our language, and our culture. The same thing was true in school, where we were expected to speak monolingual English and were often physically reprimanded when we did not. Away from home and school, among our friends, we grew used to communicating in a third variety as we code switched between English and Spanish, meshing the two languages together as is typical in situations where diglossia occurs, that is, where two dialects or languages are used by a single language community, one an everyday vernacular language and a second highly codified variety used in formal education and other specialized settings (Ferguson 1959). Although we did not have the words to describe it, what we were experiencing was a consequence of the ongoing battle among what scholars in the field today refer to as *monolingual, multilingual,* and *translingual* ideologies of language. Because language and culture are so intimately connected, we became increasingly aware that whatever languages and dialects we elected to speak would contribute to and in time inform whatever identities we eventually developed.

It's the summer of 1967 and I've returned to Chicago to live with my older sister Bertha and her six-year-old daughter Yvonne. The summer before when I came for a visit, she lived in a racially mixed neighborhood called Edgewater on the north side of the city. She now lives in an all-white, mostly Polish and German neighborhood called Avondale on the northwest side. Because it's late in the afternoon on a Sunday when I arrive in Chicago, we go straight to my sister's apartment and don't get a chance to see, much less meet, any of the new neighbors. After I get settled in and we have dinner, Bertha shows me where I'll be sleeping in the small studio apartment she is renting. Although I don't know it at the time, I will end up staying with her after this second summer and will spend my senior year at Carl Schurz, an overwhelmingly white, Northwest Side, public high school of almost four thousand students, where I will be one of a small handful of Latinx and African American students.

Before I go to bed, Bertha calls me over to the kitchen table so she can fill me in on what I will likely encounter the next day and thereafter in the neighborhood. Up to this point, all my friends where I grew up in south Texas were Mexican or Mexican American, which means I have not yet had an Anglo friend. Because she knows that this is likely to change in the coming days and that Chicago at that moment in history is considered the most segregated city in the nation, Bertha prepares me for it. "So, Juan," she says as she offers me a final piece of advice before I go to bed, "if anybody in the neighborhood asks you what your name is, just tell them it's John."

For the next year and a half, everyone in the neighborhood comes to know me as John, a name foreign to me while I was growing up but clearly necessary for survival in an all-white neighborhood in Chicago in the late 1960s. As I make new friends in the neighborhood, some of the kids occasionally ask me about my last name. I tell them it's Spanish and that my family comes from Mexico. None of them seems affected by what I reveal to them and our relationship does not change noticeably. In the summer of 1968, however, everything changes completely. It's a couple of months before I will enroll as a first-year student at the University of Illinois at Chicago Circle (UICC) after receiving a $500 scholarship provided by a Mexican American businessman who operates a string of jukeboxes in the city. As I enter a hamburger/hot-dog joint owned by the parents of a girl I know in the neighborhood and whose home I have visited many times in the company of her boyfriend, her father ignores me as I walk past him.

I walk in and find his wife—whom many of the young men who eat there, including me, call Mom—cleaning up the place. I describe what just happened and ask if she knows why her husband refused to acknowledge my presence when he passed me on his way out. "Did I offend him in some way?" I ask. "Oh, don't worry," she says, "he's just having a

bad day." Unmoved by her explanation, I ask her again. She finally suc-
cumbs and says, "It's just that, uh, he found out this morning that you're
Mexican." I'm so struck by her words that I immediately leave and go
home to an apartment I moved into with an Anglo friend after moving
out of my sister's apartment earlier that summer and ponder the revelation. The next day I tell every friend I run into that I don't want them
to call me John anymore. "Call me Juan," I tell them, "because that's
my name."

MY LIFE AS A DOUBLE AGENT IN THE ACADEMY

After four years at UICC, I earn a BA in English in June 1972 and take
a job as a clerk typist III in the Department of Criminal Justice, where I
had been a work-study student for three years. I later learn that, as was
true at the high school I graduated from, I was one of a small handful of
Latinx and African American undergraduates enrolled at the university
at the time out of a total population of more than ten thousand students. As I wait out the year to see if I'll get drafted and sent to Vietnam
before I apply for a different job, I decide one day in December to walk
across the street to the English Department during my lunch hour to see
if I run into anyone I know.

As happenstance would have it, I run into Frederick Stern, one of my
former professors, who asks me about my job. After I tell him, he laughs
and says, "You should be teaching!" "Yeah," I say in response, "like
that's an easy thing to do." He waves me over to a long, narrow window
in University Hall—the twenty-eight-story building where the English
Department is located—and points down toward another building
across the way. "You see that building over there? Go to the twelfth floor
and tell them you want to apply for the teaching job they've advertised."
Having nothing else to do, I say goodbye to Professor Stern, head over
to an office on the twelfth floor of the Science and Engineering Offices
and ask the receptionist for an application for the teaching job. "What's
your name?" she asks. "And what did you get a degree in?" She pauses
after each of my answers, then asks me to wait for a moment as she steps
away from her desk.

She returns a minute or two later with Paul Vega, the assistant director for what I later learn is the Educational Assistance Program, a unit
established on campus five years earlier to provide academic advising
and specialized classes in reading, writing, mathematics, and study
skills to underrepresented minority students recruited into the university through a special admission program. After Paul asks me a few

follow-up questions in his office, he smiles broadly and leaves the room. He returns and introduces me to Chuck Anderson, the associate director of the program. Chuck asks me many of the same questions, turns, and smiles at Paul, then asks if I can wait while they chat in his office.

Five minutes later, they return to Paul's office, and Chuck asks me an unexpected question: "Can you start tomorrow?" What I learn afterwards is that they're interested in hiring me to teach basic writing in the program, both because my English BA qualifies me for the position and also because I'm the only Latinx likely to apply. After I accept the position on the spot, they tell me that I will need to work as a recruiter and community liaison for the first nine months of the following year but should plan to start teaching basic writing in September 1973.

Imagine now, if you will, teaching writing at a major university to open-admission students just three years after the first graduate programs in rhetoric and composition studies were established at the University of Iowa, the University of Massachusetts at Amherst, The Ohio State University, and Texas Woman's University (Chapman and Tate 1987, 128) and four years before Mina Shaughnessy publishes *Errors and Expectations: A Guide for the Teacher of Basic Writing* (1977). There I am, and remain for the next seventeen years, teaching basic writing with a dozen other colleagues who, like me, are trying to figure out how best to address the writing needs of underrepresented minority students from Chicago's worst inner-city public schools who enroll in the three sections each of us teaches every quarter.

Like the students that Shaughnessy writes about, our students have difficulty putting together a sentence in Standard Written English, much less a single paragraph or a five-paragraph essay. Like Shaughnessy, we are caught in the tension between the English Department's expectation that we deploy the current traditional paradigm and the specific needs of multidialectal and multilingual students that we know we will not be able to meet by teaching the five-paragraph essay. It should come as no surprise that only 30 to 40 percent of the students in the special-admit program succeeded in passing an impromptu essay exam at the end of each quarter monitored by the English Department that determined whether or not they would be permitted to enroll in a second, more advanced writing course on doing research that they would also have to pass to graduate.

I tell this story in the first few pages of an essay titled "Putting Literacy in Its Place: Nomadic Consciousness and the Practice of Transcultural Repositioning" (Guerra 2004), and I add that the teaching situation I just described provided us with an incredible opportunity to imagine and test new ways to teach writing to a diverse pool of students who spoke various languages and dialects but were not yet equipped to write in Standard American English. As you can imagine, it was very frustrating to be constricted by the demands of the five-paragraph essay, especially with a relentless focus on grammar, syntax, spelling, mechanics, and punctuation, so much so that I thought about quitting more than once. Fortunately, many of my colleagues were as curious as I was about looking for new ways to teach writing, so we joyfully embraced each new pedagogy as it emerged: expressivist, problem solving, social constructivist, critical, and a mash of all of them put together.

What my colleagues and I learned over time was that hard as we tried, we were never going to find the silver bullet, the pedagogical approach to the teaching of writing that would once and for all equip us with the tools we desperately needed to address the myriad of challenges our students faced. Another thing we learned after experimenting with so many different pedagogical approaches was that we as writing teachers were not in a position to empower our students. The best we could do, we came to realize, was to create conditions in the classroom under which students could empower themselves—if they so choose. Since then, no one else in the field has come up with a single pedagogical approach that addresses the needs of all, much less multilingual, students because frankly there is no such thing. As we also learned, the best we could do was to make every effort to develop pedagogies in-the-moment to address the emerging needs of whatever group of students happened to be in our writing classroom at any given time.

For example, when the basic writing program at UICC experienced an unexpected influx of Latinx immigrant students in 1976, one of my colleagues in the writing program and I asked the writing director for permission to develop and teach a writing course bilingually in English and Spanish. No doubt because of the persistence of the postmonolingual condition in this country, it is likely one of the few times anyone has ever taught a bilingual writing course at a major university. At the time, my colleague Elías Argot and I concluded that we needed to build on what our students brought to the classroom—what we nowadays refer to as their *learning incomes*—in our case the repertoire of rhetorical and literacy skills that Latinx immigrant students had acquired in Spanish and English.

The course we developed encouraged students enrolled in our two special sections to speak, read, and write in whichever language they wished so long as the final series of writing assignments they completed were in English since that was the language on which they would be assessed by the English Department when they wrote the two-hour, five-paragraph impromptu essay they would have to submit at the end of the quarter. While the typical passing rate in my classes over the previous three years had averaged between 30 and 40 percent, 80 percent of the students in my bilingual class that quarter passed the impromptu written exam. Unfortunately, the passing rate in Argot's class did not improve as dramatically. Although he was Mexican educated and had developed most of the curriculum for the course, because Elías was openly gay, several male Latinx students in his class disrupted the class continuously because of their homophobic views. This made it very difficult for the other students in the class to learn what Argot was teaching. As a consequence, our grand experiment ended as suddenly as it began.

It is the early autumn of 1978 and Carol Severino—a colleague in the basic writing program—wants to pursue a master's degree in a graduate program specializing in language, literacy, and rhetoric that the English Department at UICC had established a couple of years earlier. "Why don't you come and work on a master's degree with me, Juan? I'd love to have a partner in crime who is also doing it part time." "Thanks, Carol," I respond, "but I really enjoy teaching basic writing, and I doubt I'll have time to devote to my studies." "Come on, please," she begs, "I really don't want to do it by myself." Eventually, I break down and agree to do it. After we complete the part-time master's program three years later, Carol approaches me and says, "Hey, Juan, let's go for a PhD, okay?" "What the hell do I want with a PhD, Carol?" I ask half kiddingly. "I'm perfectly happy with what I'm doing now." "Oh, come on, please," she begs. "We can take a course a quarter like we did with the master's degree, and the university will pay for it. What more could you want?" Again, I break down and agree to do it, although this time I'm not sure I'll make it past the course work. But we both do, and in 1990, the two of us go on the job market and get tenure-track positions, Carol at the University of Iowa and I at the University of Washington.

As a new, untenured professor at the University of Washington in Seattle, I know I have five years to translate my dissertation into a monograph and publish a few articles in refereed journals and edited collections to make sure I will be able to stay. One thing I am not planning to do until Carol suggests it is to coedit a collection of essays on writing pedagogies. After we send out a call for papers and receive eighty proposals, Carol and I make a conscious effort to select twenty relatively diverse proposals. In so doing, we "[strive] for balance and diversity" in terms of race, ethnicity, and institutional setting. We also look for essays that "[feature] the writing and perspectives of students whose voices are seldom heard, especially students of color and students who are speakers of other languages and dialects" (Severino, Guerra, and Butler 1997, 6). Finally, we ask contributors to the edited collection to address questions we are still asking today: How different from or similar to one another are we? How fluid or fixed are such differences? How different are students' discourses from academic discourses? What rights and opportunities should students have to maintain and express their own native discourses or native-language discourse patterns? (5–6). In a review a few years ago, Jaime Mejía described *Writing in Multicultural Settings* (1997), the book Carol and I eventually co-edited with Johnnella Butler, as "an extraordinary collection of essays [that] came at the tail end of what was arguably then the 'era of multiculturalism'" (Mejía 2011, 145). Describing the book as "clearly way ahead of its time," Mejía notes that it presents "a quite diverse array of both rhetorical and pedagogical approaches that, when taken together, represent a power-ful response to this nation's and our profession's proclivity of seeing the world only through Western blue eyes" (147).

As the conversation shifted over the next few years from the multicul-tural to the transcultural and from the multilingual to the translingual, like many of my colleagues in the field, I, too, began to question the limitations of the former and immersed myself in trying to understand how what we do in the writing classroom has changed and how our theoretical views have been transformed as scholars have introduced a whole new nomenclature, including the concepts of translingualism and translanguaging, to our vocabularies of motive. I also came to bet-ter understand how language and culture operate in a world that is no longer bounded, no longer constrained by institutional efforts to limit the range of rhetorical and literacy practices admissible in that space. Because I was interested in studying this phenomenon, I developed a graduate course in 2013 titled Writing across Difference in which stu-dents and I reflected on and reviewed emergent literature in the field that focused on theoretical and pragmatic efforts to reimagine the place of four key factors in the teaching of writing. This interest eventually led to my writing a monograph titled *Language, Culture, Identity and Citizenship in College Classrooms and Communities* (Guerra 2016a) that I hoped would help explain the crucial role of the four dimensions I men-tion in the title. I also wanted to understand the roles that the three lan-guage ideologies scholars have identified—monolingual, multilingual, and translingual—play in our collective effort to transform what we are doing in the writing classroom.

TRANSLATING THEORY INTO PRACTICE

There is no question that the personal and professional aspects of our daily lives play a critical role in helping us understand who we are, what we value and believe, and how we choose to act on those values and beliefs. As the vignettes I have shared with you demonstrate, our lived experience informs the choices we make when we reach a point in our lives at which we decide on a profession and our profession in turn shapes our lived experience because so much of our time is spent fulfilling personal and professional obligations. In my case, the profound connection between the two led to my current interest in deploying translingualism (also referred to as *translinguality*) as a counter ideology that, as many of my colleagues hope as well, will provide us with a pedagogical orientation that not only acknowledges the learning incomes of the students we serve in the writing classroom but also integrates them into the writing process in university classrooms and beyond. The bilingual class I taught in 1976 and an essay I published in 1997 titled "The Place of Intercultural Literacy in the Writing Classroom" accent my efforts to find ways to address the needs of multilingual students pedagogically. More recently, however, my efforts at updating the pedagogical perspective I developed over the years have lagged because like many of my colleagues, I shifted my focus to theorizing challenges to monolingual and multilingual ideologies and put aside the equally important and more difficult task of translating those theoretical reflections into pedagogical practice. In closing, I discuss efforts by several theorists interested in translating the recent explosion of ideas related to translinguality into pedagogical practices designed to provide students with opportunities to produce writing translingually, that is, writing that counters the oppressive constraints monolingual and multilingual ideologies impose on us all.

Before I review some of the pedagogical practices associated with translinguality that have emerged in the last few years, I would first like to touch on what I see as a more recent critical shift in our understanding of translinguality from an orientation best suited to address the needs of multilingual students to one best suited to address the needs of all students—including mainstream, monolingual ones. For many of us who have taught multilingual students for many years, translinguality first emerged as an ideological orientation more likely to contribute to the establishment of a level playing field by acknowledging the power inherent in all language practices, especially those that were historically marginalized by the unrelenting imposition of a monolingual set of expectations in every writing classroom. Vershawn Ashanti Young's conception of code meshing as an alternative to code switching (2009), A. Suresh Canagarajah's description of shuttling as a way for multilingual students to manage and negotiate movement across two or more languages (2006), and my introduction of transcultural repositioning as a way for disenfranchised students to establish agency in the linguistic choices they make (2004) all signaled a focus on the needs of multilingual students who possess broad repertoires of linguistic practices that include the so-called nonstandard languages and dialects they deploy in their everyday lives but that are typically quarantined in the writing classroom. Bruce Horner, with the support of a number of colleagues, however, has posited an alternative conception of language difference in writing, one that "recognizes difference not as a deviation from a norm of 'sameness' but as itself the norm of language use" (Lu and Horner 2013, 584). As Horner and Min-Zhan Lu argue in an essay they coauthored, "Until we see translinguality as relevant to and operating in the learning and writing of all writers, whether marked by the dominant as mainstream or nonmainstream, the art and struggle of writers from subordinated groups will always be dismissed as irrelevant to the work of mainstream learners" (586). I will have more to say about this in my closing remarks.

In reviewing the range of pedagogical approaches our varied conceptualizations of translinguality have produced, we begin to see how and why it matters where we put the accent when it comes to difference. In the case of proponents of code meshing, for example, we are encouraged to provide students in our writing classrooms with opportunities to self-consciously call on and integrate various elements from their repertoires of multilingual abilities in ways that disrupt the standardization of language promoted by a monolingual ideology. As Young (2009), who coined the term *code meshing*, points out, the ideology behind code meshing "holds that people's so-called 'nonstandard' dialects are already fully compatible with standard English. [Thus,] [c]ode meshing secures their right to represent that meshing in all forms and venues where they communicate" (62). Writing teachers who practice this approach typically encourage their multilingual students to intermingle aspects of the languages and dialects in their repertoires in much the same way Gloria Anzaldúa does in *Borderlands/La Frontera: The New Mestiza* (1987). In a recent essay titled "Cultivating a Rhetorical Sensibility in the Translingual Writing Classroom" (2016a), I describe an assignment in which I encouraged my students to code mesh in their midterm and final essays, and I point out that I failed miserably because "I inadvertently assumed that students can ignore the circumstances they face in the new rhetorical situation (an assigned essay in a classroom) and can easily transfer their language practices from one site to another" (231). It is simply not enough, I conclude, to "[expect] students to produce a particular kind of writing that mimics what we call code-meshing" (228).

In his work, Canagarajah has written extensively about shuttling and code meshing as tactics multilingual students can deploy in their writing. In an essay titled "ESL Composition as a Literate Art of the Contact Zone," Canagarajah (2014) outlines a course for multilingual students designed to develop their capacity as translinguals, that is, to develop "a competence that focuses on communicating in contexts where there are multiple norms of English, appropriating dominant norms according to one's own purposes and values, and even bringing together competing norms for voice" (28). He later describes how his course "is designed to encourage shuttling among languages, genres, and knowledge traditions to develop a translingual writing competence." While the key assignment for the class is a twelve-to-fifteen-page autoethnography that can accommodate "different voices and rhetorics within the body of the same text" (29), not every text that students in his class produced involves code meshing. Above all, Canagarajah wants his students to develop a good understanding of "the writing process, language awareness, and rhetorical sensitivity" (36). Like everyone who professes to teach from a translingual perspective, Canagarajah considers how "we can build on the strengths and resources multilingual students bring with them" rather than "building competence from scratch" (40). And like most translingual approaches, Canagarajah's focuses more "on the language awareness and metalinguistic competence that enables students to negotiate diverse semiotic resources from their own interests and voices, and not on a fixed type of textual product" (35).

Over the years, I have engaged in efforts similar to the ones Young and Canagarajah describe in their work. As I note earlier, in the bilingual writing class Elías Argot and I taught more than forty years ago, our primary goal was to encourage students to integrate learning incomes related to Spanish and English they had acquired in the course of their lives into the work they were doing in the monolingual English writing classroom. Because they were free to intermingle English and Spanish in some of their assignments, our students produced the kind of code-meshed texts colleagues regularly encourage their students to produce in writing classrooms today. The multilingual course I taught and wrote about in 1997 did much the same thing, as I made every effort to "implicitly [encourage] them to be seduced by the voice of Inclination in their personal essays" while my "explicit instructions and the assignments demanded that they instead fulfill the expectations of the voice of Institution" (Guerra 253). At the time, I argued that our goal as teachers of writing "is to find ways to help students develop 'intercultural literacy,' that is, an ability to consciously and effectively move back and forth among as well as in and out of discourse communities they belong to or will belong to" (258). I concluded by suggesting the following: "Whereas the monocultural-literacy approach is hegemonic and restrictive and the multicultural-literacy approach suggests that people are literate in a number of segregated, divided, and distinct cultures, the intercultural-literacy approach not only encourages students to accept commonalities and differences but also gives students an opportunity to engage and integrate them into their lives" (259). What I describe in my most recent book, *Language, Culture, Identity and Citizenship in College Classrooms and Communities* (2016), is not much different from what I described and did in the classroom more than twenty and forty years ago, respectively. What has changed is the vocabulary of motive many of us find more persuasive today.

As I noted earlier, the work Bruce Horner and a number of his colleagues are currently doing on translinguality actively challenges the views of everyone whose work I have described thus far, that is, everyone who focuses on the place of multilingual students in the writing classroom. Horner and his colleagues want to expand translinguality so that it encompasses the language practices of all students, mainstream and nonmainstream, monolingual and multilingual. In an essay Horner coauthored with Laura Tetreault (2016), they shift the focus by arguing that "treating all writing as translation allows us to see writers as always engaged in a process of negotiating and reworking common language practices, and to direct our attention and that of our students to exploring the responsibilities entailed by specific translational/ writing practices for reproducing and revising languages and language relations" (18). In a different essay, Horner (2017) explains why he chooses not to teach examples of code meshing "as a means of adding to the range of allowable language practices (a.k.a. the students' language repertoires) in what would then reinforce [what he calls] an 'additive' model of multilingualism [that would retain] key tenets of monolingualist ideology's identification of languages as discrete from one another and tied indelibly to the identities of particular groups of language users" (92). Instead, Horner elects to use such examples of writing to help his students and himself "rethink what differences might be made through and in all writing practices, whether marked by the dominant as conventional writing or as unconventional, by treating all these emergent practices located in time as well as space" (92). In choosing to conceive of all writing as translation, Horner and Tetreault (2016) conceive of it "not merely as a distinct form of writing but also as a feature and outcome of all writing—a feature that entails difficulty and friction—labor—and that produces rather than bridges or erases difference" (14). For this reason, they choose to ask students "to read different translations of a text and to examine what narratives are activated by different choices, and how they see those narratives connecting to larger ideologies" (20). In addition, they ask students to engage in paraphrasing, "not as a mechanical act of transferring meaning from one set of words to another . . . but instead as an act of reshaping meaning through an act of translation engaging, and producing, difference" (25).

While there is general agreement among the scholars I have cited about the theoretically fluid and emergent nature of language/communication as conceived by translinguality, there is clearly broad disagreement about how it manifests itself in practice and in pedagogical terms. The disagreements I have highlighted are actually a healthy consequence of the fact that translinguality is by its very nature emergent and unstable and, as a consequence, difficult to pin down. While I agree with Horner that teaching students to mimic particular forms of writing described as code meshing is not likely to take us far, we clearly disagree about how we each see the role of language repertoires in our conceptions of translinguality. Where I firmly believe that it is important to think of multilingual students as metaphorically bringing rich repertoires similar to the ones I describe in my own language use in the first section of this essay, Horner (2017) dismisses them as latent markings that retain "the key tenets of monolingualist ideology's identification of languages as discrete from one another and tied indelibly to the identities of particular groups of language users" (92). I frankly refuse to see the languages and dialects students bring from their communities of belonging as discrete and closed formations. In my view, a multilingual student's multifaceted language repertoire is dynamic, in constant flux, the languages continuously intermingling with one another to the point where they become indivisible. Together and as one, they reflect the rich and evocative nature of their lived and on-going linguistic and cultural experiences.

Moreover, while I may believe that it is useful for our students to discuss language ideologies in the classroom, I agree with Horner (2017) that it is dangerous to "teach a translingual approach as a choice," which he understandably frames as a failure "to understand its character as an ideology (like monolingualism) and therefore to underestimate what is entailed in encouraging the former and breaking with the latter" (95). Like the rest of us, our students do not always get to choose the ideologies they wish to invoke either. Ideologies often choose us instead, especially when we are not aware of their presence and influence in our everyday lives. Several of the vignettes I present in the first section of this essay illustrate the degree to which I often found myself being managed by an ideological uptake before I was aware of it. Suddenly discovering I was thinking monologically in English at the age of eleven, for example, was a surprise. The reason is understandable: from the time I had started school three years earlier, I had been increasingly immersed in daily circumstances in which forces conspired to get me to speak English more continuously than I realized. On the other hand, when I suddenly became aware of the price I was paying after changing my name to John at my sister's urging, I immediately challenged that particular ideological tendency. Like so many other choices that we find ourselves having to make in life, how we use language is not something always under our control. By flipping the meaning of Ahmad's description of how a body that is not at home in the world is better able to create sweaty concepts, we can also remind ourselves that our bodies often find themselves in worlds not designed for them, especially when they are worlds that foreclose and block our language, culture, and, at times, our entire way of being. Under such circumstances, we may well want to call on what H. Samy Alim and Django Paris (2017) refer to as "culturally sustaining pedagogies" to provide our students with the tools they need to respond proactively to ideological and postmonological conditions designed to dismiss them so that their bodies may, in turn, feel more at home in the world.

REFERENCES

Ahmed, Sara. 2017. *Living a Feminist Life*. Durham, NC: Duke University Press.

Alim, H. Samy, and Django Paris. 2017. "What Is Culturally Sustaining Pedagogy and Why Does It Matter?" In *Culturally Sustaining Pedagogies: Teaching and Learning for Justice in a Changing World*, edited by Django Paris and H. Samy Alim, 1–21. New York: Teachers College Press.

Anzaldúa, Gloria. 1987. *Borderlands/La Frontera: The New Mestiza*. San Francisco: Aunt Lute Books.

Bou Ayash, Nancy. 2019. *Toward Translingual Realities in Composition: (Re)Working Local Language Representations and Practices*. Logan: Utah State University Press.

Barad, Karen. 2007. *Meeting the University Halfway: Quantum Physics and the Entanglement of Matter and Meaning*. Durham, NC: Duke University Press.

Canagarajah, A. Suresh. 2006. "Toward a Writing Pedagogy of Shuttling between Languages: Learning from Multilingual Writers." *College English* 68 (6): 589–604.

Canagarajah, Suresh. 2014. "ESL Composition as a Literate Art of the Contact Zone." In *First-Year Composition: From Theory to Practice*, edited by Deborah Coxwell-Teague and Ronald F. Lunsford, 27–48. Anderson, SC: Parlor.

Chapman, David W., and Gary Tate. 1987. "A Survey of Doctoral Programs in Rhetoric and Composition." *Rhetoric Review* 5 (2): 124–86.

Christian, Barbara. 1987. "The Race for Theory." *Cultural Critique* 6 (Spring): 51–63.

Ferguson, Charles A. 1959. "Diglossia." *Word* 15 (January): 325–40.

Guerra, Juan C. 1997. "The Place of Intercultural Literacy in the Writing Classroom." In *Writing in Multicultural Settings*, edited by Carol Severino, Juan C. Guerra, and Johnnella E. Butler, 248–60. New York: MLA.

Guerra, Juan C. 2004. "Putting Literacy in Its Place: Nomadic Consciousness and the Practice of Transcultural Repositioning." In *Rebellious Readings: The Dynamics of Chicana/o Literacy*, edited by Carl Gutierrez-Jones, 19–37. Santa Barbara: University of California, Santa Barbara, Center for Chicano Studies.

Guerra, Juan C. 2016a. "Cultivating a Rhetorical Sensibility in the Translingual Writing Classroom." *College English* 78 (3): 228–33.

Guerra, Juan C. 2016b. *Language, Culture, Identity and Citizenship in College Classrooms and Communities*. New York: Routledge.

Horner, Bruce. 2017. "Teaching Translingual Agency in Iteration." In *Crossing Divides: Exploring Translingual Writing Pedagogies and Programs*, edited by Bruce Horner and Laura Tetreault, 87–97. Logan: Utah State University Press.

Horner, Bruce, Min-Zhan Lu, Jacqueline Jones Royster, and John Trimbur. 2011. "Opinion: Language Difference in Writing: Toward a Translingual Approach." *College English* 73 (3): 303–21.

Horner, Bruce, and Laura Tetreault. 2016. "Translation as (Global) Writing." *Composition Studies* 44 (1): 13–30.

Lu, Min-Zhan, and Bruce Horner. 2013. "Translingual Literacy, Language Difference, and Matters of Agency." *College English* 75 (6): 582–607.

Mejía, Jaime Armin. 2011. "Ethnic Rhetorics Reviewed." *College Composition and Communication* 63 (1): 145–61.

Severino, Carol, Juan C. Guerra, and Johnnella E. Butler, eds. 1997. *Writing in Multicultural Settings*. New York: MLA.

Shaughnessy, Mina P. 1977. *Errors and Expectations: A Guide for the Teacher of Basic Writing*. Oxford: Oxford University Press.

Van Dijk, Teun A. 1998. "Discourse Semantics and Ideology." *Discourse and Society* 6 (2): 243–89.

Yildiz, Yasemin. 2012. *Beyond the Mother Tongue: The Postmonolingual Condition*. New York: Fordham University Press.

Young, Vershawn Ashanti Young. 2009. "'Nah, We Straight': An Argument Against Code Switching." *Journal of Advanced Composition* 29 (1/2): 49–76.

2

"GATHERING DUST IN THE DARK"
Inequality and the Limits of Composition

James Rushing Daniel

In an article for *The Baffler*, writer and track laborer John Tormey (2019) describes the plight of those like himself for whom higher education has not permitted entry into the middle class:

> There are more people out there with stories like mine than you'd expect. Now they work as electricians, carpenters, laborers, plumbers, mechanics, and tin-knockers, but in their history are some years spent in college, racking up debt that would in no way contribute to increasing their yearly income. For a few, there's a college degree hidden somewhere in the back of [a] closet at home, gathering dust in the dark.

Growing up in a "white, Irish-Catholic, union-affiliated household" in the 1970s, Tormey was influenced by the era's rhetoric of social mobility that esteemed the middle class while disparaging manual labor. Because of the pervasive belief that "working with your hands is for those kids who lack the brainpower to do otherwise: burnouts, fuckups, the products of asshole parents, kids without options," he went to college, majored in English, got an MFA in creative writing, and taught for several years. However, as for many of us, Tormey's teaching life was financially unsustainable. In the end, he quit teaching, giving up on his aspirations for a middle-class life, and got a job with the commuter rail.

What Tormey describes is an increasingly common experience for working-class college graduates. As Thomas Piketty (2020) contends, working-class Americans have seen a dramatic decline in their purchasing power and standard of living since the 1950s, currently claiming about half the share of national income they did between 1960 and 1980 (523). While the wealthiest decile of Americans has enjoyed an explosion of wealth since 1980, outpacing the average income of the bottom 50 percent by twenty-five times in 1980 and more than eighty times in 2015 (525), the purchasing power of the minimum wage has declined 30 percent over the same period (521). This gap continues to widen even

https://doi.org/10.7330/9781646421732.c002

though attainment of higher education has increased substantially over the past half century, with less than 10 percent of the US population attaining a college degree in the 1960s versus 30–40 percent today (535). An added complication is that educational investment in the United States has declined over the past four decades (535), creating vast inequalities between top-tier private institutions and underfunded public ones (537). Admission to top universities remains starkly unequal, privileging legacy students (538) with high parental income (536). Accordingly, while a top degree continues to be a path to employment and privilege, it remains the privilege of an elite few. Less prestigious degrees, alternatively, no longer offer the protection against underemployment they once did (Habibi 2015). As Gary Roth (2019) notes, two out of five college graduates currently work jobs that do not require a degree (14).

Such conditions challenge the claims of numerous compositionists striving to draw lines between education and empowerment.[1] In her canonical 1996 essay "Freshman Composition as a Middle-Class Enterprise," Lynn Z. Bloom credits college writing with "enabling the transformation and mobility of lives across boundaries, from the margins to the mainstreams of success and assimilation on middle-class terms" (668). James Thomas Zebroski (2006b), one of the field's leading scholars of social class, frames the composition classroom as enabling "'studying up' the social ladder" (27). In his 2014 CCCC chair's address, Howard Tinberg (2014) congratulated those in the field for striving "to ensure that all students have equal access to *empowering literacy education*" (332). Against these assertions, data on economic inequality present a view of US universities as sites of stark and intractable difference, either in the preservation of privilege, as in the case of elite universities, or in the inability to support the social mobility of the working class, in the case of less prestigious public institutions.

As the divisive effects of the new economy have become increasingly apparent, more scholars in composition have turned to issues of class and political economy, discussing pedagogical approaches foregrounding working-class methods and perspectives (Carter and Thelin 2017; Welch 2008), assigning writing about late-capitalist working conditions in the composition classroom (Scott 2009; Seitz 1998), cultivating feminist, antiracist, and anti-capitalist methodologies (Banks 2011; Kynard 2007; Stenberg 2015), and critiquing austerity and the casualization of faculty labor in neoliberal contexts (Kahn et al. 2017; McClure, Goldstein, and Pemberton 2017; Welch and Scot 2016). Nevertheless, the field has generally refrained from directly contending with the diminished capacity of a college education to ameliorate material differences. While composition courses can certainly communicate a variety of skills to students that are directly applicable to professional contexts and offer a host of *nonmarket* intellectual goods, they can ultimately do little to help low-income students attain middle-class jobs. Because of this, I believe compositionists must more explicitly register the limits of our capacity to empower students in the short term. In this respect, I agree with John Marsh (2011) that "we cannot teach or learn our way out of inequality" (179) as the economic goods higher education confers cannot overcome the pervasive opportunity hoarding of the economically privileged. However, while Marsh looks for solutions beyond pedagogy, I remain committed to the notion that the writing classroom can continue to be a deeply important site, particularly insofar as it can support students' interrogation of difference and opposition to systems of inequality. Following David Coogan's (2006) defense of service learning as a site of social change, I argue that teachers of writing can begin to combat the broader effects of inequality by shifting their focus away from materially empowering students and toward orienting students to the enduring work of economic justice and social change, particularly with respect to confronting the logics and conditions of precarity. While admittedly a disheartening acknowledgment of our ineffectualness in the face of mounting precarity and inequality, particularly for those students who most need economic empowerment, I believe such a shift in focus is necessary if compositionists are to honestly assess both the limitations and the possibilities of our work in twenty-first-century economic contexts.

In what follows, I first demonstrate how many of the field's discussions of social mobility have relied upon a reductive model of social class that presumes inequality can be remediated through such simple programmatic strategies as rectifying deficits in cultural knowledge for working-class students and promoting equity at the university. After articulating these arguments and the criticisms against them in the field, I present economic evidence to complicate the field's solutions to inequity and to demonstrate the resistance of contemporary economic inequality to pedagogical intervention. Finally, I propose a pedagogy of long-term social change rooted in public writing, advocacy, and service learning, discussing my own recent work in service learning focused on engaging students in social justice work in the Seattle area.

DISCIPLINING CLASS

While scholars in composition have noted the limited capacity of education to promote social mobility (Bousquet 2007; Scott 2009), many suggest that pedagogical strategies in the composition classroom can assist students in shifting their economic position. These approaches consistently focus on social class, contending either that a college degree can assist working-class students in entering the middle class or that obtaining a college degree *itself* confers a shift in class (Harris 2000; Zebroski 2006a). Because in these constructions social class is invariably framed as conscious, avowed, and performed, relatively minor shifts in language, credentials, or even self-assessment are often presented as capable of precipitating a shift in class.

Zebroski, whose extensive theoretical work on the issues of class in the context of composition promotes greater sensitivity to working-class culture, language, and values at the university, has long offered one the field's most vocal defenses of the strong links between discourse and social class. In "Social Class as Discourse: Mapping the Landscape of Class in Rhetoric and Composition," Zebroski (2006a) opposes a material view of social class based in "one's position in the hierarchies of income, education, and occupation" (525), as such a perspective, in his view, celebrates those at the top of the economic hierarchy while ignoring the conditions that allowed them to prosper (525). He accordingly advocates an approach that regards class as emergent in "regulated language practices, which include language practices within and across institutions" (535). In Zebroski's conception, our class standing is effectively the way "we are positioned" (542) by class discourses that construct the subjectivity and values of class actors (559–65). Elsewhere, he develops this perspective, noting that viewing social class as discourse "presents a rationale and opportunity for 'studying up' the social ladder" (2006b, 27), as class is ultimately a matter of discourse, that is, how one performs class and is figured by class discourses. Accordingly, he promotes "the *dual need* to teach the conventions of ruling discourse *and* critique those conventions through new forms" (27). Acknowledging the problems of retaining low-income students, Zebroski contends these students must be taught to adopt the discursive conventions that will allow them to join the ranks of more privileged classes and to challenge these conventions. The presumption of such a statement is that the discourse of the ruling class is the dominant mechanism of difference between classes, not wealth or income. As I contend, this construction of class difference as resting in discourse, while it may critique the presumption of the ruling class as permanent or natural, offers the illusory prospect of transcending class through social performances.

Several additional composition theorists share Zebroski's contention that class resides largely in one's relationship to discourse. Nancy Mack

(2007) seconds Zebroski's approach of examining language as "a classed social relation among interested groups" (332) and critiques the privileging of the middle class that pervades discourses of class, calling for more equitable means of capturing and relating to economic difference (338). Similarly, Donna LeCourt (2006) constructs social class as "economically structured and culturally fluid" (45), acknowledging class's material valence but asserting its discursive variability. David Borkowski (2004) likewise views class as a matter of one's cultural linkages, codes, and attitudes—for example, the privileging of heteronormativity (95) and the distrust of academic elitism (97). In his assessment, transforming one's relationship to these norms and embracing the norms and practices of the middle class can facilitate a shift in one's class standing: "Books train working-class kids in the cultural practices of the elite. . . . [and] can sometimes provide upward mobility" (103). While, like Zebroski, these critics acknowledge class position has a material basis, their view of class as largely a social enterprise similarly suggests that shifts in discourse, knowledge, and performance can effect changes in one's class position.

Many additional composition scholars similarly contend social mobility can be granted through mastering the professional managerial class's discourse. In his canonical essay "Inventing the University," David Bartholomae (1985) advocates equipping writers with the relevant registers or "codes" (156) to better prepare them for alternative class discourses: "To speak with authority, student writers not only have to speak in another's voice but through another's 'code'; and they not only have to do this, they have to speak in the voice and through the codes of those of us with power and wisdom" (156). Donald Lazere (1992) similarly critiques the openly radical approach of Leftist academics who reject the value of teaching such class codes, noting, "Teachers may unavoidably have to 'coerce' students and 'lay on' academic culture and standard English in the cause of showing that they contain the potential to be a force for *either* conformity or nonconformity" (19–20; emphasis in original). Michael Gos (1995) suggests teaching working-class students to "overcom[e] social class markers" (32), as does Joseph Harris (2000), who contends the university fails to offer students an education in what it means to belong to the middle class. While Harris does indeed locate the notion of class within a group's "social and material interests" (46), he nevertheless contends that the essence of one's social class is ultimately a matter of cultural capital, "a set of skills and knowledges" (50) that must be acquired by each individual and constantly renewed (50).

While such emphasis on adopting class codes has recently lost ground to perspectives supporting students' own language practices,[2] in his recent afterward to Genesea M. Carter and William H. Thelin's (2017) edited collection, Zebroski (2017) again addresses the necessity for working-class students to acquire the normative trappings of the dominant class discourse: "To be sure, they will need to take up [Lynn Z.] Bloom's middle-class discourse, but—and it is a big but—that does not mean they must eliminate, eviscerate, or otherwise cast off their working-class culture or identities" (322). Here, once again, class is a matter of identity and language rather than materiality. Zebroski continues to maintain that discourse and performance remain crucial arbiters of class. Notably, in the same volume, Thelin and Carter (2007) outline a comparatively more heterogeneous model of class that nevertheless remains largely tied to the concept of social codes. As they contend, instructors must "develop an awareness of and appreciation for the diverse factors that shape the students who enter their classrooms" (4), acknowledging how exploitative relations between owners and workers construct "the class system" (5). However, they additionally note that the working and middle classes are often distinguished by the "elaborate codes" (8) through which students express themselves and by important differences in behavior among classes. Ultimately they defend "working-class pedagogy" (9) rooted in a "working-class ethos" (9), contending that the working class is ultimately a matter of identity rather than materiality and that this identity must be better attended to in order to support student success. As they note, "Much care must be incorporated into pedagogies and curricula so as to respond to our students' identities and our students' needs" (14).

This focus on student need speaks to an additional means of providing social mobility that emerged in force in the 1990s, namely increasing access and inclusivity. However, like the teaching of class codes, many proponents of this strategy frame class as overwhelmingly cultural, discursive, and identity-based rather than structural and have focused their pedagogical approaches accordingly. David Seitz (1998) explores how the perspectives of critical pedagogy have often favored dissensus and exploration of differences in identity in ways that neglect the perspectives of minorities and historically underserved populations. Steve Parks and Nick Pollard (2010) similarly ask how writing programs might "provide community support for working-class students in elite writing classrooms" (477). The justification for such support, however, is not in the material differences between working- and middle-class students but in differences in cultural perspectives. Working-class students, in their view, come from places "where occupations have a pre-hi-tech sound, such as truck driver or waitress" (477) and hence "often find their own voice and experiences elided or passed over" (477). Acknowledging that social mobility is increasingly elusive for low-income college students and that working-class students are progressively less represented in higher education, Mary Soliday (1999) similarly contends that solutions to these problems lie in greater inclusivity and institutional diversity: "If we are serious about sustaining diversity, then we must examine and challenge the barriers the academy places in the way of working class students" (737–38). Opposing remediation and assessment as potential barriers, Soliday instead advocates "mainstream[ing] basic writers with freshman students" (738).[3]

Notably, some critics have proposed alternative class models based in material conditions rather than discourse and identity. In his 2007 essay on class taxonomy, Marc Bousquet critiques Zebroski's "oversimplified versions of class relations" (316) and the way Zebroski "switches from discussing class relations as discourse to evaluating a rhetoric of class relations as an organizing tool" (316). Bousquet is particularly censorious of Zebroski's lack of engagement with Marxist and post-Marxist theory and his neglect of the material valence of social class, specifically noting that Zebroski overlooks "the steady proletarianization of intellectual workers" (318) and accordingly fails to consider the implications of this process for a performative theory of class. Jennifer Beech (2007) similarly critiques Zebroski for the way he "excludes the primary body of practitioners of first-year writing instruction" (294) and glosses the question of how such a group remains economically marginalized despite their education and obvious mastery of class codes.

Several additional composition theorists have also advanced theories of class that contest strictly cultural models and offer more expansive and ambitious solutions. Nancy Welch (2008) notably questions the identity-based construction of class and calls for the discipline to "rhetoricize social class to shift our definition of working class from a focus on cultural identity to a focus on one's available means for exercising decision-making power" (11). Tony Scott (2009) also addresses composition's deployment of class as "a social identity, an aspect of culture examined in isolation from the political economics of production" (110). Citing the field's aversion to the potential of class conflict—Zebroski's (2006a) stated objection to the class analysis of Marxist sociologist Erik Olin Wright rests on the grounds that Wright's model promotes an "us/ them" (546) relationship—Scott (2009) critiques the field's tendency to focus on "descriptions of dialects, habits of communication and consumption, and isolated instances of social embarrassment" (113). He additionally notes how such a view leads to a problematic model of writing education as cultural "embourgeoisement" rather than "as ongoing material *praxis* carried out by real people in real locales under real material terms" (117). Echoing Walter Benn Michaels's (2016) claim that "we like to talk about the differences we can appreciate, and we don't talk about the ones we can't" (6), Scott (2009) contends that class "is not genetically produced; it isn't something we celebrate with festivals and parades or give its own official month. . . . It is ultimately about unequal relations of power" (120).

To build on these critiques, I contend that Zebroski and similarly aligned critics are ultimately misconstruing class as a fundamentally rhetorical enterprise with consequences for material wealth and patterns of work rather than as an expression of material inequality with links, albeit uneven and inconsistent, to discourse. This is perhaps most clearly expressed in Zebroski's view of the role of discourse in transitioning away from the working class. He writes, "When we who are first generation college students . . . decided to leave working class culture and make the crossing to the university and the middle class culture of the professions, what sorts of language acts helped us imagine that action before it happened?" (2006a, 565). Here, Zebroski problematically suggests that enrolling in the university and entering the business world are themselves acts of transcending class because, presumably, the individual moves from one discursive class context to another. However, missing from this claim is any acknowledgment that such discursive moves may represent no *material* shift in one's class position, such as was the case with John Tormey (2009). Moreover, for Zebroski, the possibility of the move itself is discursive insofar as *imagining* such movement is an effectively discursive act involving the individual thinking beyond the bounds of the class discourses that have constructed them. Absent here as well is any regard for the structural constraints that hold individuals in particular class positions regardless of thought or discourse. His perspective, accordingly, fails to explain how education might contend with the *material* stagnation of social mobility for college graduates.

Several factors further trouble the solutions frequently presented by composition scholars. The first solution, that inequality can be amended through the teaching of cultural codes and discourses, underestimates the material conditions that lock individuals within economic brackets. In a recent study, Tim Bartik and Brad Hershbein found that a college degree "does not equalize the lifetime earnings of people from different economic backgrounds" (*New York Times*, May 23, 2018). In other words, while a college degree typically means a higher income for a graduate than they would have had with only a high-school diploma, for those not born into wealth, obtaining a college degree will do little to shift their class position or overall economic status. Troublingly, Bartik and Hershbein also report that a college education is least beneficial for racial minorities; on average, low-income African Americans who obtained a college degree remained in the lowest income bracket of college graduates. In a separate study, Hershbein (2016) found college graduates from families whose income was 185 percent over the federal poverty line earned substantially more than students whose family income was below this threshold, 33 percent more in graduates' early careers and 50 percent more in their late careers. While such a study admittedly does not examine graduates' mastery of class codes, it suggests exposure to the presumptively middle-class environment of higher education is not sufficient to equalize inequality for low-income students. In a more concerning statistic, a 2018 report from the US Census Bureau found that the poverty rate of college-educated people increased 0.3 percent between 2016 and 2017 (Fontenot et al. 2018, 11), bringing the total number of college graduates living in poverty to 3.6 million. While this group only represents around 1 percent of the US population, this statistic likewise suggests that, for many, the knowledge conferred by a college degree, and often the credential itself, is insufficient to overcome economic inequality.

The second major disciplinary argument, that improving inclusivity at the university promotes social mobility, among other goods, is also troubled by the exclusionary nature of contemporary institutions. To be sure, institutional elitism and social exclusion based on class, race, and other factors do indeed exist and contribute enormously to the alienation of minority and low-income students at prestigious universities.[4] However, current economic data suggest that inclusivity initiatives alone are unlikely to impact the broader problem of inequality. One reason for this is that low-income and working-class people are simply absent from elite schools (Leonhardt, *New York Times*, January 18, 2017). A survey conducted in 2017 concluded that at thirty-eight US colleges, "more students came from the top 1 percent of the income scale than from the entire bottom 60 percent" (Aisch et al., *New York Times*, January 18, 2018). The study additionally reported that while one in four of the wealthiest students in the United States attend an "elite college," defined as eighty of the most selective institutions, less than 0.5 percent of children from the poorest quintile of US families attend one. These numbers, notably, are diverging—the population of extremely wealthy students at top schools has steadily grown since 2002 (Aisch et al. 2018).

Evidence additionally suggests that a college degree, even from an elite university, is worth significantly less in the hands of those who are not white and wealthy. Sociologist S. Michael Gaddis (2015) reports that being a racial minority significantly diminishes the professional opportunities of college graduates from prestige schools (1453), with Black job candidates being hired at rates similar to graduates from less selective schools (1453). An additional study found that while the overall employment rate for college graduates declined between 1990 and 2018, minority college graduates faced substantially higher unemployment and underemployment than their white peers (Gould, Mokhiber, and Wolfe 2018). This is not at all to suggest compositionists should neglect serving disadvantaged students and revising grading methods to enact socially just practices to confront the racial and class prejudices imbedded in higher education (Inoue 2019), but rather to assert that the conditions of class and inequality are far more structural and obdurate than many composition scholars currently acknowledge and to suggest what we are doing is not enough.

TEACHING FOR SOCIAL CHANGE

My intervention of orienting students toward social justice through public-oriented pedagogy responds to the work of composition scholars in the areas of critical pedagogy, service learning, and the social turn. I specifically seek to build upon Welch's (2008) promotion of teaching working-class methods in the college writing classroom to combat neoliberal encroachment and her assertion that "though we can't call a strike or launch a social movement from a classroom, we can teach and learn the attitudes, relationships, and practices that are the preconditions for imagining oneself and others as participants in social policy making and agents of social change" (5). My turn to long-term solutions regarding inequality additionally responds to the field's theorization of service learning as a mode of practical engagement with publics and community partners, specifically Paula Mathieu's (2005) conception of "tactical" (xiv) service learning that rejects normative or instrumental conceptions and instead embraces the situated nature of service and its long-term potential for orienting students toward community engagement. As she writes, "A tactical orientation needs to be grounded in hope, not cast in naïve or passive terms, but hope as a critical, active, dialectical engagement between the insufficient present and possible, alternative futures" (xv). Building on this work, I suggest that public engagement, specifically in the form of service learning, has the capacity to interest and involve students in the conditions of inequality and to allow them to gain a practical introduction to the necessary task of combatting economic inequality in an age in which social mobility is increasingly unattainable.

I undertook this work in a recent undergraduate writing class specifically focused on issues of race, ethnicity, and class.[5] Working with the Carlson Center at the University of Washington, I developed a service-learning component in which each student was placed with a Seattle-area community partner—these included North Seattle Boys & Girls Club, East African Community Services, Aki Kurose Middle School, the Prison Scholar Fund, and others. These community partners were selected for their work with minority groups and because of their ability to offer students opportunities to engage in tutoring, writing, and community literacy in ways that would complement the course's writing focus. Negotiating my own misgivings about higher education's limited ability to combat rising inequality and declining social mobility, the course design reflected my attempts to better respond to these conditions by retreating from the common narrative of literacy, writing, and critique as unequivocally empowering enterprises. Rather, the course chiefly presented these goods as capable of supporting students' reflection on social issues and sustaining long-term social justice work and social change.

The first unit, prior to the start of service learning, was devoted to developing a critical framework to help students understand their subsequent service and to provide them with an opportunity for personal reflection on the issues of race, ethnicity, inequality, and social class. I assigned Malcolm X's (1994) speech "The Black Revolution," asking students to draft an essay considering the leader's call for Black revolution, a call that speculates on the possibility of "a revolution without violence or bloodshed" (56–57). I asked the students to reflect on the question "What, if anything, has changed with respect to racial inequality since Malcolm X's speech?" and to consider the extent to which his call "remain[s] relevant for the contemporary world." In starting the course with such an assignment, I sought to engage students in the ongoing crisis of racial, social, and economic inequity that predominated during, and indeed after, the Trump administration and to prompt them to consider how these issues were present in their own lives in order to elicit reflective writing connecting individual experiences of discrimination with larger social forces. In doing so, I sought to invite students to share a variety of experiences that could form the basis of a comparative conversation.

As students began volunteering, the writing I assigned shifted toward the analysis of community partners and students' service learning experiences in ways meant to foreground the value of long-term work and community partnership. In addition to writing weekly reflections, students wrote two longer essays in which they drew links between their service learning and the broader theoretical concerns of the course. One assignment asked students to research and write about the history, purpose, and day-to-day operation of their community partners. I prompted students to consider the work of the organizations through the framework of race, ethnicity, and economic inequality. Here, I again asked students to consider the expansive utility of long-term social justice work, specifically focusing on how community-based organizations can support underserved communities. Adding further nuance to students' analyses, another assignment asked them to employ the concept of intersectionality developed in their reading of Yen Le Espiritu's (2012) essay "Race, Class, and Gender in Asian America" to analyze their community partners and the community they serve. I specifically encouraged the students to consider class as they investigated how minority populations in the Seattle area are marked by startling inequality and marginalization. Informed by Scott's (2009) notion of class as "unequal relations of power" (120), the assignment encouraged students to interrogate the subordinating and materially disempowering aspects of social class in local communities. More broadly, the assignment aimed to press students to think critically about the structural conditions of late capitalism in which those who occupy multiple minority groups often experience compounded marginalization. However, the assignment was also intended to encourage students to reevaluate some of their preexisting assumptions regarding links among race, ethnicity, gender, ability, sexuality, and class and to reorient them towards more pluralistic and inclusive modes of thinking. Also undergirding this assignment was an attempt to foster the kinds of nuanced self-critique Mathieu (2005) suggests are necessary for improving one's tactical service: "admitting one's failures, seeing one's work as insufficient" (19).

The course concluded with a two-thousand-word essay asking students to consider their work throughout the quarter through the framework of resistance. Drawing from bell hooks's (1992a, 1992b) essays "Talking Back" and "marginality as a site of resistance," essays that present resistance as the refusal to be silent and marginality as imbued with power and the potential for solidarity, students were asked to utilize class discussions, readings, service-learning experiences, and contemporary events to support an argument defending the greatest contemporary threat to marginalized people and the most effective means of combatting it. I also asked the students to consider an attendant set of questions: How are minority populations disempowered? What are the effects of this marginalization? What kinds of action are possible from marginal positions? In choosing this topic, I sought to bring the course to a close by orienting students towards long-term social change, specifically asking them to consider how their community partners and their own service learning work could be understood as engaging in resistance against various forms of inequality.

Students produced impressively sophisticated analyses that acknowledged their own capacity to intervene in injustice through public work. In one paper, a Latinx student wrote about the systematic oppression and silencing of minorities, conditions, he noted, he had previously been largely inattentive to beyond his own ethnic group. An international student similarly discussed how the suppression of minorities could be combatted though solidarity and the strengthening of communities based in common interest, work he observed in a youth-development program. Another student focused on the threat of forced assimilation and the loss of cultural identity, specifically in ELL programs for the children of immigrants. She noted how multicultural educational policies and translingual approaches to ELL, like those she practiced in her work with an elementary school, could combat the trend of minority populations losing their cultural identities.

In thinking critically about their service learning as part of an ongoing, community-based initiative against inequality, students left the class understanding they could play a meaningful part in social change. Nevertheless, these modest successes in no way offset the distressing reality that most low-income students, particularly those belonging to minority groups, are now effectively unable to change their own life circumstances through education. While scholars can develop pedagogical and assessment practices to support underprivileged students at universities to which they've already been admitted and improve students' facility with writing, the hardening of economic inequality increasingly entails that college teachers cannot redress difference simply by preparing students to compete for jobs. For this task, far more expansive and creative initiatives are needed.

CONCLUSION

As I argue throughout this chapter, composition has struggled to offer solutions to people like Tormey (2019), for whom a college education was not enough to allow passage into the middle class. For many compositionists, the solutions lie in overly sanguine notions of class and social mobility that presume the capacity of a college education, and training in writing specifically, to change graduates' economic positions. Zebroski and others, as I detail, have pursued solutions that theorize the potential of individual agency to promote economic mobility. While these solutions, to their credit, attempt to think beyond the material bind many underprivileged students find themselves in today, they nevertheless neglect the impediments to climbing the economic ladder. For Marsh (2011), the crux of the problem lies in society's flawed framing of education as the great social equalizer, a role it cannot possibly fulfill given the pervasiveness of inequality. But while I believe Marsh is right to question the faith we have placed in the university to drive social mobility and to look for solutions beyond pedagogy, my contention in this chapter is to suggest pedagogy still has a valuable part to play in preparing students to seek the social changes necessary to support low-income and minority students. I focus specifically on the intransigent problem of economic inequality and the necessity of promoting public methods, a mild rebuke of those in the field who continue to insist the composition classroom remains capable of elevating the life chances of some of the most underprivileged students. I argue, rather, that composition scholars must heed the call of the field's more economically engaged voices and orient students to ambitious and forward-thinking forms of public engagement. One difficult problem this raises, however, is resistance. When tasked with this work, privileged students may balk at being asked to invest themselves in redressing conditions that have benefitted them. Moreover, focusing on social change rather than more immediate "needs" may feel like a bait-and-switch for underprivileged students who hope to obtain bankable skills in their college courses.

My response to this problem is twofold. First, as I suggest throughout this chapter, orienting the classroom to redressing inequality in the long term need not neglect writing education and the inclusion of underprivileged students. In working with community partners and analyzing inequality, students can grow as writers and be well positioned for subsequent academic and professional work, arguably more so because of their negotiation of the real-world challenges presented by service learning. Such a study of inequality and social change may also have the additional benefit of helping students navigate the unequal scenes of the university and the workplace. Second, the enormity of economic inequality and the clear inability of the university to address it demands acknowledgment and intervention. While students may prefer a course that *feels* supportive of class mobility, and indeed may feel thrust into the work of social justice and social change, our inability to offer many students what they enter our classes to obtain, a middle-class life, means addressing this problem is critical. As I have suggested, one possible solution is teaching this crisis, orienting our students to the problem of inequality and convincing them of its consequence.

NOTES

1. Notably, a modest number of composition scholars have indeed interrogated disciplinary assumptions regarding educational value. Harvey J. Graff (2010) has questioned the arguments that have long correlated literacy and social mobility: "There is little evidence that increasing or high levels of literacy result directly in major economic advances" (640). Chase Bollig (2015) has also explored the issue of educational value, acknowledging that the economic conditions of contemporary higher education—namely debt, precarity, and greater socioeconomic stratification (158)—trouble the economic success of graduates. He counters, however, that value, broadly conceived, may follow from the cultivation of critical "citizen-worker[s]" (168) who are "conscious of how power relations (racial, gendered, classed, abled) bear on their understanding of themselves in rhetorical workplaces" (168).

2. While this conversation is explicitly concerned with social class, it converges with parallel disciplinary conversations on the interrelation of race, ethnicity, language, and class in the context of teaching writing. Steve Parks (2013) explores these issues in *Class Politics: The Movement for the Students' Right to their Own Language.* Carmen Kynard (2007) notably takes Parks to task for depoliticizing Black language. As she notes, the purpose of the movement "is to fully inhabit the little bit of theoretical space that we have left to enact what Smitherman was advocating through SRTOL . . . that black styles are revolutionary . . . they move black working-class audiences to new levels of social awareness, solidarity, and political activism" (379).

3. Pegeen Reichert Powell questions institutional motives behind retention initiatives. Contending that complex personal and economic conditions inform students' lives in ways that make efforts purely grounded in retention not necessarily beneficial to students, she advocates adopting pedagogical methods that "propel students into writerly behavior beyond the classroom" (2014, 386).

4. As Anthony Abraham Jack (2019) contends, low-income, minority students at elite colleges who attended underfunded public high schools, a group he terms "doubly disadvantaged" (11), face significant obstacles as they attempt to acclimate to the university (28).

5. As a lecturer with the University of Washington's Interdisciplinary Writing Program (IWP), I teach writing courses "linked" with large lecture courses in numerous departments across the university. The writing course I describe in this chapter is such a course and was linked with a lecture in the Department of American Ethnic Studies and utilized course readings from the lecture.

REFERENCES

Banks, Adam J. 2011 *Digital Griots: African American Rhetoric in a Multimedia Age.* Carbondale: Southern Illinois University Press.

Bartholomae, David. 1985. "Inventing the University." In *When a Writer Can't Write: Studies in Writer's Block and Other Composing Problems,* edited by Mike Rose, 134–65. New York: Guilford.

Beech, Jennifer. 2007. "So Much Depends Upon the Route." *JAC* 27 (1/2): 290–303.

Bloom, Lynn Z. 1996. "Freshman English as a Middle-Class Enterprise." *College English* 58 (6): 654–75.

Bollig, Chase. 2015. "'Is College Worth It?': Arguing for Composition's Value with the Citizen-Worker." *College Composition and Communication* 67 (2): 150–72.

Borkowski, David. 2004. "'Not Too Late to Take the Sanitation Test': Notes of a Non-Gifted Academic from the Working Class." *College Composition and Communication* 56 (1): 94–123.

Bousquet, Marc. 2007. "White-Collar Proletariat: The Case of Becky Meadows." *JAC* 27 (1/2): 303–29.

Carter, Genesea M., and William H. Thelin, eds. 2017. *Class in the Composition Classroom: Pedagogy and the Working Class.* Logan: Utah State University Press.

Coogan, David. 2006. "Service Learning and Social Change: The Case for Materialist Rhetoric." *College Composition and Communication* 57 (4): 667–93.

Espiritu, Yen Le. 2012. "Race, Class, and Gender in Asian America." In *South Asian Feminisms,* edited by Ania Loomba and Ritty A. Lukose, 135–41. Durham, NC: Duke University Press.

Fontenot, Kayla, Jessica Semega, and Melissa Kollar. 2018. "Income and Poverty in the United States." US Census Bureau, Current Population Reports. https://www.census.gov/content/dam/Census/library/publications/2018/demo/p60-263.pdf.

Gaddis, S. Michael. 2015. "Discrimination in the Credential Society: An Audit Study of Race and College Selectivity in the Labor Market." *Social Forces* 93 (4): 1451–79.

Graff, Harvey J. 2010. "The Literacy Myth at Thirty." *Journal of Social History* 43 (3): 635–61.

Gos, Michael W. 1995. "Overcoming Social Class Markers: Preparing Working Class Students for College." *The Clearing House* 69 (1): 30–34.

Gould, Elise, Zane Mokhiber, and Julia Wolfe. 2018. "Class of 2018." Economic Policy Institute, May 10. epi.org/publication/class-of-2018-college-edition/.

Habibi, Nader. 2015. "America Has an Overeducation Problem." *New Republic*, December 2. https://newrepublic.com/article/124943/america-overeducation-problem.

Harris, Joseph. 2000. "Meet the New Boss, Same as the Old Boss: Class Consciousness in Composition." *College Composition and Communication* 52 (1): 43–68.

Hershbein, Brad. 2016. "A College Degree Is Worth Less If You Are Raised Poor." Brookings, Feb. 19. https://www.brookings.edu/blog/social-mobility-memos/2016/02/19/a-college-degree-is-worth-less-if-you-are-raised-poor/.

hooks, bell. 1992a. "marginality as a site of resistance." In *Out There: Marginalization and Contemporary Cultures,* edited by Russell Ferguson, Martha Gever, Trinh T. Minh-ha, and Cornel West, 441–44. Boston: MIT Press.

hooks, bell. 1992b. "Talking Back." In *Out There: Marginalization and Contemporary Cultures,* edited by Russell Ferguson, Martha Gever, Trinh T. Minh-ha, and Cornel West, 337–40. Boston: MIT Press.

Inoue, Asao. 2019. *Labor-Based Grading Contracts: Building Equity and Inclusion in the Compassionate Writing Classroom.* Fort Collins, CO: WAC Clearinghouse.

Jack, Anthony Abraham. 2019. *The Privileged Poor: How Elite Colleges Are Failing Disadvantaged Students.* Cambridge, MA: Harvard University Press.

Kahn, Seth, William Lalicker, and Amy Lynch-Biniek. 2017. *Contingency, Exploitation, and Solidarity: Labor and Action in English Composition.* Fort Collins. CO: WAC Clearinghouse.

Kynard, Carmen. 2007. "'I Want to Be African': In Search of a Black Radical Tradition/African-American Vernacularized Paradigm for 'Students' Right to Their Own Language,' Critical Literacy, and 'Class Politics.'" *College English* 69 (4): 360–90.

Lazere, Donald. 1992. "Back to Basics: A Force for Oppression or Liberation?" *College English* 54 (1): 7–21.

LeCourt, Donna. 2006. "Performing Working-Class Identity in Composition: Toward a Pedagogy of Textual Practice." *College English* 69 (1): 30–51.

Mack, Nancy. 2007. "Being the Namer or the Named: Working-Class Discourse Conflicts." *JAC* 27 (1/2): 329–50.

Malcolm X. 1994. "The Black Revolution." In *Malcolm X Speaks: Selected Speeches and Statements*, edited by George Breitman, 45–57. New York: Grove.

Marsh, John. 2011. *Class Dismissed: Why We Cannot Teach or Learn Our Way Out of Inequality.* New York: Monthly Review.

Mathieu, Paula. 2005. *Tactics of Hope: The Public Turn in English Education.* Portsmouth, NH: Heinemann.

McClure, Randall, Dayna V. Goldstein, and Michael A. Pemberton, eds. 2017. *Labored: The State(ment) and Future of Work in Composition.* Anderson, SC: Parlor.

Michaels, Walter Benn. 2016. *The Trouble with Diversity: How We Learned to Love Identity and Ignore Inequality.* New York: Picador.

Parks, Steve. 2013. *Class Politics: The Movement for the Students' Right to their Own Language.* 2nd ed. Anderson, SC: Parlor.

Parks, Steve, and Nick Pollard. 2010. "Emergent Strategies for an Established Field: The Role of Worker-Writer Collectives in Composition and Rhetoric." *College Composition and Communication* 61 (3): 476–509.

Piketty, Thomas. 2020. *Capital and Ideology.* Translated by Arthur Goldhammer. Cambridge, MA: Harvard University Press.

Roth, Gary. 2019. *The Educated Underclass: Students and the Promise of Social Mobility.* London: Pluto.

Reichert Powell, Pegeen. 2014. *Retention and Resistance: Writing Instruction and Students Who Leave.* Boulder: University Press of Colorado.

Scott, Tony. 2009. *Dangerous Writing: Understanding the Political Economy of Composition.* Logan: Utah State University Press.

Seitz, David. 1998. "Keeping Honest: Working-Class Students, Difference, and Rethinking the Critical Agenda in Composition." In *Under Construction: Working at the Intersections of Composition Theory, Research, and Practice*, edited by Christine Farris and Chris Anson, 65–78. Logan: Utah State University Press.

Soliday, Mary. 1999. "Class Dismissed." *College English* 61 (6): 731–41.

Stenberg, Shari. 2015. *Repurposing Composition: Feminist Interventions for a Neoliberal Age.* Logan: Utah State University Press.

Tinberg, Howard. 2014. "2014 CCCC Chair's Address: The Loss of the Public." *College Composition and Communication* 66 (2): 327–41.

Thelin, William H., and Genesea M. Carter. 2017. Introduction to *Class in the Composition Classroom: Pedagogy and the Working Class*, edited by Genesea M. Carter and William H. Thelin, 3–15. Logan: Utah State University Press.

Tormey, John. 2019. "Known Assailants." *The Baffler*, January. https://thebaffler.com/salvos/known-assailants-tormey.

Welch, Nancy. 2008. *Living Room: Teaching Writing in a Privatized World.* Portsmouth, NH: Heinemann.

Welch, Nancy, and Tony Scott. 2016. *Composition in the Age of Austerity.* Logan: Utah State University Press.

Zebroski, James Thomas. 2006a. "Social Class as Discourse: Mapping the Landscape of Class in Rhetoric and Composition." *JAC* 26 (3/4): 513–83.

Zebroski, James Thomas. 2006b. "Social Class as Discourse: The Construction of Subjectivities in English." In *Identity Papers: Literacy and Power in Higher Education*, edited by Bronwyn T. Williams, 19–28. Logan: Utah State University Press.

Zebroski, James Thomas. 2017. "An Afterword to *Class in the Composition Classroom*: First-Year Writing as a Social Class Enterprise." In *Class in the Composition Classroom: Pedagogy and the Working Class*, edited by Genesea M. Carter and William H. Thelin, 320–35. Logan: Utah State University Press.

3

DESCONOCIMIENTO
A Process of Epistemological Unknowing through Rhetorical Nepantla

Iris D. Ruiz

A NEPANTLERX IN ACTION

My psyche resembles a bordertown. When I enter into acts of academic writing, I feel I'm entering into a crossroads. I strive to decolonize while engaging in acts of colonial epistemic violence. I resist erasure of my difference. Yet, I'm pushed to defer to normatives while striving to communicate the differences I encounter without seeming "abnormal." What this process feels like for someone like me, a Chicana (Indigena/Mexicana/Latina/Americana), is like crossing the border: the border of consciousness operates like a rough-edged mental schism with peaks that jaggedly slide back and forth through rules, limitations, conventions, identities, experiences, traumas, languages, discourses, and histories while hitting bricks and jumping barbed wire along the way and between transitions. There is violence that takes place. There's no refuge for me between these spaces—no words, no concepts, no not in English, no not even in Spanish. So, I embrace the contradictions, and I imagine comfort in these in-between spaces. If I imagine a comfort, I can transcend the violence of these constraints. If I can vocalize what it feels like, I make this process of navigating differences materialize and represent my reality through discursive possibilities. This is *nepantla.* I have found comfort here. Here, I can breathe in the crossroads of contradiction.

I am Chicana. It's not a bad word. I am both European and Indigenous. I have a genocidal past in my blood. I have trauma in my DNA. I am native. My ancestors resisted violence, colonization, dispossession, modernization, and exploitation of their lands. In "The Coloniality of Gender," María Lugones (2010a) reminds us that "women of Color feminists have made clear what is revealed in terms of violent domination and exploitation once the epistemological perspective focuses on the

https://doi.org/10.7330/9781646421732.c003

intersection of these categories" (369). We must embrace contradictions as Chicanas. European colonizers had no choice but to dehumanize and differentiate themselves from those of a mixed race or not of pure blood (Lugones 2010a; Ríos 2016). Differentiations occurred through both religion and skin color and resulted in both ideological and material consequences, further justifying the colonization of the Americas (Ruiz 2016a). Part of this colonial mission based upon differentiations, whether real or imposed, was rhetorical in that new terms were created to account for new peoples, cultures, and material gains. The naming of peoples, places, and things gave rise to a new colonial order that was premised on consolidating power for Europe—in this case Spain. To ensure this consolidation, rhetorics of religion, blood, and skin color were employed to impose broad classification schemas that had brutal moral, economic, ecological, material, and political consequences (Lugones 2010b; Quijano 2000).

In reference to the rhetorical and material effects of coloniality as a process of dialogic and dialectical intersubjective experience of domination on occupied territories, Lugones (2010b) notes that while European colonials presupposed that they encountered "free real estate" when they "discovered" the New World, she notes that "the global, capitalist, colonial, modern system of power that Anibal Quijano characterizes as beginning in the sixteenth century in the Americas and enduring until today met not a world to be formed, a world of empty minds and evolving animals" (747). On the contrary, colonials met existing flora and fauna in this area: humans, animals, elements, and deciduousness and different philosophical and ontological matrices of established knowledges belonging to pre-Hispanic cultures, but they were not called this by the Indigenous inhabitants; they were named thus by the colonists. Centuries of oppression began in this manner. Why does this matter? This is what I write back to un-know my oppression.

Oppressive circumstances called for those who bore the "mark of difference," like me and my ancestors, to experience an erasure—an imposed physical (redistribution and gutting of land), spiritual (mass Christianization), and mental amnesia. This amnesia occurred through the purposeful erasure and destruction of previous social structures, the devaluation of those structures, and the resulting negation of those structures: think cosmology and a rhetorically grounded, Nahuatl holistic view of nature—an advanced ecological understanding of the universe, time, the elements, for example, and even the advanced mathematical, medicinal, and psychological language (Léon-Portilla 1990) of previous civilizations and their histories, which also includes the burning of treatises and intricate documentation of precolonial educational systems. As a way to confront this traumatic existence through writing, I occupy the space of a *nepantlerx*—a space of the disenchanted—and I simultaneously seek to know what was imposed upon me and to un-know at the same time. I have become a master navigator of *desconocimiento* (the feeling of being lost in the unknown). I've found comfort here.

For many Chicanxs, performing rhetorical acts of a nepantlerx demonstrates why subaltern narratives are necessary and will endure. Narratives for the subaltern are always subversive and sometimes decolonial. It is not only through narrative that the decolonial consciousness can speak (Baca 2008) through spaces of colonial erasure, and narrative means more than a genre of the personal with no research foundation. Writing about the decolonial turn and the vulnerability of knowledge and shifting epistemologies, Gerrie Snyman (2015) states, "A decolonisation of knowledge is needed whereby the epistemic perspective, cosmologies, and insights of critical thinking from the subalternized racial/ethnic/ sexual spaces and bodies of what is termed 'the Global South' are taken seriously" (267). This chapter is dedicated to being taking seriously while demonstrating how I engage a decolonial narrative, also known as *rhetorical nepantla*. I'm writing this chapter because nepantla rhetoric has not been a focus common in rhetorical theory classes in composition and rhetoric, and Gloria Anzaldúa has only been operating on the margins of "colored/subaltern rhetorics" often found at the end of syllabi for rhetorical theory courses. I won't go into the specifics of this work, as it is discussed in my book *Reclaiming Composition* (Ruiz 2016b), which problematizes the placement of "people of color scholarship" (146–47) within rhet/comp (Anzaldúa 2012; Baca 2008; Keating 2006; Licona and Chávez 2015; Lugones 1992, 2010a, 2010b; Moraga and Anzaldúa 198).

In this chapter, I demonstrate how I've engaged in acts of academic writing as a nepantlerx. Through the process of rhetorical nepantla and as a nepantlerx (Anzaldúa 2012), I explore what it means to be a nepantlerx, one who actively lives, breathes, and thrives in the margins of spaces of the forgotten and the overtly seen, in this case as a Chicana navigating the territories of mainstream, white hegemonic, colonial rhetorical archetypes. Last, I act as a nepantlerx who engages in "deep reflections [that] move us along through a journey towards self-awareness, enabling us to maintain what is useful and discard what is problematic" (DeNicolo and Gónzalez 2015, 113). I also demonstrate how using nepantlerx rhetoric provides a space to bridge the gap between theoretical junctions, such as in *Decolonizing Rhetoric and Composition: New Latinx Keywords for Theory and Pedagogy* (Ruiz and

Sánchez 2016), in which Latinx authors demonstrate various acts of nepantla by engaging the in-between space that resides in the interstices of unproblematized and common keywords such as *race* and *writing* and decolonial delinking, a.k.a. decoloniality. This collection is an active example of an engagement with epistemological possibilities brought upon by entering into nepantla space (Mignolo 2000, 2).

CONOCIMIENTO AND NEPANTLERXES: KNOWING AND UN-KNOWING

We think we know things because we all went to school. In the United States we are taught US history in K–12 education, but what we learn, if we go beyond the limited images etched into our psyches as European history tied to the beginning of enlightened, philosophical thought, is that History is a rhetorical illusion for both the colonized and the colonizer. It operates on the presupposition of linearity and myth (Foucault 1969; Ruiz 2016b; Trouillot 1995) and as one digs deeper into pre-Hispanic histories, for example, one becomes more aware of what one does not know. However, even though the contingency of historical accounts might be easy enough to accept as the field has shown through its various Octalogs I (Berlin et al. 1988), II (Enos et al.1997), and III (Agnew et al. 2011), one must go a step further to consider the consequences of not being a part of a story, especially if it's the story everyone is taught. The story of progress as told in US history classes, for example, is a very enticing and fantastical story Damián Baca alludes to in his book *Mestiz@ Scripts, Digital Migrations, and the Territories of Writing* (2008). Such stories create archetypal figures such as the heroine, the villain, and the trickster, just to name three (Jung 1959, 4–8).

Another not so obvious archetype that is a result of the same linear and progressive narrative of the East to West trajectory is one I occupy as a colonized Chicana who has also been archetyped as a student and a scholar of color who studies "colored scholarship," a.k.a. marginalized scholarship. One must only comb the databases of rhet/comp journals and books to realize how marginal decolonial theory is and what and whom it engages. I've often wondered about the consequences of challenging these rhetorical constructs and divisions and their accompanying archetypes. I know I've liked the opaqueness of poststructuralism and the possibilities it opened up for me, but why? Well, I was already navigating the academy as a bicultural and bilingual Chicana, and theories that provided a door into disrupting canonical texts are my oxygen in colonial spaces. I cannot be contained within static structures.

Because I am a writer of color, poststructural theories opened the door for me, but decolonial theory has provided the possibility for an epistemological rupture of the territorial and colonial nature of the field, one that stems largely from an East to West Eurocentric vantage point. In doing so, I have had to confront what it means to "enter" into a discursive space that has been hostile to my own history, or my story, if you will. We all have a story, and good stories are always welcomed in most circles, but in our field, only certain stories are paid attention to and gain mainstream currency, and in these rigid disciplinary stories, materialized through legitimized publication venues, I am often cast as what I call a "colonial archetype," an "outsider looking in." I've had to learn how to survive in the margins of academia.

Surviving by being a nepantlerx is an act of decolonial intervention. More specifically, it is an act of epistemic delinking and disobedience (Mignolo 2009). I've successfully delinked from mainstream histories of rhet/comp, for example, and I've exposed how the field has predicated its burgeoning disciplinary status upon Eurocentric histories tied to literary and educational histories—a colonial-settler venture. I became a nepantlerx by treading both physical geographical borders and figural epistemological margins, and, contrary to the critiques of decolonial gazing as creating new vantage points of analysis or as uncritically creating centers of hegemonic vantage points, one is only able to expose such epistemological dis/junctions from spaces in-between the colonizer and the colonized. A nepantlerx feels at home in this space. Nepantla allows one to both know and un-know—to confront restrictive colonial archetypes, to displace them in an effort to "disidentify," or *desconocer*, the ties that bind one into a fictional colonial story in a never-ending thread of limiting archetypes referred to below as "models of identity." AnaLouise Keating (2006), borrowing from Anzaldúa's musings and writings about nepantla, describes it as follows:

> During nepantla, our worldviews and self-identities are shattered. Nepantla is painful, messy, confusing, and chaotic; it signals unexpected, uncontrollable shifts, transitions, and changes. Nepantla hurts!!!! But nepantla is also a time of self-reflection, choice, and potential growth—what Anzaldúa describes as opportunities to "see through" restrictive cultural and personal scripts. (9)

And to be a nepantlerx basically means knowing nepantla and how to "do" nepantla. The *x* signifies no gendered boundaries.

I take many of my narrative cues from the nepantla state occupied by Anzaldúa, a nepantlerx who doesn't receive enough attention in composition studies and rhetorical theory. Damián Baca has referenced her work heavily in his book *Mestiz@ Scripts* (2008). In his book, Baca defines mestiz@ as a fusion of "cultures [that] emerged across the Western Hemisphere in the late fifteenth century as a consequence of 'mestizaje', the fusion of bloodlines between American Indians and Spanish Iberian conquerors under colonial situations" (2).

In his book, Baca notes that in *Borderlands/La Frontera: The New Mestiza* (1987), Anzaldúa "advances her new mestiza consciousness as one that is 'perpetually transitioning between worldviews (cultural, economic, spiritual, gendered, and erotic), mestiza consciousness offers the possibility of 'thinking and writing from' the intersection of Mesoamerican and Western perspectives, where their collective expressions merge" (Baca 2008, 5), not for the practice of complete assimilation but for the process of true syncretism—a syncretism that inhabits decolonial definitions of those terms, names, and phenomena that attempt to define colonials by limiting their ability to be epistemically disobedient. Nepantlerxes operate in the interstices of syncretic processes.

Anzaldúa, although underacknowledged in rhet/comp, is a master nepantlerx and carried the notion of nepantla—syncretic negotiation—into the United States: a colonialist society. As I enter into the space of the nepantlerx and accompany Anzaldúa's practice, I must acknowledge that a nepantlerx would betray her practice if she caved to the colonial textual practice that asks her to identify a thread of texts that will give her a legitimate disciplinarity identity, one characterized by mainly white voices, though caving exposes the coloniality of scholarly publications and imperial scholarship practices (Delgado 1984). Such an imperial scholarship practice risks the imposition of a violent, colonial, epistemic trauma that corroborates with the earlier experience mentioned above regarding the destruction of histories and knowledges associated with the native Mexicans or Aztecs of Tenochtítlan. Through occupying the space of nepantla, exposure of epistemological hegemony occurs through the process of unknowing and delinking. This is *desconocimiento*: unknowing to re-know and re-member.

From a path of desconocimiento, one sees what is reified by not only publication practices but also by educational institutions—colonial institutions of normalization (Ortego y Gasca and Ruiz 2017), or as the French would call it, the *ecolé normale* (Fitzgerald 2001; Ruiz 2016b)— embedded in colonial and Eurocentric matrices of power (Mignolo 2011). Nepantlerxes, in the spaces of colonial history, see that US schools have served to create, maintain, and disseminate normal behavior; early land-grant institutions were called *normal schools*. Publication practices are no different (Ruiz 2017).

As a nepantlerx seeking to displace scholastic hegemony at the expense of colonized bodies and bodies of knowledge—places where I often don't see myself—I'm hyperaware when I am performing rhetorical moves of legitimacy by citing Europeans. It is only through the practice of nepantla that a nepantlerx can fuse the action of both knowing and unknowing simultaneously.

On one side of the nepantla state, the side of the Chicana rhet/comp academic situated within a canonical, disciplinary history of poststructuralists, I acknowledge that in 1987, Linda Brodkey, my late graduate school mentor, published *Academic Writing as Social Practice.* Brodkey called herself a Foucauldian who very much believed in the power of language to disrupt oppressive effects of language associated with "isms" such as racism, classism, and sexism, and as such she believed in language as a vehicle to create consciousness. She believed language, in this case Standard English, was tied to its accompanying ideological discourses (Berlin 1982; Pennycook 1994) embedded in institutionalized power structures interested in keeping current colonial relations intact (read: Eurocentric hegemony as postulated by Samir Amin [2010]). In her book, Brodkey (1987) cites Michel Foucault (1969) from his famous text *The Archaeology of Knowledge.* I quote Brodkey and Foucault at length because one must first know in order to un-know:

> "Words and things" is the entirely serious title of a problem; it is the ironic title of a work that modifies its own form, displaces its own data, and reveals, at the end of the day, a quite different task. A task that consists of not—of no longer—treating discourses as groups of signs (signifying elements referring to contents or representations) but as practices that *systematically form the objects of which they speak.* Of course, discourses are composed of signs, but what they *do* refer to *more* than the use of signs to designate things. It is this *more* that renders them irreducible to the language (*langue*) and to speech. It is this "more" that we must reveal and describe. (Brodkey 108; emphasis added)

Within Brodkey's chapter, she uses this quote to foreground a discussion on the material effects of discourse in efforts to "create and sustain a reality in the words they use" (108). She claims, "Materialism suggests that it is the potential for social action in language interactions, the sheer desire to critique and change an unsatisfying social reality, that brings people to speech and writing" (109). People use language to alter reality. As a discursive, decolonial nepantlerx, I can do the same.

On the other side, my nepantla process of un-knowing builds upon Brodkey's position that writing creates worlds, and those of us who love to read know this well. This side offers readers a way to escape in a moment's notice into alternative realities, possibly delving into a storm where kings desire to colonize the savage of the island, as in Shakespeare's *The Tempest* (2015). In this play, the archetype of the savage, Caliban, resembles the Indigenous of colonized spaces who are regarded as savages and barbarians both in fictional plays such as this one and through nonfiction accounts of conquest such as that written by Bartolome de las Casas (Ruiz 2016a). Within and through performative texts and historical treatises, it can be said that a colonized reality, also known through one's consciousness of being or ontological existence, is woven through discursive threading (a.k.a. nepantla) and ideological dispositions made concrete and material through conquest, violence, genocide, and annihilation of Indigenous cultures, tribes, knowledges, lands, and spiritual foundations. All of this constitutes the ways stories are embedded with power: they subject, classify, and limit the archetype of the savage, but the nepantlerx in me knows that in the process of unknowing, the opposite can take place.

Consciousness is a type of knowing, so to *desconocer* (un-know) for the colonized is to simultaneously see and unsee the colonial processes that manifest through material, physical, psychological, epistemological, and spiritual warfare and negation. In order to perform this process successfully, the nepantlerx sees that the colonizer must mentally create and regard the colonized as nothing, a thing, an animal: "[t]o colonize is to destroy and to create, a gratuitous act and an expression of an arbitrariness and terror of whim and desire" (Mbembe 2001, 188–89). This is where the nepantlerx resides: on the border of destruction/survival.

Fanon (2008, 2) gave this nothingness a name, the *zone of nonbeing*: "an extraordinary sterile and arid region, an utterly naked declivity . . . [a] descent into real hell" (268). I've sometimes heard my fellow colleagues of color say they feel they live in hell. Sometimes I agree with them. This world and this space of nepantla is painful; it is hostile to the colonized nonbeing. For in order to be, we must accept the colonizers' impositions of our ontological presence when we decide to "be" anywhere regarded as an institution of the nation-state (Anderson 1983). When we do decide to be, we tend to have to make a choice of which subjective archetypes to occupy, many of which have been dismissed as creations of identity politics—the scholar of color, the minoritized scholar, the marginal scholar, the scholar who works on antiracism, the scholar who works on social justice—and identity politics name but a few of these archetypal ontological possibilities for colonized scholars within the field of composition and rhetoric. The nepantlerx, however, learns how to navigate them well. These archetypes can also be referred to as *racialized expectations*, as there are those who do "race work" and those who do "empirical research." It is often a struggle to break free of this type of epistemological branding, which has received harsh criticism lately due to an increasing backlash against identity politics work (Azerrad 2019; Fukuyama 2018).

NEPANTLA AND THE PROCESS OF RE-MEMBERING

I have chosen to do "race work" and practice decoloniality. In doing so, I have engaged in multidisciplinary work. Some of this work has materialized as a process of historical recovery I refer to in this chapter as a process of re-membering my psyche, my spirit, and my identity. What I have to re-member is that out of colonial necessity, Europeans linguistically and rhetorically constructed newly conquered Indigenous tribes as ungodly, backwards, and uncivilized. These constructions were inseparable from the physical features of the newly conquered tribes. The "brown people" became those to be enslaved and controlled, while the white people became God's chosen people who controlled, converted, and exploited the brown folk (Ruiz 2016a). This rhetorically based social construction created an initial concept of race (Chou 2017), which has now become naturalized by scientific rhetoric in our US hegemonic memory and has simultaneously produced material consequences. Michael Omi and Howard Winant (2015) argue that "race is a relatively modern phenomenon. When European explorers in the New World 'discovered' people who looked different than themselves, these 'natives' challenged their existing conceptions of the origins of the human species, and whether all could be considered in the same 'family of man'" (10). As a result, Europeans *experienced an extreme case of* cognitive dissonance, and their creation stories became questionable. Religious uncertainty for Europeans called for artificially imposed religious, humanist discursive distinctions between Europeans and natives. Europeans thought of themselves as children of God, while the natives were deemed ungodly, forced to be slaves, subjected to genocide, and denied property and political rights. Their humanity became disposable, as Europeans denied New World natives the right to be considered human beings with redeemable souls. At stake were not only the prospects for religious conversion but also the types of treatment to be accorded to the Indigenous people in the form of material consequences (Mignolo 2002; Quijano 2000).

In "The Enduring Enchantment: (Or the Epistemic Privilege of Modernity and Where to Go from Here)," Walter Mignolo (2002) calls this type of colonialist imposition of both the economic and intellectual realms a "geopolitical" organization of the world. He claims that through this type of organizational scheme, "the 'modern/colonial' world was founded and sustained through a geopolitical organization of the world that, in the last analysis, consisted of an ethnoracial foundation" (934). He also notes that

> in the sixteenth century race did not yet have the meaning it acquired in the eighteenth and nineteenth centuries. However, the racial classifications from the eighteenth century based on skin color rather than on blood purity cannot be understood without the former. The transformation from blood purity to skin color runs parallel to the transformation from the hegemony of religious discourses grounded in faith to the hegemony of secular discourses grounded in reason. (935)

As a nation-state, the United States was cleared by the sixteenth-century-induced geopolitical system of power relations, based on skin color and mixed religious myths such as blood purity, to enter into a system already positioned against the Other. This inherited positionality for Europeans presented a locale that already existed in automatic tension and resistance to the Other and gave way to the social construction of both the term "scholar of color" and the corresponding archetypes of the scholar of color. However, before Spanish and English colonialism, Indigenous tribes had their own educational systems and their own students and they were brown students because they were Indigenous students.

According to Miguel Léon-Portilla (1990), the Americas, before European colonization, had students because there were schools. These schools differed from how we might conceive of a university today, but they existed for the same purpose: to "norm" students into society and teach them about the importance of history and religion. However, since the alphabetic language had not yet entered into and tainted the cultures of Mesoamerica, these students/scholars were known as *momachtiani, momachti, momachtihquētl,* or *momachtiqui* in the Aztec language, Nahuatl. In the Aztec culture, schools were called *calmecacs* and *telpochcalli,* and their teachers were known as *telpochcaltins.* Through these two Aztec educational systems, the first for commoners and the second for Aztec nobility, teachers facilitated the momachti interaction with legal, military, and religious aspects of Aztec life. Calmecacs (schools) also gave their students the opportunity to learn intellectual subjects such as art, astronomy, astrology, genealogy, and history. However, the normalizing function of the calmecacs was given mostly to parents. In fact, parents and schools shared equally in the teaching of strength and self-control, the fundamental aspects that underpinned a person's character. The overall goal of the interaction between parents and telpochcaltins was to create a good-natured young man.

Calmecacs and *telpochcallies* introduced young people to the Aztec state's institutions and heavily emphasized respect for others and obedience to administrators, elders and priests. José de Acosta, a sixteenth-century Jesuit, said the Aztec educational system was so grounded and effective that "it should be used by the Spanish to introduce young people to Catholicism" (Acosta 2002, 374). Furthermore, Friar Bernadino de Sahagún (1985) proclaimed that the order and discipline imposed in Aztec schools was so impressive that after the conquest of Mexico in 1521, the destruction of Aztec educational philosophy at the hands of the Spanish left youths without respect for the new colonial system. The first educational institution founded after the conquest was Colegio de la Santa Cruz and was made of stones from the greatest of the Aztec pyramids, nowadays called the Templo Mayor. The Colegio was founded in 1536 and was used by Nahuas (Aztecs) of noble descent.

What this history proves is that students of color have a much longer history than that accorded to them by Western colonial understandings of students of color, in the oppressive sense, of the nineteenth through the twenty-first centuries. It also shows that Western, American exceptionalism is a rhetorical falsehood in service to colonialism. Educational systems in the United States have long sought to erase these facts from history books provided to students in middle and high schools in efforts to erase the history of students of color and the sense of historical accomplishments that may lead to empowerment and alternative ways of knowing and seeing the universe.

To illustrate this point further, I turn to Victor Villanueva's analysis of rhetorical exchanges between European religious figures such as Franciscans and Incan and Aztec philosophers in his essay "On the Rhetoric and Precedents of Racism" (1999). I do so because in the introduction to this essay, Villanueva recounts verbal exchanges that occurred between a Franciscan and an Incan philosopher to show that Incans did not understand the developmental mindset of the Franciscan, and that the European colonials' misunderstanding and intolerance of the Incan's "prolixity" of argumentation resulted in the theft of the Incans' gold, silver, and precious stones (646). Next, in a more developed and nuanced manner, Villanueva turns to an exchange among twelve Spanish Franciscans and Aztecs whose delegation consisted of a group of *tlamatinime*, or philosophers. Villanueva confirms what I have noted above—that somewhere between the ages of six and nine, young Aztecs "which might have included women" left their families to join the calmecac community. "There, they received a rigorous education based on discussions with teachers, or wise ones (Huehuetlatoli). The discussions will allow the young Aztecs to acquire the wisdom already known (momachtique), a wisdom which is to be rendered in the adequate word (in quali tlahtolli). This, then, was the Aztecan trivium, displayed in the rhetoric called the flower-and-song (in xochitl in cuicatl)" (Dussel 2013, 95–97, quoted in Villanueva 1999, 646).

What Villanueva is doing here is a practice of decolonial epistemic disobedience. He is turning the gaze of the Indigenous back on their colonizers with the use of Greco-Roman rhetorical devices in order to refute claims that Indigenous people were a people without a history and without a language, unworthy of the kingdom of God. In doing so, he calls the rhetorical device of the flower-and-song "the Aztec trivium" and continues his decolonial analysis of Aztec rhetorical practices.

The Greek understanding of trivium is referred to as the lower division of the seven liberal arts comprising grammar, rhetoric, and logic. Of course, the Aztecs would not have known of these terms because they did not use an alphabetical language and possessed a drastically different worldview. Nevertheless, the act of reclaiming rhetorical practices that have been undermined, burned, and devalued necessitates looking at these Indigenous rhetorical practices through the lens of Western terms that have been borrowed from a Greco-Roman understanding and language. Villanueva proceeds with his analysis and labels each portion of the Aztec/Spanish exchange with five terms: salutation and introduction, narratio, dispositio, refutatio (including authority, ideology, a worldview, and antiquity), and conclusio (647). In the end, Villanueva's analysis is telling of how even with the use of rhetorical devices and the necessary presence of a translator, there was a complete lack of communication between the Europeans and the Aztecs. He states, "No multiculturalism there, no cultural hybrid possible, though some try to reclaim the Incan or Aztecan, try hard to be more than the Eurocentric criollo of Latin America" (647). Interestingly, the "trying" he refers to above is exactly what I am attempting to do in this portion of this chapter, trying to reclaim a lost history, a lost sense of linguistic and rhetorical Indigenous practices, a lost sense of self and culture.

These losses are detrimental for students of color who are not aware that these pre-Hispanic "students of color" had their own methods for understanding the world and proclaiming that worldview through the use of their own rhetorical devices or *in xochitl in cuicatl.* These were the *first* students of color. I re-member (Vázquez). Re-membering is healing. A type of medicinal history (Ruiz and Arellano 2019).

READING THROUGH NEPANTLA: THE US EDUCATIONAL MISSION

In order to understand how old-world, pre-Hispanic knowledge was replaced with a Eurocentric and settler-colonial education tradition, I turn to Lawrence Cremin's *American Education: The Colonial Experience, 1607–1783*, written in 1970. As would any critical historian who practices decolonial epistemic disobedience, I read this book with the intent of reading "between the lines" as a nepantlerx and accounting for unfilled crevices and cracks and with the intent to "fill the spaces left" in tandem with composition scholars such as Jacqueline Jones Royster (1999), Villanueva (1999), and Christina Ramírez (2015). As with any historical account of colonialism, it is important to consider these spaces, absences, cracks, and contingent crevices because the colonized are subjects to be talked about and negotiated while being compromised and silenced. In this case, the silenced are those students of color (or potential students of color) who were included to a minimal degree in seventeenth-century educational institutions or excluded from them altogether. As one can see in the following historical accounts of the establishment of English colonies in the New World, including Virginia and New England, natives (also referred to as Indians in this source) are only talked about but not talked to. Their voices are not included; in this account we only see European sources and hear from a European author.

In order to understand the Industrial Revolution and the age of scientism and their relation to the students of color in eighteenth-century colleges, it is important to know that in the seventeenth century, during early English colonial ventures and conquests, that Native Americans were permitted into institutions of higher education and schools in general. The reason for this integration, as they attended schools alongside their English colonial peers, was to civilize Native Americans and have them assimilate to the cultural and religious beliefs that were composed of a scattered mosaic of different English colonial cultural customs and beliefs. Although English culture has been perceived as monolithic and stable, looking at this historical treatment of the creation of English educational institutions shows the process was one that endured many cultural influences, failures, and triumphs. Cremin (1970) establishes that the process of colonization quickly led to the need for English settlers to produce staples instead of search for precious metals, and this transition led to the need for cheap labor and English hegemonic control. Disappointment with the lack of precious metals available in Virginia during the early seventeenth century made it necessary for English settlers to concentrate upon the cultivation of labor and land.

> Slowly, the interest of the settlers shifted from the search for gold to
> the production of staples—grain, grapes, silk grass, and especially
> tobacco—and a broadside of 1616 sketched a happy pastorale in which
> the food problem had been solved and preparations were in progress
> "to set upon minerals, whereof there are many sorts." (John Smith 1907,
> quoted by Cremin 1970, 10)

This account, which Cremin describes, is partially borrowed from "A
Map of Virginia" by Capt. John Smith (1907) in *Narratives of Early Virginia, 1606–25*, edited by J. Franklin Jameson Scribner. These types of
documents show the colonial exclusion of Native Americans in any plans
to dispossess them of their lands and account for the ways educational
grants were maintained on the premise that these institutions would cure
the Native Americans of their false religion, backwards virtue, and incivil-
ity. It was because of Sir George Yeardley, governor of Virgina, that the
real transformation of Virginia into a self-sustaining agricultural community was effected in 1619. Cremin quotes Sir Yeardley's instructions
to Virginia to "lay the foundation for a 'flourishing state'" (11). These
instructions "ordered that a hundred acres of glebe land . . . be reserved
in each of the four boroughs for the maintenance of ministers and ten
thousand acres at Henrico for the endowment of a college to train up
the children of the infidels 'in true religion, moral virtue, and a civility
and for other godly uses'" (quoted in Cremin 11). It is apparent that
part of this mission to colonize and settle Virginia was also about creating
an "ordered community" by establishing civil institutions and a political
body. Cremin (1970) notes that Sir Yeardley also brought documents
calling for the establishment of a council of state and a general assembly
in the colony; as a result, the first representative body of North America
was Virginia, which was created to attract new English immigrants to
populate the territory and establish its economic structure (14). English
immigrants came in great numbers to Virginia and by

> the 1620's [*sic*] the English had moved farther than any other Western
> power toward conceiving of colonies, not as exploitative bands of transient
> men, but as permanent, self-sustaining communities; and their concept of
> colonial communities came gradually to embrace families, churches, mis-
> sions, print shops, and **schools**, which would methodically propagate English
> customs, ideas, language, laws, and literature. (22; emphasis added)

However, some colonial missions failed due to misbehaved first waves
of English immigrants, which called for more support for Puritan and
Pilgrim influence in both Virginia and New England. What is not mentioned, however, is whether or not Natives were open to these missions
or whether there was any consideration in any of these plans about

whether Natives desired to enter or participate in these institutions. Surprisingly, what is mentioned is the Indian massacre of 1622, which halted the first attempts to establish educational institutions that were assimilating machines that functioned to achieve intellectual as well as political hegemony. With no one to assimilate, what would be the purpose of such institutions?

Cremin's book, although dated 1970, mentions the syncretic process of colonial education, visible to the nepantlerx reader, as one that has been established, and he reveals the messy colonial cultural collisions among peoples, lands, and ideas. He notes that

> education was itself part and parcel of the process of cultural transmission. It linked the colonies to the metropolis, affording them access to the accumulated political, moral, and technological wisdom of the West; and it furnished them with the means of modifying, refining, and extending that wisdom in the solution of new and unprecedented problems. Indeed, it is in the relationship between the knowledge the colonists developed for coping with the New World and the agencies they established for transmitting that knowledge, or, alternatively, between the historical processes whereby the colonial character was formed and the institutional processes whereby the colonists sought to form character, that one finds the key to the colonial experience, and the origins of American education. (24)

As this quote discusses the remaking through the remixing of cultures, it is important to see the connections in this type of colonial knowledge matrix through a decolonial, nepantlerx lens. This lens shows how the colonial process allowed for very little influence from Native Americans in colonial educational missions while at the same time, reduced their understanding of the "New" World as one that could produce material gain in a one-way direction: for English colonials. There is a syncretic process alluded to here, but it does not allow for any agency on behalf of those being colonized. There is no possibility of agency for the disenfranchised; there is a hint toward intersubjectivity, but the natives remain passive, as their goods and resources are credited with "influence."

> Finally, the transmission of culture was a reciprocal process, and from the first years of settlement—in fact, from the earliest voyages of exploration—the New World exerted its influence on Europe. It is not merely that American products, such as white potatoes and maize and persimmons and raspberries and tobacco, were enthusiastically adopted by the English; the very existence of the New World stirred the imagination of the Old, requiring it to rethink many of its time-honored beliefs. From More to Locke, philosophers located their utopias in America; and a steady flow of information concerning the realities of the colonial world—the Indians, the plants and animals, the terrain—worked a transforming influence on

English political, religious, and scientific ideas. Indeed, the very traditions that later seventeenth-century English migrants brought with them to America had themselves been modified by American influences. (24)

While Cremin notes the American influences on English migrants, there is no real attention paid to how the Natives felt about all this imposition on their land, their bodies, their minds, and their souls. Their personhood is totally sidestepped in this historical account, and this is a stark representation of the colonial intentions of the seventeenth century and the ways students of color were fathomed in early colonial America. They were a nonissue, yet, as the nepantlerx sees, they were also an archetype in the making. Their substandard position began with colonialism.

RE-KNOWING: DELINKING FROM COLONIAL ARCHETYPES

In "Epistemic Disobedience, Independent Thought and De-Colonial Freedom," Mignolo (2009) describes epistemic delinking as a disobedient process of both decolonizing knowledge and producing a type of epistemology known as decolonial knowledges as they relate to colonial relations between Native Americans and Anglo Americans. "The need for political and epistemic delinking here comes to the fore, as well as decolonializing and de-colonial knowledges, necessary steps for imagining and building democratic, just, and non-imperial/colonial societies" (2). Such archetypal discursive constructions create what Mignolo refers to as the "colonial matrix of power," which is predicated on Eurocentered knowledges and history; the relations of power interpret the powerful as superior and the powerless as inferior as they have done with Native Americans and Anglo Americans. It is through the process of epistemic delinking that one can start to question the points of origin that create the intelligibility of colonial archetypes as either superior or inferior. Thus, to perform epistemic delinking, à la Mignolo, is not necessarily to relink to any other supposed point of origin—Latin American thought, history, and culture as an example—but to search out various points of origin that serve to delink from dominant epistemologies, which are inherently biased and skewed to serve their own political, economic, and cultural ideologies.

Mignolo explains this process in his own words:

My humble claim is that geo- and body-politics of knowledge has been hidden from the self-serving interests of Western epistemology and that a task of de-colonial thinking is the unveiling of epistemic silences of Western epistemology and affirming the epistemic rights of the racially devalued, and de-colonial options to allow the silences to build arguments to confront those who take "originality" as the ultimate criterion for the final judgment. (4)

Western epistemology is taken as the locus of analysis, interrogation, and legitimacy. It is the ideological chain to be delinked from in order to produce many epistemologies that challenge "original" Western-, white-, and European-derived epistemologies and resultant colonial archetypes. In order to contest colonial archetypes of inferiority, I continually act as a nepantlerx by performing an epistemically disobedient (Mignolo 2009) praxis and engaging nepantla and disengaging from these limitations.

THE FUTURE OF NEPANTLERX RHETORIC

The result of this continued colonial project and the intermixing of Indigenous people and Europeans has produced the Mestizo/a/x individual. However, ontologically speaking, many of us have adapted to and embraced this term. Today, in our field, many Latinx comp/rhet scholars focus on a variety of topics that can be seen as addressing symptoms of not only this colonial past but also of the continued project of colonial claims to Eurocentric superiority and disciplinarity, which places us, by default, on the margins of these colonized spaces. For nepantlerxes to effectively decolonize disciplinary archetypes, promulgated by calls to make rhetorical moves such as to "situate oneself in the field" as a Latinx rhet/comp scholar, it should be noted that the field, when viewed from my nepantlerx gaze, can be seen as being deeply embedded within Western exceptionalism (Said 1979).

For example, critical composition scholars Patricia Bizzell (1992), Linda Brodkey (1987), and Raúl Sánchez (2017) all acknowledge the interested nature of discourses of disciplinarity in purporting a supreme language, discourse, and consciousness, as so many other composition-ists do; this is a commonplace assumption. Furthermore, disciplinary historians have created a disciplinary consciousness at the expense of marginalizing others with no rights to claim humanity equal or superior to Europeans (Ruiz 2016b). In particular, Bizzell, in *Academic Discourse and Critical Consciousness* (1992), notes that the belief in our disciplinary consciousness stems from the conviction that students are in need of acculturation and assimilation and that they must be gifted with the superior intellectual skills and cognitive development a Standard English literacy education can provide. She states that the field "attempts to justify the goals of composition to justify sacrificing students' home languages for a higher, perhaps morally and intellectually

superior academic discourse of Standard English" (130). She also cites
E. D. Hirsch's (1977) book *Cultural Literacy*, included in *The Philosophy
of Composition*, as believing individual potential can only be thoroughly
developed through cultivation in the most cognitively rich and efficient
means of communication (130). In other words, we serve the rather
traditional goal of instruction in Standard English and the resulting superior consciousness through grooming those with an inferior
consciousness tied to inferior or inept linguistic and literacy practices
(my definition of literacy is borrowed from James Paul Gee [1998]).
This belief is colonial education 101. Adopting the narrative praxis of
nepantlerxes, how can we, as a field, disassociate from this colonial consciousness and transition to valuing genres and pedagogical practices
based upon Chicana Feminism (Zepeda 2016) that "know" and "see"
me and other nepantlerxes through a deep process of conocimiento?
Engaging the works mentioned herein would be a strong beginning to
that process of unknowing to re-know and re-member.

REFERENCES

Acosta, José de. 2002. *Natural and Moral History of the Indies*. Durham, NC: Duke University Press.
Agnew, Lois, Laurie Gries, Zosha Stuckey, Vicki Tolar Burton, Jay Dolmage, Jessica Enoch, Ronald L. Jackson II, LuMing Mao, Malea Powell, Arthur E. Walzer, Ralph Cintron, and Victor Vitanza. 2011. "Octalog III: The Politics of Historiography in 2010." *Rhetoric Review* 30 (2): 109–34.
Amin, Samir. 2010. *Eurocentrism*. New York: Monthly Review.
Anderson, Benedict. 1983. *Imagined Communities*. New York: Verso.
Anzaldúa, Gloria. 2012. *Borderlands/La Frontera: The New Mestiza*. San Francisco: Aunt Lute Books.
Azerrad, David. 2019. "The Promises and Perils of Identity Politics." *Heritage Foundation*, January 23. https://www.heritage.org/progressivism/report/the-promises-and-perils-identity-politics.
Baca, Damián. 2008. *Mestiz@ Scripts, Digital Migrations, and the Territories of Writing*. New York: Palgrave MacMillan.
Berlin, James A. 1982. "Contemporary Composition: The Major Pedagogical Theories." *College English* 44 (8): 765–77.
Berlin, James, Robert Connors, Sharon Crowley, Richard Leo Enos, Victor Vitanza, Nan Johnson, Susan Jarratt, and Jan Swearingen. 1988. "Octalog I: The Politics of Histori- ography." *Rhetoric Review* 7 (1): 4–49.
Bizzell, Patricia. 1992. *Academic Discourse and Critical Consciousness*. Pittsburgh: University of Pittsburgh Press.
Brodkey, Linda. 1987. *Academic Writing as Social Practice*. Philadelphia: Temple University Press.
Chou, Vivian. 2017. "How Science and Genetics Are Reshaping the Race Debate of the Twenty- First Century." Harvard University Graduate School of Arts of Sciences, Science in the News, April 17. http://sitn.hms.harvard.edu/flash/2017/science-genetics-reshaping-race-debate-21st-century/.

Cremin, Lawrence. 1970. *American Education: The Colonial Experience, 1607–1783.* New York: Harper and Rowe.

DeNicolo, Christina Passos, and Mónica Gónzalez. 2015. "Testimoniando en Nepantla: Using Testimonio as a Pedagogical Tool for Exploring Embodied Literacies and Bilingualism."

Journal of Language and Literacy Education 11 (1): 109–26. http://jolle.coe.uga.edu/wp-con tent/uploads/2015/04/Passos-DeNicoloGónzalez_Final.pdf.

Delgado, Richard. 1984. "The Imperial Scholar: Reflections on a Review of Civil Rights Literature." *University of Pennsylvania Law Review* 132 (3): 561–78.

Dussel, Enrique D. 2013. *Ethics of Liberation: In the Age of Globalization and Exclusion.* Translated by Eduardo Mendieta. Durham, NC: Duke University Press.

Enos, Richard Leo, Janet M. Atwill, Linda Ferreira-Buckley, Cheryl Glenn, Janice Lauer, Roxanne Mountford, Jasper Neel, Edward Schiappa, Kathleen Ethel Welch, and Thomas P. Miller. 1997. "Octalog II: The (Continuing) Politics of Historiography." *Rhetoric Review* 16 (1): 22–44.

Fanon, Frantz. 2008. *Black Skin, White Masks.* Translated by Richard Philcox. New York: Grove.

Fitzgerald, Katheryn. 2001. "A Rediscovered Tradition: European Pedagogy and Composition in Nineteenth-Century Midwestern Normal Schools." *College Composition and Communication* 53 (2): 224–50.

Foucault, Michel. 1969. *The Archeology of Knowledge.* Translated by A. M. Sheridan Smith. London: Routledge.

Fukuyama, Francis. 2018. "Against Identity Politics: The New Tribalism and the Crisis of Democracy." *Foreign Affairs* (September/October). https://www.foreignaffairs.com/arti cles/americas/2018-08-14/against-identity-politics-tribalism-francis-fukuyama.

Gee, James Paul. 1998. "What Is Literacy?" In *Negotiating Academic Literacies: Teaching and Learning Across Literacies and Cultures,* edited by Ruth Spack and Vivian Zamel, 51–60. Abingdon: Routledge.

Hirsch, E. D., Jr. 1977. *The Philosophy of Composition.* Chicago: University of Chicago Press.

Jung, Carl Gustav. 1959. *The Archetypes and the Collective Unconscious.* Edited and translated by Gerhard Adler and R. F. C. Hull. Princeton, NJ: Bollingen.

Keating, AnaLouise. 2006. "From Borderlands and New Mestizas to Nepantlas and Nepantleras: Anzaldúan Theories for Social Change." *Human Architecture: Journal of the Sociology of Self-Knowledge* 4 (3): 5–16.

Léon-Portilla, Miguel. 1990. *Aztec Thought and Culture: A Study of the Ancient Nahuatl Mind.* Translated by Jack Emory Davis. Norman: University of Oklahoma Press.

Licona, Adela C., and Karma Chávez. 2015. "Relational Literacies and Their Colonial Possibilities." *Peitho* 18 (1): 96–107.

Lugones, María. 1992. "On *Borderlands/La Frontera*: An Interpretative Analysis." *Hypatia* 7 (4): 31–37.

Lugones, María. 2010a. "The Coloniality of Gender." In *Globalization and the Decolonial Option,* edited by Walter D. Mignolo and Arturo Escobar, 369–90. Abingdon: Routledge.

Lugones, María. 2010b. "Towards a Decolonial Feminism." *Hypatia* 25 (4): 742–59.

Mbembe, Achille. 2001. *On the Post Colony.* Berkeley: University of California Press.

Mignolo, Walter D. 2000. "Introduction: From Cross-Genealogies and Subaltern Knowledges to Nepantla." *Nepantla: Views from South* 1 (1): 1–8.

Mignolo, Walter D. 2002. "The Enduring Enchantment: (Or the Epistemic Privilege of Modernity and Where to Go from Here)." *South Atlantic Quarterly* 101 (4): 927–54.

Mignolo, Walter D. 2009. "Epistemic Disobedience, Independent Thought and De-Colonial Freedom." *Theory, Culture & Society* 26 (7–8): 159–81.

Mignolo, Walter D. 2011. *The Darker Side of Western Modernity: Global Futures, Decolonial Options.* Durham, NC: Duke University Press.

Moraga, Cherrie, and Gloria Anzaldúa. 1983. *The Bridge Called My Back: Writings by Radical Women of Color*. New York: Kitchen Table/Women of Color Press.

Omi, Michael, and Howard Winant. 2015. *Racial Formation in the United States*. 3rd ed. New York: Routledge.

Ortego y Gasca, Felipe de, and Iris D. Ruiz. 2017 "The Syllabus, a Vehicle for Academic Colonialism?" *Latino Literary Magazine* (August): 1–22.

Pennycook, Alastair. 1994. "Incommensurable Discourses?" *Applied Linguistics* 15 (2): 115–38.

Quijano, Anibal. 2000. "Coloniality of Power, Eurocentrism, and Latin America." *Nepantla: Views from South* 1 (3): 533–80.

Ramírez, Christina Devereaux. 2015. *Occupying Our Space: The Mestiza Rhetorics of Mexican Women Journalists and Activists, 1875–1942*. Tucson: University of Arizona Press.

Ríos, Gabriela Raquel. 2016. "Mestizaje." In *Decolonizing Rhetoric and Composition: New Latinx Keywords for Theory and Pedagogy*, edited by Iris D. Ruiz and Raúl Sánchez, 109–21. New York: Palgrave MacMillan.

Royster, Jacqueline Jones. 2012. *Feminist Rhetorical Practices: New Horizons for Rhetoric, Composition, and Literacy Studies*. Carbondale: Southern Illinois University Press.

Ruiz, Iris D. 2016a. "Race." In *Decolonizing Rhetoric and Composition: New Latinx Keywords for Theory and Pedagogy*, edited by Iris D. Ruiz and Raúl Sánchez. New York: Palgrave MacMillan.

Ruiz, Iris D. 2016b. *Reclaiming Composition for Chicano/as and Other Ethnic Minorities: A Critical History and Pedagogy*. New York: Palgrave MacMillan.

Ruiz, Iris D. 2017. "A Decolonial Conference Review: Meditations on Inclusivity and 4 C's '17 in Portland, Oregon." *Latino Rebels*, March 29. https://www.latinorebels.com/2017/03/29/a-decolonial-conference-review-meditations-on-inclusivity-and-4-cs-17-in-port land-oregon/.

Ruiz, Iris D., and Sonia C. Arellano. 2019. "*La Cultura Nos Cura*: Reclaiming Decolonial Epistemologies through Medicinal History and Quilting as Method." In *Rhetorics Elsewhere and Otherwise: Contested Modernities, Decolonial Visions*, edited by Romeo García and Damián Baca, 141–68. Champaign, IL: NCTE.

Ruiz, Iris D., and Raúl Sánchez, eds. 2016. *Decolonizing Rhetoric and Composition: New Latinx Keywords for Theory and Pedagogy*. New York: Palgrave MacMillan.

Sahagún, Fray Bernadino de. 1985. *Historia general de las cosas de Nueva España*. Mexico, D.F.: Editorial Porrúa. https://books.google.com/books/about/Historia_general_de_las_cosas_de_Nueva_E.html?id=JBpuAAAAMAAJ.

Said, Edward W. 1979. *Orientalism*. New York: Vintage.

Sánchez, Raúl. 2017. *Inside the Subject: A Theory for Identity for the Study of Writing*. Champaign, IL: NCTE.

Shakespeare, William. 2015. *The Tempest*. Edited by Barbara Mowat and Paul Werstine. New York: Simon & Schuster.

Shor, Ira, Eugene Matusov, Ana Marjanovic-Shane, and James Cresswell. 2017. "Dialogic and Critical Pedagogies: An Interview with Ira Shor." *Dialogic Pedagogy: An International Online Journal* 5: S1–S21. https://dpj.pitt.edu/ojs/index.php/dpj1/article/view/208/147.

Smith, John. 1907. "A Map of Virginia." In *Narratives of Early Virginia, 1606–25*, edited by J. Franklin Jameson. New York: Charles Scribner's Sons.

Snyman, Gerrie. 2015. "Responding to the Decolonial Turn: Epistemic Vulnerability." *Missionalia: Southern African Journal of Missiology* 43 (3): 266–91.

Trouillot, Michel-Rolph. 1995. *Silencing the Past: Power and the Production of History*. Boston: Beacon.

Vázquez, Rolando. 2009. "Modernity Coloniality and Visibility: The Politics of Time." *Sociological Research Online* 14 (4): 109–15.

Villanueva, Victor. 1999. "On the Rhetoric and Precedents of Racism." *College Composition and Communication* 50 (4): 645–61.

Zepeda, Candace. 2016. "Chicana Feminism." In *Decolonizing Rhetoric and Composition: New Latinx Keywords for Theory and Pedagogy*, edited by Iris D. Ruiz and Raúl Sánchez, 137–51. New York: Palgrave MacMillan.

4

EXPLORING DISCOMFORT USING MARKERS OF DIFFERENCE
Constructing Antiracist and Anti-ableist Teaching Practices

Stephanie L. Kerschbaum

Preface. This chapter contains numerous questions and invitations to story, inviting you to recall moments of pedagogical discomfort. Some of these questions may spur memories that may affect or trigger you, depending on your experiences.

In this essay, I invite you to join me in considering how we story ourselves as teachers and what possibilities this storying may open up or close off for developing antiracist and anti-ableist writing pedagogies. More specifically, I suggest how marking difference can help us learn to listen to our own pedagogical narratives, taking an especial focus on narratives of discomfort, in order to challenge our own complicity in privilege and oppression in higher education. Before going further, however, let me say some things about audience and my imagined positioning as I write to and with audiences reading this chapter. I envision a broad audience for this collection, including educators who have had many different kinds of experiences in the classroom. But I also imagine that the people who will most benefit from critically examining their own discomfort and who probably should be more uncomfortable more often are those who, like myself, must account for and recognize their own privilege. In this chapter, then, I focus on able-bodied privilege and white privilege, even as these forms of privilege are affected by multiple axes of identity and identification. In what follows, I encourage you to spend time reflecting upon and working with your own stories. I hope you'll use these stories to push back, engage with, and consider what it would look like for your teaching to move towards greater inclusivity and to challenge racism and ableism in your classrooms and pedagogy.

To move towards antiracist and anti-ableist practices, we first need an understanding of racism and ableism, as well as how they are

https://doi.org/10.7330/9781646421732.c004

interconnected. In building my own understanding of these concepts, I have been strongly influenced by the work of lawyer and social justice activist Talila A. Lewis (2021), who stresses that any approach to ableism—discrimination and oppression based on disability—is incomplete without also attending to its relationships to racism. Lewis's working definition of ableism is grounded in community work and conversation with disabled Black and other negatively racialized folk, including Dustin Gibson. This definition explicitly connects ableism to anti-Blackness and racism, describing it as

> a system that places value on people's bodies and minds based on societally constructed ideas of normality, intelligence, excellence, desirability, and productivity. These constructed ideas are deeply rooted in anti-Blackness, eugenics, misogyny, colonialism, imperialism and capitalism.
>
> This form of systemic oppression leads to people and society determining who is valuable and worthy based on a person's language, appearance, religion, and/or their ability to satisfactorily [re]produce, excel and "behave." You do not have to be disabled to experience ableism.

Historian Ibram X. Kendi's 2016 *Stamped from the Beginning* further reinforces the connections Lewis offers between racism and capitalism, noting that arguments about and definitions of racism have shifted to suit the needs, desires, and greed of white people who have benefited from its structures and systems. It is important to remember racism is not just about stereotypes or discriminatory or exclusionary behaviors; it also involves the ability to exert control or power over others. Lewis's working definition emphasizes that ableism is tied up in reinforcing and perpetuating racism and other valuations of people based on beliefs about productivity and worth. Thus, moving towards an anti-ableist and antiracist teaching practice entails challenging these valuations, unearthing the social structures that have taught us to dehumanize others, and changing our behaviors towards humanizing possibilities for all of us.

Let's get started. Take a moment to reflect on how you have encountered, perpetuated, and/or challenged such valuations, structures, and behaviors in your teaching. There's some blank space right below. Go ahead and jot down notes toward a story, or record a memory that has stuck with you, or narrate a pedagogical moment of discomfort. This might be a story of success or achievement, but more likely (and more usefully for the purpose of this chapter), it will be a moment you have puzzled over or wondered about. It might be an instance of failure you want to learn from; it might be a memory that makes you cringe or that you wish you could erase. It can be anything that hangs around in your memory. Tug at that thread of memory and restitch it below. (If this is not your personal copy of the book, do it on a scrap of paper, on a sticky note, in your teaching journal, as an annotation on your syllabus, as a voice note on your computer or phone.) As you write down this story, imagine whatever audience you like, and try to include as many details as you can: relate not only what happened but also how you felt, who else was there, what else was going on in the space you were in.

I'm asking you to take this pause before you move into the rest of the chapter; it really is important that you document something of this memory before continuing to read. This documentation is important not only as a record of what comes out of you but also as a record you can revisit and reconsider at a later time to gain new perspective and to connect with the self and other characters you have recounted in this story. If you're reading this chapter for a second or third time, feel free to write down a different story, retell the same story, or just add new details to an earlier story.

I admit I'm curious about what kind of story you chose to write, what came out of you as you sat down (or stood, or lay down, or used your body in any way that worked for you) to narrate this story. I wonder whether you told a familiar story, one you've told bunches of times, or if this is the first time you've recorded this story outside your memory. I wonder how the story makes you feel. I wonder whether it is a story you told willingly or a story you can only tell here and now because just the pages of this chapter and you are listening right now. I wonder how this story fits into the broader context of your teaching experience. Do you have a long history of teaching and consequently many stories? What brought *this* story to mind at *this* time? Are your teaching experiences relatively new and the stories fresh? What moments are highlighted in your memory? What memories refuse to go away even if you wish you didn't have to recall them? Are there stories you've needed or wanted to tell but just haven't been able to? Is this one of those stories?

In what follows, I suggest a method for recording, listening to, and retelling stories I've been dwelling with over the last fifteen years. I first forwarded this process at the end of the third chapter of *Toward a New Rhetoric of Difference* (Kerschbaum 2014) when I suggested teachers could pay attention to their pedagogical narratives for what they reveal about self- and other positioning and interactional possibilities. Analyzing these stories draws upon the concept of marking difference, a means by which people make ongoing rhetorical decisions about how to present themselves and respond to others in everyday interactions. Marking difference developed out of my careful listening to students' talk during small-group peer-review sessions. I wanted to learn more about how students acknowledged differences between themselves and their classmates, so I paid close attention to how they named and described themselves and others and how they characterized actions and choices they'd made in their writing and research. This work led me to the concept of "markers of difference," which I defined as rhetorical cues that signal the presence of difference between two or more interlocutors (see Kerschbaum 2014, chapter 2).

Story emerged again and again as students made claims about why their peer-review comments should be given weight or about how they experienced an author's argument or a peer's writing. These were almost always stories about how students wanted themselves to be perceived by others and that depended on others participating in those self-constructions. Students marked themselves as particular kinds of people and situated themselves against and alongside other characters in their stories. We as teachers use story too, in ways that have significant consequences for our own ongoing identity constructions, our interactions with students, our relationships with our colleagues, and the classroom environments we create.

Here's one of my own stories, a memory from almost twenty years ago:

As a graduate teaching assistant learning how to teach, my fellow TAs and I would frequently talk together—during office hours in our shared offices, over drinks in the Union, during regular professional-development sessions—about what we do in the classroom and how we do it. Class discussion is a commonly raised topic. Sometimes I am quiet during these conversations, especially when they occur in front of the whole teaching staff. Almost everyone seems to have as an ideal the classroom where conversation proceeds "naturally," where they don't have to tell students to raise their hands. In these moments, I lean back and slink down in my seat and try to push away the creeping feeling of shame I feel because I can't—I just cannot—do a classroom where people just talk whenever they want. I have to have an order for students' contributions, and I have to be able to visually recognize who wants to talk. For a long time—a long, long time—I think this means I'm not as good as my peers at teaching. I think "good teachers" are all excellent at leading lively classroom discussions where everyone in the room just jumps in and talks and everything proceeds very smoothly without explicit intervention from the teacher.

Marking difference provides a useful set of rhetorical tools for reflecting on this story. First, notice how I name and describe myself. I share my title and rank: "graduate teaching assistant." I share that I am "learning how to teach." My graduate student self in this story does not mention a disabled identity. In fact, the closest thing to a reference to my deafness in the narrative is an elliptic mention of what I cannot do: "I can't—I just cannot—do a classroom where people just talk whenever they want." I find this striking, especially because I first wrote down this story while drafting a keynote talk for a conference, writing as a tenured associate professor who regularly publishes in disability studies and actively claims a deaf identity in just about every sphere of her professional life.

In addition to not mentioning disability explicitly, my graduate student self in this narrative also doesn't claim a raced identity. But, like disability, race is also woven into this narrative. Not mentioning my racial identity does not mean race is not relevant to the scene unfolding in the story above. Many discussions of privilege draw on metaphors of labor and work to highlight what is involved in crafting an identity, building relations, and forwarding a particular kind of self within higher education environments saturated with racism and ableism. For example, Staci M. Perryman-Clark and Collin Craig (2019), writing about writing program administration work, assert that "WPA discourse, as an amalgamation of experiences, bodies, labor, policies, rules, departments, and documents, is always and already race work" (9). This understanding of race work is not limited to administration: teaching and occupying space in a classroom is to occupy a racialized space, one where teachers may find themselves aligning with, drawing upon, and making use of institutional and cultural images of who a teacher is, what a teacher looks like, and how a teacher behaves in order to bolster or reinforce desired teaching selves vis-à-vis students. Too, teachers may find themselves, within those same racialized structures, required to do additional emotional and intellectual labor simply to persist in the classroom. Or teachers may find these structures lead them to perform differently than they might want because of how others in the classroom respond to and perceive them. Perryman-Clark and Craig elaborate: "Comporting blackness to minimize white anxiety is race work. Deciding how one chooses to be visible on campus is race work. . . . What we decide to teach is race work. How we dress is race work. Achieving legibility in front of panoptic white administrative gazes is race work," and the list goes on (10).

I did not explicitly name my whiteness in the story above, but it is nevertheless present: my institutional context was overwhelmingly white and my white identity was not something that significantly motivated fears and anxieties about my teaching. Put another way, I did not worry about being a bad teacher because I was white; whiteness was not called to the forefront of my awareness when I thought about what kind of teacher I was. As a consequence, naming and describing my pedagogical identity as raced (and gendered, and classed, and later, as disabled) has been a learned practice. My whiteness makes it easy or possible for me to tell some kinds of stories and to explicitly mark myself in some ways while leaving others unmarked, as this story reveals.

One way to read this story is to understand it as marking a difference between the teaching self I wanted to put forward and the teaching self I actually could put forward for my students. My notion of a desired teaching self was informed by a variety of things, including (but not limited to) narratives and images of "ideal teachers" that circulated in my graduate program, the lore around teaching shared among teaching assistants, and even my experiences in graduate seminars with the faculty who were teaching me how to teach. The disconnect between my imagined version of the teacher I should be and the teacher I actually performed in front of the classroom led to intense feelings of discomfort whenever we had conversations about classroom discussion.

I also recognize thick threads of ableism marked in this narrative. For example, the ideal classroom exchange I describe using terms like "jump in" and "lively" is ableist, as is the idea that talking should be the dominant mode of participation in a classroom. The very notion of natural or smooth communication valorizes and privileges one particular type of contribution while devaluing many other possible means of participating and engaging in classroom dialogue. I had internalized these ableist ideas and was using them to compare myself to others and find myself wanting for not being able to conduct classrooms in this way.

This is not a story I would have, or perhaps even could have, shared when I was a graduate student instructor, or even as an untenured assistant professor. I felt too vulnerable: I not only felt intense fear of not being good enough but I also worried that these inadequacies could prevent me from landing an academic job or, after getting a job, securing tenure. It was much easier for me to focus my conversations about pedagogy on arenas in which I felt more confident and less uncomfortable, such as responding to student drafts or holding writing conferences. This is not because I thought I was the best at these activities but because in these arenas, I was confident I could learn better ways of doing this work or learn to change my pedagogy. In contrast, there was no change or improvement I could imagine that would make it possible for me to follow a classroom of twenty students well enough to have a rollicking unmanaged-by-me conversation.

Our pedagogical lives are shaped by the stories we tell about teaching. These stories help us to maintain and sustain particular versions of who we are as teachers. Through story, we invest in desirable selves we put forward to ourselves and to others. We cannot separate the stories we tell from where they are told, when they are told, to whom they are told. The pedagogical environments you experience shape the stories you remember and share, and the kinds of colleagues and the professional interactions you have influence which stories seem relevant to tell or which are heard by others, what details are prominent and which ones are backgrounded, and how you feel about those details.

In what follows, then, I ask you to remember—and as often as possible, to record—stories that may lead you to feel less secure, less comfortable, less confident in portraying a desired self. I don't ask for this discomfort easily—and I've felt uncomfortable again and again trying to write this chapter. I keep at it, however, because I believe these stories of discomfort and friction offer space for us to continue the ongoing work of unearthing the racist and ableist structures that shape how we move in the classroom and, consequently, the relationships we build with our students, our colleagues, and even with ourselves.

EXPLORING DISCOMFORT BY TELLING STORIES

I have a lot of stories about feeling uncomfortable in front of the classroom. Attending to these moments of pedagogical discomfort can help us unpack relations of privilege and oppression, as well as notice what we are valuing and devaluing in ourselves and others. In moments when I am uncomfortable, I often find myself just wanting to escape and be anywhere but in that space of discomfort. Reflecting on these moments later and trying to trace patterns in them has helped me develop a practice of listening to what my discomfort is trying to tell me: Why am I uncomfortable in this space, at this time?

I mention earlier my sense of self-consciousness around not being able to perform teaching during class discussions the way I imagined every other teacher was doing. In that case my self-consciousness emerged as I judged myself negatively. Self-consciousness emerging out of negative judgment can manifest for a lot of reasons. For example, a bad-hair day can generate intense self-consciousness, as can an outfit that just isn't working, as can a feeling of being out of place, no matter how that out-of-placeness is signaled. Historian Tanisha Ford's 2015 book *Liberated Threads* shows how Black women purposefully used fashion and style to perform resistance and activism during the civil rights movement. Ford reveals how clothing choices and hair styles are entwined with how we perform ourselves on a daily basis and that such choices are far from neutral. These performances are highly gendered, raced, classed, sized, and even disabled: the clothes we can wear, that we want to wear, that we need to wear, that we have to wear, the clothes designed for us or not designed for us all contribute to whether we feel comfortable as we move through our daily lives. Cultures around "professional" dress at different institutions also impact how different teachers experience themselves as fitting or not fitting. Ford's work again and again emphasizes that attention to clothing and hair, far from being a superfluous concern, is integral to the messages we send about who we are, who we want others to see us as, and our own sense of fitting or misfitting (Garland-Thomson 2011) in an environment.

When was the last time you experienced self-consciousness in the classroom? When were you last reminded, whether by others' behaviors or your own feelings of discomfort, of your body or appearance in the classroom? Tell that story.

When and where and how do you feel out of place? When are you reminded you don't fit or don't fit in? Another way we are reminded about our fit or lack thereof is through microaggressions. This scholarly term has actually moved into common parlance; there are many places to learn more about microaggressions, but I like Derald Wing Sue and Lisa Beth Spanierman's 2019 book *Microaggressions in Everyday Life.* Microaggressions are everyday slights, snubs, or insults, whether intentional or unintentional, that communicate negative messages to people about group identifications they share. Microaggressions are one way people learn something about how others perceive or don't perceive them, and they occur with regularity for people who are part of marginalized or minority groups. Examples of microaggressions involve having your name mispronounced, being mispronouned, having your racial identification erased or denied, being ignored or overlooked as part of a group, having a stereotype amplified, or being asked to respond to inappropriate comments or questions.[1]

Have you experienced microaggressions as a teacher? What happened? Fill in the surrounding context—What happened before? What happened after? How did you respond? How did other people in the scene behave or respond?

Yet another form of discomfort for me emerges when I am raising or engaging course content and conversations around current events, particularly rhetorics of racism, misogyny, homophobia, and ableism that regularly appear in the news and in public discourse. When these topics come up, I want to engage them in authentic and sustaining ways, especially for students who are vulnerable in the face of these political and cultural forces, students whose lives are at risk of being erased, denied, or ignored. In these conversations, I feel acutely aware that I am a white faculty member at a predominantly white educational institution. Too, I am conscious that being deaf does not give me particular insight into others' disability experiences. I feel uncomfortable in these moments for lots of reasons, many of which have to do with how I want to be perceived by my students, by my colleagues, and in my own personal accountings to myself of what I do in the classroom. I do not want to get it wrong. And my position at the front of the classroom means I have quite a bit of authority to manage and direct these conversations. I want to do that in ways that create a space where my students can grow and learn. But I also know I have failed at this in the past, and those failures still feel painful and can come to the forefront when I'm trying to lead these conversations.

In these moments, I am compelled to notice just how powerful whiteness is as a racial habitus. In *Antiracist Writing Assessment Ecologies*, Asao Inoue (2015) draws on Pierre Bourdieu's work to explain a racial habitus:

> Racial habitus places an emphasis on the continual (re)construction of race as structures, as sets of dispositions that are discursive, material, and performative in nature. We speak, embody (are marked materially), and perform our racial designations and identities, whether those designations are self-designated or designated by others. (43)

Inoue describes how ways of moving and being in the world are continually structured by patterns, opportunities, discourses, and environments (see also Inoue 2019). To put this another way, the choices available to people are not choices they have created for themselves: the choices have already been structured, given to people to choose from. With the concept of racial habitus, Inoue is calling upon faculty—and perhaps particularly white faculty—to recognize that our presence and ways of moving in different kinds of spaces and our degrees of comfort or discomfort are tied to these racial structures. For example, if you are white and regularly move in environments composed largely, if not solely, of other white people, you are replicating and participating in a dominant white racial habitus simply by moving easily through that space and subsequently recreating and replicating those patterns that enable comfort and ease for white people.

A dominant racial habitus—and generally in the United States, the dominant racial habitus is a white racial habitus—specifically invites white people not to notice many things about it: indeed, its invisibility is part of what enables its perpetuation. Here, I'm getting at the issue of discomfort from another angle. If you are in a majority, or if you find yourself occupying different minority or majority stances in the different circles you move through, ask yourself about the various spaces and circles and environments you move in and out of and through: When and where are you able to not notice your environment? When and where do you move easily and comfortably in a space? In theorizing kairotic spaces in her book *Mad at School*, Margaret Price (2011) draws explicitly on notions of comfort and discomfort to show how power is exchanged within social encounters. It is not typically the more powerful interlocutor who is uncomfortable within kairotic spaces. If you rarely find yourself feeling uncomfortable within the everyday spaces in your life, ask who else regularly moves in and through these spaces. In your teaching, how do you create spaces that make you comfortable as a teacher, and how might some of those spaces be experienced similarly or differently by your students?

Reflect back to the beginning of the current term or the last term during which you taught. How did you experience the classroom environment? Who shared that classroom space with you? What aspects of the institutional context or classroom context do you find yourself noticing, paying attention to, and/or wanting to describe? How do you perceive the students in the classroom? What resources or materials do you use to learn something about those in the classroom with you? What kind of classroom space do you imagine (some of) your students experiencing?

Discomfort manifests for me, too, at particular times: times of the semester, times of the month, times of the year, times of the day. There are relationships and positions that contribute to discomfort: students I cannot understand well (for a wide range of reasons); classroom dynamics that lead me to worry I am the butt of the joke; students who make particular kinds of requests or behave in ways I do not expect. I experience discomfort when the responses I anticipate from students are not the ones I actually do get, or when I feel I have not been my best self in the classroom. Despite my best efforts to build positive, productive working relationships with all my students, each semester students and even fellow teachers and colleagues respond to my presentations of self in ways that feel threatening to the self I want to forward.

Tell a story about a time *when you felt discomfort in your classroom. What kind of time was it? Is it a recurring time, was it a singular time, is there a rhythm to the discomfort you can identify? Do you remember a specific memorable episode, or a type of event that generates discomfort when it occurs? Are there persistent or consistent elements across the moments of classroom discomfort you find yourself recalling?*

Thus far, I've mentioned numerous sources of discomfort that might manifest in your teaching, and I've invited you to record some of those moments on these pages. I've mentioned the built environment, as well as how feeling as if you are presenting the self you want to be presenting and having that self recognized by others matter to feelings of (dis)comfort. I've pointed to ease or difficulty of movement, as well as to different levels of comfort in environments that anticipate or exclude particular kinds of raced and disabled bodies. And as I have been writing this chapter and documenting my own experiences and stories of comfort and discomfort, it has been far easier for me to identify (and imagine sharing in print) moments of discomfort associated with disability than it has been for me to identify (and imagine sharing in print) moments of discomfort related to my whiteness. This is not surprising: my white identity is a dominant, privileged identity I am not as often called upon to pay attention to through others' behaviors or reflections of me back onto myself. But when I revisit my stories—when I think about what I call to mind, what details emerge in the stories I tell, my whiteness, white privilege, and the racist apparatus of white supremacy are visceral presences. In the next section, then, I suggest some ways you can read across your stories and consider ways to tell them differently.

ANALYZING OUR PEDAGOGICAL STORIES, MOVING TOWARD NEW STORIES

As a white graduate student concerned with issues of social justice and equity and language practice, I found myself caught up in recurring dilemmas regarding how to respond to and grade student writing. I knew I wanted to recognize and affirm all my students' ways of writing, thinking, and engaging while supporting them as they grew in new directions as writers and thinkers. And yet, it became patently clear I didn't value all my students' discourses in the same way when it came down to assigning grades. I'll never forget one student from my first-year teaching whom I ended up failing in my course. He was the only student I assigned an F to, in fact. It took me years to realize I'd made some judgments of his thinking and his writing that depended upon notions of academic discourse that were anything but natural or necessary. At the time he was in my class, I could not see what that student was doing with his writing and thinking because all I noticed was what he was not doing. It took me much longer than it should have to realize how deeply I had internalized value judgments and associations with particular styles and approaches to language, to recognize those value judgments for what they were, and to unlearn them.

The stories we tell—of the classroom, of ourselves as teachers, of ourselves as people—are a big part of how we perform pedagogy and orient to our students. We are always figuring ourselves out, and we are always coming to know who we are with every new group of students (Kerschbaum 2014). As we move into teaching new courses, in new socio-political contexts, with different things happening in our professional and personal lives, new insights and relational possibilities take shape. Each class, each new group of students, then, has something to teach us about where and how we experience discomfort. For many of us, in order to be our full selves, we may need to start telling, recording, or writing our stories differently. To be more fully inclusive in the classroom, we may need to imagine telling different kinds of stories about ourselves as teachers. We may need to recognize where we may be performing "whiteliness" (see Condon 2012, 34) or where we may need to shift or change patterns, resist institutional cultures, and enact change in our teaching.

Doing this work is not just about telling one story or two. It is about examining the accumulation of stories; it is about digging through sedimented layers of stories; it is about acknowledging the stories we hold on to and protect, as well as the stories we must let go of and start telling differently. As you do this work, you might answer some of the following questions:

- What teaching identities do you notice yourself being invested in, wanting to protect?
- What resources are you using in your storytelling to defend, protect, reinforce, or conserve power?
- How might your stories move away from self-defense in order to open up different kinds of possibilities, different kinds of inclusion for your classroom?
- Whom do you tell stories to?
- When do stories factor into your conversations or your correspondence or your personal or professional writing?
- What happens when you tell the same story to different audiences or in different contexts?
- What different stories do you find yourself telling at different times and places?

- Try telling a counterfactual story: What would happen if . . . ?
- What details do you resist telling, details you just feel you can't write down in these stories?
- Notice the teaching self you might be protecting or feeling invested in. Why are those identities being protected? What is at stake for you in those self-constructions?

You've already started this process by recording (some of) your stories over the course of reading this chapter. At first it doesn't matter how you record them or what modes or forms of production you use. The essential point is that your story must be one you are able to revisit, retell, and maybe even revise. Some stories we tell are familiar ones that get told over and over again—to cement a relationship, reinforce a self, build an identity. These familiar stories are important. But over time, in order to grow and change, we must write down new stories to move our behaviors and practices in new directions.

When I finally wrote down the story of my graduate student self and my imagined ideal of classroom discussion, I realized narrating my graduate student self involves very different resources for storytelling than the ones I use to narrate my current pedagogical self. The cultural material that served as touchpoints for my new-to-teaching self predominantly framed disability as an individual problem: something for me, personally, to deal with and overcome, something for me to make as completely unproblematic for other people as possible. Being white meant I could give over more of my energy to focusing on minimizing my disability while not worrying (as much) about whether those around me were similarly perceiving and negatively judging my racial self-presentation. Writing down that story while trying to remember what it was like when I was a brand-new teacher enabled me to begin pulling out some of the assumptions underlying the story's structure and apparatus.

Was the only version of the story—of the deaf teacher trying to lead class discussion—really one about my personal failure to foster an imagined *Dead Poets Society*-esque classroom environment? Certainly not. As I moved through the early years of my career, I largely went to disability-related panels at the conferences I attended. Some of you might be thinking, "Of course you did, that's exactly what your academic expertise is." But the truth is, I started going to disability-related talks not because they were the ones I would select based on my intellectual interests. Instead, it was those conferences' inaccessibility when I first started attending that led me to attend disability panels because they were usually the only sessions I could attend and expect to receive even a modicum of access, such as being able to read along with a presenter's script.

Engaging with disability studies scholars helped me learn there are different ways to tell a story about not being able to follow a free-flowing class discussion. My original story positioned me alongside versions of other composition teachers that, frankly, only existed in my imagination. And my imagination was constrained by the cultural models of teachers that were readily available to me, almost none of whom were deaf teachers in classrooms populated almost entirely by hearing students. In order to tell a better story, I needed to imagine other possibilities, other ways of telling a story about teaching, and to identify new story lines for my teaching self.

In the same way orientations to disability influenced the story lines I created for my teaching self, so too did orientations to race and ethnicity. Inoue's work on the effects of a dominant racial habitus underscores that for many white people, myself included, the path of least resistance, the easiest choice to make, is often one that backgrounds a white racial identity or that does not explicitly acknowledge whiteness. For me, learning how to talk about whiteness (something I am still learning how to do) has meant in part noticing how much whiteness saturates the environments in which I teach and write and work. This noticing has pushed me to seek out other kinds of storying around race and to refuse to treat whiteness as invisible or as the absence of color. When I do not explicitly address race and whiteness, my discussions of disability do not openly attend to the ways whiteness has structured how I experience deafness and disability. Perhaps the most prominent influence here involves being able to hold disability up front and center when engaging around accommodation and access questions and not having to simultaneously negotiate negative judgments of me based on my whiteness. In this way, white privilege reinforces and supports my ability to publicly engage in advocacy work. When I do not acknowledge white privilege at work, I contribute to the presumption that these privileges are natural, just how things are, rather than explicitly constructed and reinforced by a cultural apparatus that holds up whiteness as a privileged identity (see Condon 2012; Martinez 2018). White cultural logics and performances of privilege are often put to work to maintain white privilege and power, even by the most well-intentioned white people. I have to check myself often.

This is where engaging with other voices—research, digging into data, analyzing sources, situating perspectives alongside one another, developing connections and exploring contradictions and new questions that emerge—becomes central. The stories we tell are often aimed at representing reality and various forms of lived experience in some way. But we also must remember our stories never reflect the full range of possibilities and experiences.

There is much to learn from teachers and scholars in rhetoric and composition regarding how to tell stories differently. Aja Martinez's work on critical race counterstory (2014, 2016, 2018) emphasizes the value of a critical race theory framework for upending typical academic narratives. Cruz Medina (2018) describes the importance of culturally relevant digital storytelling for challenging borders and boundaries around academic literacy. Scholars such as Carmen Kynard (2006, 2018, 2019), Victor Villanueva (1993, 2006), and Melanie Yergeau (2010, 2013, 2018)—among many others—weave tapestries of their experiences in the academy alongside deep theorizing across those stories and experiences, often in ways that are damning for dominant perspectives. And in *Teaching Queer*, Stacey Waite (2017) uses her own and her students' stories to brilliantly unpack how teachers' and students' perceptions of one another's bodies and presence in classrooms matter significantly to the learning process. Unsurprisingly, this theorizing emerges prominently from scholarship produced by people who experience being on the margins of many aspects of academia. White and/or nondisabled teachers and scholars have much to learn as we situate ourselves and our stories in this work. This is not an easy process; it is (will be) an ongoing lifelong path, as Frankie Condon (2012) illustrates.

As you practice telling stories, it is important that you also acknowledge how you are positioned and the sorts of stories you tell. If a storyline is commonly or widely amplified through mass-media channels or in your social circles, it may be important to wonder about the dominance of those stories and how those stories and experiences might look very different from another perspective. The scholars cited above all help us ask, What is glossed over or left out of these stories? Who is erased or invisible? Some stories are easier or more readily available to tell than others. Of these stories we might ask, What social or cultural structures support or invite or facilitate some stories while making others more challenging or difficult to tell? Sometimes whether a story is easy or difficult to tell depends on the audience—What happens when you move your story and tell it somewhere, somewhen else? As we record our own stories and grapple with our own vulnerabilities and discomfort, this grappling may make it possible for us to create space for others to be their own full selves and for us to listen to them in the ways they—and we—want to be heard.

APPENDIX 4.A

QUESTIONS FOR REFLECTION AND ANALYSIS ACROSS YOUR STORIES

1. What are the stories of your pedagogical life? What types of events or moments do you find yourself chronicling and recording about your teaching?

2. How do you appear as a character in your stories?

3. How do you story your students in relation to you? What other characters populate your pedagogical narratives?

4. How do the material environments in which you teach and the material resources of your teaching performances figure into your storying?

5. What aspects of your identity do you call out, explicitly negotiate, or describe in your stories? What do you find yourself *not* describing or engaging?

6. How do you describe your students and other characters in your stories? What do you find yourself noticing or deeming relevant as you include them in your stories?

NOTE

1. For example, in "They Call Me Dr. Ore," Ersula Ore recounts her (typical) experience of having white male students question her credentials on the first day of class.

REFERENCES

Condon, Frankie. 2012. *I Hope I Join the Band: Narrative, Affiliation, and Antiracist Rhetoric.* Logan: Utah State University Press.

Ford, Tanisha. 2015. *Liberated Threads: Black Women, Style, and the Global Politics of Soul.* Chapel Hill: University of North Carolina Press.

Garland-Thomson, Rosemarie. 2011. "Misfits: A Feminist Materialist Disability Concept." *Hypatia* 26 (3): 591–609.

Inoue, Asao B. 2015. *Antiracist Writing Program Assessment Ecologies.* Fort Collins, CO: Parlor.

Inoue, Asao B. 2019. "How Do We Language So People Stop Killing Each Other, or What Do We Do about White Language Supremacy." YouTube video, 46:23. https://www.youtube.com/watch?v=brPGTewcDYY&feature=youtu.be.

Kerschbaum, Stephanie L. 2014. *Toward a New Rhetoric of Difference.* Urbana, IL: NCTE.

Kendi, Ibram X. 2016. *Stamped from the Beginning: The Definitive History of Racist Ideas in America.* New York: Nation Books.

Kynard, Carmen. 2006. "Y'all are Killin' Me up in Here: Response Theory from a Newjack Comp Instructor/Sistuhgirl Meeting Her Students on the Page." *Teaching English at the Two Year College* 33 (4): 361–87.

Kynard, Carmen. 2018. "Stayin Woke: Race-Radical Literacies in the Makings of a Higher Education." *College Composition and Communication* 69 (3): 519–29.

Kynard, Carmen. 2019. "Administering While Black: Black Women's Labor in the Academy and the 'Position of the Unthought.'" In *Black Perspectives in Writing Program Administration: From the Margins to the Center,* edited by Staci M. Perryman-Clark and Collin Lamont Craig, 28–50. Urbana, IL: NCTE.

Lewis, Talila A. 2021. "January 2021 Working Definition of Ableism." Talila A. Lewis, January 1.https://www.talilalewis.com/blog/january-2021-working-definition-of-ableism.

Martinez, Aja Y. 2014. "A Plea for Critical Race Theory Counterstory: Stock Story versus Counterstory Dialogues Concerning Alejandra's 'Fit' in the Academy." *Composition Studies* 42 (2): 33–55.

Martinez, Aja Y. 2016. "Alejandra Writes a Book: A Critical Race Counterstory about Writing, Identity, and Being Chicanx in the Academy." *Praxis: A Writing Center Journal* 14 (1). http://www.praxisuwc.com/martinez-141.

Martinez, Aja Y. 2018. "The Responsibility of Privilege: A Critical Race Counterstory Conversation." *Peitho* 21 (1): 212–33.

Medina, Cruz. 2018. "Digital Latinx Storytelling: Testimonio as Multimodal Resistance." In *Racial Shorthand: Coded Discrimination Contested in Social Media,* edited by Cruz Medina and Octavio Pimentel. Computers and Composition Digital Press. https://ccdigitalpress.org/book/shorthand/chapter_medina.html.

Ore, Ersula. 2014. "They Call Me Dr. Ore." *Present Tense: A Journal of Rhetoric in Society* 5 (2). https://www.presenttensejournal.org/volume-5/they-call-me-dr-ore/.

Perryman-Clark, Staci M., and Collin Lamont Craig. 2019. "Introduction: Black Matters: Writing Program Administration in Twenty-First-Century Higher Education." In *Black Perspectives in Writing Program Administration: From the Margins to the Center,* edited by Staci M. Perryman-Clark and Collin Lamont Craig, 1–27. Urbana, IL: NCTE.

Price, Margaret. 2011. *Mad at School: Rhetorics of Mental Disability and Academic Life.* Ann Arbor: University of Michigan Press.

Sue, Derald Wing, and Lisa Beth Spanierman. 2019. *Microaggressions in Everyday Life.* New York: Wiley.

Villanueva, Victor. 1993. *Bootstraps: From an American Academic of Color.* Urbana, IL: NCTE.

Villanueva, Victor. 2006. "Blind: The New Racism." *Writing Center Journal* 26 (1): 3–19.

Waite, Stacey. 2017. *Queer: Radical Possibilities for Writing and Knowing.* Pittsburgh: University of Pittsburgh Press.

Yergeau, Melanie. 2010. "Circle Wars: Reshaping the Typical Autism Essay." *Disability Studies Quarterly* 30 (1). http://dsq-sds.org/article/view/1063.

Yergeau, Melanie. 2013. "Clinically Significant Disturbance: On Theorists Who Theorize Theory of Mind." *Disability Studies Quarterly* 33 (4). http://dsq-sds.org/article/view/38 76/3405.

Yergeau, Melanie. 2018. *Authoring Autism: On Rhetoric and Neurological Queerness.* Durham, NC: Duke University Press.

PART II

Classroom and Curricular Praxis

5

WHOLE-SELF RHETORIC
Teaching the Justice Situation in the Composition Classroom

Nadya Pittendrigh

Worldwide, and even in the United States, there are many possibilities and justifications for response to wrongdoing. Bruce Western's 2018 *Homeward: Life in the Year After Prison* provides an example of this diversity. In a village in Ethiopia, a small child is struck and killed by a German researcher's car and elders in the village decide on a proper response to the death: to make up for the child's loss, the researcher must give the family a small sum and also effectively become a part of the deceased child's family. He is told he will need to visit from time to time and that "if they are going through problems, you should help them just as a member of their own family would" (xiv). The author tells this story exactly because it challenges common assumptions about what to . do when someone has caused catastrophic harm.

According to conventional assumptions about justice, situations of extreme aggrievement must be met with a pay schedule of punishment responsive to egregiousness or proportional to injury. The person who burns a barn might be expected to pay for the damage, while a person who recklessly or intentionally burns the barn would pay a more severe penalty. Within such a framework, we expect the family that loses a child under the circumstances described may well revile the person responsible or simply never want to see them again. Yet surprisingly, the researcher here is neither expelled nor rejected but instead is expected to join the family, almost as a kind of replacement. This scenario challenges conventional expectations in the same way restorative justice challenges our assumptions about justice. Like restorative justice, which puts perpetrators of crime into dialogue with those who have been harmed, the villagers' response to the lost child depends on a commitment to a shared future with the very person who caused the problem in the first place. The analysis presented in this chapter explores the implications of such an impulse and its relevance to rhetoric and composition pedagogy.

https://doi.org/10.7330/9781646421732.c005

The practices instantiated by the global restorative justice movement closely resemble those long practiced by many native or traditional cultures. According to traditional understanding among the Navajo, "A person who does harm to another 'acts as if he [*sic*] has no relatives,'" and repair requires a restored sense of relationality between the harmer and the harmed (Sullivan and Tifft 2005, 1). Many African nations, including South Africa, have also used an analogous approach to reconciliation in the aftermath of atrocity. Likewise, Mennonites in North America have developed restorative-justice programs, which have been adapted for use in the mainstream criminal justice system. These practices all challenge the assumption that a situation of radical conflict between the material interests of aggrieved parties must conduce to violence, expulsion, or natural war.

In the following analysis, restorative justice represents a ready-to-hand example of the mainstream US justice system attempting to incorporate alternative approaches in situations of conflict, and this analysis makes a similar move in reconceiving rhetoric in the context of navigating conflict more widely. In considering the relevance of restorative justice to the concerns of rhetoric, this chapter takes some of its inspiration from the 2018 CCCC: at the conference a striking number of panelists looked towards Krista Ratcliffe's conception of rhetorical listening, as well as Sonja Foss and Cindy Griffin's conception of invitational rhetoric, for tactical clues in navigating what I am calling *a shared future with the other*, specifically in the context of Donald Trump's then-recent election.[1] In the same spirit in which one might reach for rhetorical listening or invitational rhetoric when faced with the reality that half the country regards the views of the other as utterly anathema, this chapter reaches for restorative justice precisely when openness to the other seems unthinkable. Yet as I argue, in the name of teaching rhetorical skills for a shared future, the form of rhetoric that arises from restorative justice offers something to rhetorical pedagogy that neither rhetorical listening nor invitational rhetoric does.

The thinking that produced restorative justice applied to the composition classroom can be gathered under the heading for a form of rhetoric I am calling *whole-self rhetoric*. Whole-self rhetoric means coming to the table in a negotiation not armed and not operating from the narrow mandate of pursuing one's own material interests, but instead coming to that table with one's entire personality, very much including one's doubts about one's point of view. This argument demonstrates the contrast between such an approach and the traditional model of persuasion that continues to provide the rationale for much of composition pedagogy. Strongly influenced by courtroom rhetoric, the standard directive of persuasion encourages writing and thinking modeled on the behavior of a savvy lawyer whose overriding directive is victory and who therefore must suppress information that does not benefit the material interests of their client.

I aim to make a case for whole-self rhetoric as an undertheorized, underappreciated form of rhetoric that characterizes the rhetoric that takes place within restorative-justice dialogue and that ought to be on the table as part of our understanding in a context of conflicting values or ideas. I do not argue that it can replace all other forms rhetoric, but I offer it as an ideal towards which we can aspire and that can be engaged and developed in classrooms. In the following pages, I explore the implications and promise of engaging both restorative justice and whole-self rhetoric in rhetoric and composition classrooms and of adjusting the traditional focus on persuasion in such classrooms to make room for whole-self rhetoric.

WHAT IS RESTORATIVE JUSTICE?

Besides providing practical alternatives to punitive criminal proceedings, restorative justice offers an alternative set of framing assumptions to those provided by the mainstream criminal justice system. Criminal justice takes the situation of crime out of the hands of the people directly involved, effectively distancing them under the assumption that they have nothing to say to one another, that no further collaboration is possible between the parties, or that no one wants to listen to one another any longer. Against this tendency to isolate the harmer and the harmed from one another, restorative justice legitimates the opposite inclination, namely that sometimes the way to make things right is through a negotiation between the people involved: restorative justice provides a framework for willing parties to listen, build collaborative understanding, or find a productive path forward. In this sense, restorative justice can be understood as an extreme test case for the potential inherent in what Krista Ratcliffe (2006) calls "rhetorical listening." As Ratcliffe describes it, rhetorical listening involves "interpretive invention," offering "a way of making meaning with/in language" (17). However, restorative justice pursues collaborative interpretive invention in circumstances where the potential reasons to close the door on dialogue are admittedly much stronger than anything confronted in classrooms.

Restorative justice treats the community and its context as the medium through which meaningful repair to the social fabric might

be managed following a crime. According to the United Nations definition, restorative justice refers to "a process whereby all the parties with
a stake in a particular offense come together to collectively resolve how
to deal with the aftermath of the offense" (Sullivan and Tifft 2005, 23).
Through such processes, the people who are actually affected are called
upon to engage in dialogue in order to find a way forward, and importantly, the solution is not outsourced to the state. This essential engagement of community as a stakeholder in crime means offenders are not
excised from the community after wrongdoing. Ongoing consideration
of the offender as part of the community following a crime maintains a
potential thread of obligation on the part of the offender to the community. At the same time, that thread of obligation also extends back to
the community: the community is actively involved in finding productive
solutions after a crime and is therefore also accountable for solutions
that minimize further future harm. Thus, restorative justice often takes
the form of structured, mutually responsible inquiry, providing ritualized accountability for all parties.

Unlike criminal justice, which takes justice out of the hands of victims
and hands it over to the state, restorative justice directly engages victims'
experiences by foregrounding the attempt to address their needs and
take steps towards healing. At the same time that restorative dialogue
addresses what literally happened, what harm was caused, and the needs
of the parties involved, it also seeks to ensure offenders fully understand
"the damage they have caused" and their liability in repair (Johnstone
2011, 1). Advocates argue that even if reconciliation may not result
from a given restorative-justice dialogue, such reckonings open the
door to learning, while the criminal justice system makes such positive
transformation less accessible: the fact that a violation of law is treated
as a violation of the state effectively disengages victims from the process
while incentivizing offenders to maintain innocence rather than face
the harmful effects of their actions.

Though the restorative justice process hinges on dialogue between
the wrongdoer and those who have been impacted, the ripple effects of
that encounter extend beyond the immediate crime, potentially addressing broader ecologies of violence and need. Such discussions necessarily
include the nature of harm to the victim, the ripple effects of mistrust
and fear in the wider community, and what new harms were instituted as
a result. The point is that by coming to understand the full picture of the
reality of the other, we do the opposite of fostering violence. We lay the
groundwork for preventing future violence by creating precisely the kind
of understanding that might have prevented the crime in the first place.

Both rhetorical learning and restorative justice emphasize participants being brought back into awareness of their impact on others. This emphasis in restorative justice cultivates a capacity for communal understanding: "The hope is that those responsible for a harm will be able to acknowledge to the community and perhaps to the person(s) they harmed what they did and in some way make amends" (Sullivan and Tifft 2005, 1). Here, Dennis Sullivan and Larry Tifft (2005) emphasize understanding interpersonal harm as a community competency to be ritualized and taught. They describe an educational process of structured community response in the situation of having been harmed. Such responses ideally involve "questions to ask about the value or morality of social arrangements that manufacture and maintain structural inequities in societies . . . and that compete with restorative processes as an appropriate (healing) response to such crime" (3). In other words, restorative justice is not just an immediate response to individual harm. It engages the community in inquiry about systemic violence and inequality.

Sullivan and Tifft (2005) suggest that insofar as restorative justice focuses on meeting human needs, its relevance cannot stop at the borders of the criminal justice system. Since the criminal justice system itself infiltrates every aspect of social life, the authors argue, "restorative justice does not emerge out of a storehouse of correctional practices but out of a political philosophy of relationship" (391). As a "political philosophy of relationship," restorative justice resonates with contemporary rhetorical theory and potential implications for teaching. If students enter classrooms already enmeshed in material ecologies of power, the influence of incarceration saturates their being, which justifies inquiry into both incarceration and the paradigm of restorative justice as urgent matters for rhetorical inquiry.

RESTORATIVE JUSTICE IN THE CLASSROOM

This chapter merely scratches the surface of restorative justice's potential to enrich writing pedagogy, but my own classroom experiments (see appendix 5.A) fall into two categories: restorative justice can provide fruitful avenues of inquiry for interrogating structural inequality and the criminal justice system, or it can provide an alternative approach to communication itself. The rest of this analysis focuses on the latter, in which restorative justice provides a paradigm of collaborative inquiry (particularly in the context of conflict) with the potential to improve the polity. Though classrooms generally do not involve the degree of conflict that would motivate a restorative justice scenario, rhetoric and composition classrooms are obviously inflected by the conflicts that exist in the wider culture. As a cursory sketch of the local context where I teach, for example, gun culture is both held dear and earnestly questioned by various students on a campus where students are also allowed to bring weapons so long as they are concealed. It is also a majority-minority institution, yet in a historical moment in which the Southern Poverty Law Center (2019) records a national increase in hate crimes and hate groups, many students explicitly express the desire not to participate in discussions that engage political, racial, or material differences out of a sense of personal peril. Students of color routinely confess they do not want to know what others in the class think about high-stakes issues such as immigration, race, and policing because they do not trust each other to hold views compatible with their own continued existence in the community. Some affirm the assumption that there is no possibility of a negotiation, dialogue, or transformation when it comes to race and other issues of justice that intimately inform their own lives. Others simply decline to engage issues of racial inequality in the class with strangers. Yet if participants are prepared for it, restorative justice can provide fruitful avenues of inquiry for engaging uncomfortable issues, offer novel approaches to ethical exchange in otherwise ossified discourses of justice, and simultaneously provide an opening into the possibility for transformative dialogue in situations of severe conflict. Restorative justice demonstrates, against extreme odds, the possibility of dialogue between people whose positions may be anathema but who nonetheless find a way to listen and to be open to one another.

Making incarceration, race, policing, or punishment central to rhetorical inquiry in a composition classroom automatically enmeshes the class in fraught issues already felt acutely by our students, with collaborative rhetorical inquiry itself offered as a primary means of navigating that fraught context. Thus, any composition class that places incarceration or punishment at its center will surely feature all the widely held instincts and attitudes that justify our criminal justice system, including the intuition that the cops must be right. As one of my students argued, "I don't know why we are talking about the criminal at all. We should be worrying about the victim." Here, the instinct to side with justice guides us to think the criminal has lost the right to speak and has no standing. Students also resist the challenges that restorative justice poses to their intuitions on the grounds that when there's a crime, someone must pay: you cannot let them get away with it. One additional area of resistance comes from our natural inclination to assume the cops must have been justified in doing what did in a questionable situation because we want the psychological relief of believing what they did must be okay. We tell ourselves, "After all, Eric Garner was selling cigarettes illegally." We come up with differences between ourselves and the person shot by the police because it relieves our fear. Restorative justice challenges this inclination to neatly separate oneself not only from the dangerous person but also from the person in danger. Thus, confronting inequity through restorative justice (unlike traditional conceptions of justice, which neatly isolate the guilty) directly engages the lurking authoritarianism of the current political moment. In the classroom, criminal justice commonplaces like *If you can't do the time, don't do the crime* provide an opening to engage questions about whether or not the law is always perfect, or to what extent the society owes something to the potential criminal to help them become the kind of person who does not commit crime.

Whether as a paradigm for responding to conflict, or as an institutional response to crime, restorative justice is a hard sell in writing classrooms, where writing, not crime, provides the focus. In this sense, restorative justice functions only as an analogy for the kind of rhetoric I'm advocating as having a place in the considerations of rhetoric and composition: the restorative-justice paradigm addresses violations, not just of law but also of the wider social fabric, including violations in a given conversation. In other words, restorative justice offers rituals and practices for plural dialogue in the context of conflict, which is only analogous to issues of breaking the law. Accordingly, my own experiments with restorative justice in the classroom take restorative justice as a response to crime as a challenging provocation through which to engage intractable, "wicked" problems, perhaps particularly regarding incarceration, inequality, and rhetoric. By virtue of their intractability, such problems require collaborative inquiry, precisely because they involve multiple stakeholders with persistent, conflicting interests.

PERSUASION VERSUS RESTORATIVE JUSTICE

The rhetorical practices of restorative justice point us toward a world in which people with radically different viewpoints can in fact come together in the public square in order to deliberate for the common good. In this section, I make the case that a world in which students are routinely trained in something more like restorative justice, or as

I ultimately argue, the whole-self rhetoric it gives rise to, has a better chance than debate or persuasion of producing that world eventually.

Though many other authors have resisted a narrow or exclusive focus on persuasion as the central paradigm for teaching writing, it continues to shape priorities in the argument culture of the writing classroom. As A. Abby Knoblauch (2011) documents in "A Textbook Argument: Definitions of Argument in Leading Composition Textbooks," scholars have called for alternatives to argumentation "that explicitly focus on negotiation and understanding" (245). From Rogerian rhetoric to invitational rhetoric, the need for pedagogical alternatives to traditional argument have not only been articulated, but methods have been offered. Yet as Knoblauch shows, even when textbooks as expansive as *Everything's an Argument* (Lunsford, Ruszkiewicz, and Walters 1998) include Rogerian or invitational approaches, those approaches typically make a minor cameo in a landscape otherwise dominated by "traditional argument," which she says "privileges argument as winning and undercuts the radical potential of argument as understanding across difference" (248). Knoblauch affirms that in the most popular composition textbooks, and by extension the worldview pervading composition classrooms, such methods typically are subsumed by the framing assumptions of persuasion.

If composition textbooks and their assumptions about argument telegraph a worldview, perhaps no recent textbook operating in the persuasive paradigm has had more influence than *They Say / I Say* by Gerald Graff and Cathy Birkenstein (2006). The worldview implicit in the book's title is that one's warrant for speaking is that one is saying something different: I have discovered that the sun does not revolve around the earth, so "they" (or the world) are wrong, and I am here to set the record straight. My warrant for speaking is that what "they" say is wrong. For the purposes of teaching academic writing as conversation, the book does include argument templates for expressing ambivalence and "listening" to naysayers. Yet just as Knoblauch observes that Rogerian and invitational rhetoric are overshadowed by an overwhelming emphasis within "traditional argument" on winning, likewise, expressing mixed feelings and really listening to the other side plays a minor part in the overriding emphasis of *They Say / I Say*. Certainly, nowhere in *Clueless in Academe* (Graff 2004) nor in *They Say / I Say* do the authors explicitly say the exigence for speaking comes from a willingness to do battle, but it is implied in the overall pedagogy, which teaches undergraduate and graduate students that finding flaws in the arguments of others provides the very definition of academic argumentation.

So how do the rhetorical practices inherent in restorative justice differ from traditional argument and persuasion, or how does a classroom saturated with restorative justice differ from a classroom whose focus is persuasion? One answer is that if persuasion in the composition classroom is often about "they say / I say," in restorative justice, everyone has their say. There is no sense that one perspective in the conversation dominates or is more important than the other. The premise of a persuasion situation, by contrast, is that the speaker has nothing to learn, is in possession of the relevant facts, and is tasked with replicating themself. The persuasion paradigm says, "Right now you are different from me—you either have nothing in your head, or you have wrong things in your head. And if you have nothing in your head, great, I will fill it. If you have wrong things in your head, I will get in there with some weed killer, spray it, kill wrong things, and then plant it with healthy crops." Accordingly, persuasion allows the persuader to retreat into the sense that they are already sufficient: "What you know is good, and your task is to clone your thought because it is known that what is in the other person's head is weeds and what is in your own head is wholesome food."

If the persuasive model regards the persuader as sufficient already, in restorative justice it is vital no one approach the table in that spirit. Instead, the premise is that no one is wrong and no one is right. What we need is not that people are persuaded but rather that everyone has an expanded mind. Participants don't go into a restorative-justice scenario pressing each other into admitting the other is right. Person A doesn't try to get Person B to adopt Person A's view or replace their current view with Person A's own view. Instead, restorative justice is more about pooling resources or information. One goes into a restorative-justice scenario in a spirit of learning. Or perhaps we can understand such a scenario in terms of having some information to present to a committee. If there is an engineering firm and I am from the department of material sciences, I have information about what kind of steel is the cheapest, but it would not make sense to approach the discussion in a spirit of "I want the building to be XYZ and we must use this kind of steel" because maybe others on the committee have information that would impact the overall plan—that approach is more like restorative justice. You are a member of a committee. You have a piece of the puzzle. But you are not there to call the shots. You don't want to replace someone else's view with your view. Instead, you want to add to their knowledge, and vice versa.

Ratcliffe's (2005) conception of *Rhetorical Listening* speaks to this discussion, precisely because her explicit interest is in listening, in the name of teaching/transmitting a stance of openness. Unlike "the moves that matter in academic writing" in *They Say / I Say* (Graff and Birkenstein 2006), which urges students to find the meaning of what they have to say insofar as it contrasts with opposing claims, Ratcliffe emphasizes care in examining such identifications and disidentifications (much of it geared towards checking the abuses of whiteness within cross-cultural exchange) through listening for understanding.

Yet I have come to believe restorative justice functions differently from rhetorical listening. Ratcliffe (2005) defines rhetorical listening as a stance of openness, or a mode of understanding within cross-cultural communication, and suggests that one essential capacity to teach students involves being on the lookout, while listening to one another, for our differing cultural frames. She writes, "By focusing on claims and cultural logics, listeners may still disagree with one another, but they may better appreciate that the other person is not simply wrong but is functioning within a different cultural logic" (33). She is saying that even when you disagree with another person's stance, if you understand where they are coming from, you are in a better position to disagree with their worldview while at the same time understanding where it comes from. You are in a better position not to withdraw entirely from the person you disagree with.

Yet this is where I believe rhetorical listening falls short of what I think we currently need. In fact, Richard Spencer, infamous voice of the alt-right, can summarize the views of his enemies on the Left—he already knows the Left is operating from a different set of principles, and that is why he hates them. Perhaps the insufficiency I'm pointing to in this concept of rhetorically listening can be seen particularly vividly in the Trump era: picture a Trump supporter versus a progressive—their politics seem irreconcilable. The progressive understands Trump supporters are operating from a different set of principles, yet the progressive still finds their principles despicable, and vice versa. Instead, for the purposes of either peace or teaching, I suggest the fault does not lie in the attempt to understand the other person's point of view. Insofar as we are teaching students to anticipate counterarguments, we are actually teaching them to understand the worldview of the other the better to attack it; in that sense, we are not teaching our students to better understand one another. So my argument is that restorative justice involves something higher than just listening to the other. Restorative justice is listening with a commitment to a shared future with the perceived-as-malevolent other.

Richard Marback's (2010) analysis of vulnerability within rhetoric is worth thinking about in this connection. His essay "A Meditation on Vulnerability in Rhetoric" tracks common understandings about rhetoric, particularly our fear of being persuaded and our habitual understanding of vulnerability as a liability. He writes, "At stake in the pejorative view of rhetoric is an anxiety over influence, an awareness of experiencing oneself as vulnerable," not only to deception but also to being intervened with (2). Ratcliffe's (2005) theorization of rhetorical listening contrasts with this exaggerated image of rhetoric as interventionist when she recommends eavesdropping as a mode of rhetorical listening, which suggests just listening without necessarily "putting your oar in."[2] In these contrasting, gendered accounts of rhetoric as passive or as interventionist, we can see an image of rhetoric as action that is often intuitively troped as a kind of penetration.

And maybe penetration does offer an illuminative way of thinking about rhetoric for the purposes of distinguishing the rhetorical practices of restorative justice from persuasion: when one comes to the table for restorative justice, the expectation is not "I'm going to perform some kind of penetrating violence upon you, and then you do the same to me, and from that justice will arise." Likewise, the parties in a restorative-justice situation are not made to scold one another from radically different positions. In a restorative-justice situation, it's more like we come to the table and we fuse. I see how you are me and you see how I am you, so we can extend to each other the kind of sensible, non-psychopathic non-revenge designed to attempt to make things right. We apply to one another the same kinds of correctives we might perform on ourselves.

Restorative justice, which takes as axiomatic that the criminal did not act from pure evil and guides students to conclusions and feelings compatible with the fact that the criminal did not freely choose to be evil, or simply has a story to tell, helps students see that if they had been the criminal, they too would have done what the criminal did. Likewise, restorative justice slows down the default reaction to being harmed by others, namely the desire for the other person's suffering.

WHOLE-SELF RHETORIC

Like restorative justice, invitational rhetoric is a method for gently and humanely changing the mind of the other, with an emphasis on dialogue, not persuasion. Thus, invitational rhetoric's focus on creating an environment in which change can occur, and not necessarily on changing minds, resembles the rhetorical practices of restorative justice. Yet I argue in the immediately following pages that invitational rhetoric differs in important ways from what I am calling *whole-self rhetoric*, which is the name this analysis gives to the rhetoric that arises from a successful restorative justice scenario.

In "Beyond Persuasion: A Proposal for Invitational Rhetoric," Sonja Foss and Cindy Griffin (1995) find fault with persuasion's dominance in rhetoric, for its fixation on conquest, conversion, and advice. According to the authors, these rhetorics focus on the establishment of superiority and jockeying for position, against which the authors advocate for a mode of communication that does not intervene. They enjoin us not to seek to change the other, which imposes upon the other person's right to self-determination. Even so, the authors don't actually oppose changing the minds of others; they simply think change should be invited, not pushed for.

In what I am calling *whole-self rhetoric*, by contrast, not knowing with certainty that you are right, and not being asked to act as if you do, creates gentleness within inquiry, particularly in the context of conflict. On this point, whole-self rhetoric has the same goals as invitational rhetoric, but whole-self rhetoric differs from invitational rhetoric and rhetorical listening in its emphasis on openness to being changed. Rather than adopting a stance of certainty, whole-self rhetoric encourages each person to act like a member of a team of scientists: you are going to present your results, but others are looking at the issue with different perspectives and results. So you do have something to contribute, but you are also there to listen. The key difference between invitational rhetoric and whole-self rhetoric is that in invitational rhetoric, the first step still focuses on one's interlocutor: one turns towards the other, whereas the first step of whole-self rhetoric focuses on the speaker. In other words, part of what is emphasized in whole-self rhetoric is bringing to the table parts of yourself that have no designs on the other, which means being open to being changed.

The key distinction between whole-self rhetoric and invitational rhetoric is that whole-self rhetoric offers a first step, one that stands a chance of actually producing open-mindedness or mutual understanding. Unlike a command to be respectful or civil to the other, whole-self rhetoric offers a first step. The first step entails nonattachment to victory, meaning a willingness to explore doubt. If, in its dominant historical forms, there is a fundamental orientation in rhetoric towards a gladiatorial model, whole-self rhetoric means not bringing your idealized, weaponized self to the table, ready to cajole or to bully. Instead, whole-self rhetoric says, "Here's what I've got, including my doubts and limitations, and I fully acknowledge I don't know everything." Within such a scenario, your opponent wouldn't be your opponent, which makes more possible all parties lowering their defenses and listening to one another. Important, such an outcome could not be willed into existence by an agreement to be civil. Instead, whole-self rhetoric offers an actual procedure that makes listening possible.

Beyond the first step, whole-self rhetoric requires more than nonattachment to victory; just as important, the other person needs to know you are doing it (you are pursuing whole-self rhetoric, not the familiar victory-seeking forms of persuasive rhetoric). For the benefit of your interlocutor and in order to create a whole-self rhetoric situation, you must explicitly own your whole self, meaning the limitations of your view must be made accessible to your interlocutor. Displaying your ability to explore doubt in front of your interlocutor demonstrates to the other person that you are not in the conversation for victory, and doing so occasionally has magical effects: when someone in a conflict says, "Well okay, I can hear that," it becomes possible for the other person to be open. Suddenly, the situation becomes less a fight than an inquiry.

Whole-self rhetoric also differs from rhetorical listening, which puts its faith in knowing more: the premise of rhetorical listening is that if information were more freely transferred between conflicting parties, we would dehumanize each other less, which would guide us to cut the other person a break. Whole-self rhetoric instead asks us to impose upon ourselves the same skepticism we impose upon the world because the capacity to doubt oneself is a precondition to open-mindedness. Whole-self rhetoric does not demand that we respect the narcissism of others but instead asks that if we disrespect narcissism, we should turn that disrespect for narcissism on ourselves. Whole-self rhetoric guides us to openly own our biases; then maybe the other person can do so as well. In fact, if rhetorical listening emphasizes information exchange, it is actually possible that exchanging more information could make the conditions for dehumanization even worse. Turning on yourself, by contrast, demonstrates open-mindedness through open consideration of doubt.

Such procedures are certainly familiar to all humans and are nothing new. Yet what I am arguing is that they represent a neglected dimension of inquiry and should be part of what we explicitly teach students: the willingness and ability to side against your own advantage. Whole-self rhetoric amounts to a kind of due process conducted internally, with an emphasis on doing so justly. A reasonable internal attempt to set things right represents a huge check on the desire to punish and humiliate because we do not know with certainty we are right. We are able to hear someone out because we haven't already decided the other person is wrong.

INVITATIONAL RHETORIC VERSUS WHOLE-SELF RHETORIC

Fundamentally, whole-self rhetoric means recognizing we are all vulnerable while teaching interlocutors not to come to the table as their idealized selves. Restorative justice represents a version of this insofar as the offender's idealized self and their justifications about why it was acceptable to do what they did are not welcome at the table. In the restorative-justice scenario, the offender is not encouraged to say, "I did it because my mom did XYZ, and it's not my fault, and I'm not sorry, for reasons ABC." Such justifications are not welcome, in part because they tend to involve simplification, which effectively dehumanizes both the offender and the victim. For instance, if the offender says, "I'm not sorry for what I did," it is probably not entirely true—a part of them actually is sorry, and that part will be enlarged when they hear more about the harmed person and their experience. In resisting such simplifications, whole-self rhetoric asks the parties to arrive at the table with the idea that they don't know everything and they are not the only ones hurting, and in fact, everyone involved experiences helplessness and humiliation.

The whole-self brought forth in a restorative-justice scenario contrasts with the paradigmatic persuasion scenario—that of the courtroom. Persuasion in a courtroom means having a plan, or a severely edited self, and knowing what to edit based on the plan. The culture of the table in such a scenario is not a safe place. In a courtroom proceeding, or in a persuasion scenario taking its cue from the courtroom, the situation guides us to not trust the others at the table: one argues to win. The attorney's role is to defend a client who did or did not commit a crime and to hide everything not advantageous to victory; on the other hand, everything that is advantageous must be strengthened like a juggernaut. Given these conditions, why should a lawyer admit their client actually did anything wrong? Doing so would be like going into a battle in a T-shirt when the other side has swords and armor. Yet if both lawyers were part of a committee tasked with deriving the truth, everything we know about the armor of court would be eliminated.

That courtroom situation saturates the teaching of writing, particularly academic writing. If the guiding muse is critique, or leveraging one's own intervention against the limitations of the other arguments in the field, that approach informs our habits of explaining to students what persuasion is: persuasion means taking someone or someone's position to pieces. Insofar as the rhetor is motivated by the desire for victory over the other, persuasive rhetoric is different from whole-self rhetoric because (like invitational rhetoric) it is other-oriented.

This other-oriented, victory-focused courtroom rhetoric also exerts undue influence upon our instincts about confronting the outside world in general: "Why should I be high-minded and fair? If I take the high road, I will just be exterminated." Whole-self rhetoric attempts to reboot these excessively weaponized instincts insofar as it asks participants to engage with the equivalent of a T-shirt and no sword. The aim is to suspend the mentality that the other side is going to be unfair and that therefore I'm going to go ahead and be unfair preemptively.

Whole-self rhetoric is the opposite of courtroom rhetoric, and everything modeled on it, insofar as the negotiators resist the creation of an invulnerable version of themselves with all doubts hidden and vulnerabilities protected. It asks the rhetor to own their vulnerabilities, or to own that they are not pure, perfect, or innocent. It asks the rhetor to forego certainty as a prerequisite to working on a shared future with the other. The move is to decline to radically separate yourself from the other through a conception of either innocence or righteousness. By the same principle, whole-self rhetoric sets aside the usual social game in which one feels obligated to front invulnerability.

CONCLUSION

In evaluating whole-self rhetoric, perhaps by association with invitational rhetoric, people may mistake it for a type of rhetoric that prioritizes civility and excludes the expression of negative feelings, discomfort, and conflict. In fact, far from squashing negative, disruptive feelings within conflict, whole-self rhetoric represents a better way of engaging conflict. Calls for civility and demands for respect seem to suggest interlocutors are not allowed to be angry, or that anger simply must be swallowed in order for the aggrieved parties to move on. Importantly, this is exactly not what whole-self rhetoric represents: whole-self rhetoric does not demand of the aggrieved parties that they transcend their experiences in order to somehow magically transcend their anger. In this sense, whole-self rhetoric begins where civility leaves off. Everything is great if everyone is nice in the first place, but whole-self rhetoric begins to address the question of what to do, and how to proceed, once someone has already harmed someone.

It is important to note that whole-self rhetoric cannot simply be adopted through force of will, regardless of the conditions of the exchange. Rather, whole-self rhetoric depends upon the whole-self rhetoric scenario. Thus, it is not enough that the parties involved are willing to try. In order for the interlocutors to actually participate in whole-self rhetoric, the people involved must be able to actually see the performance of the whole self of their interlocutor. Something must be done so the people at the table really believe the other person is willing to side against themself, show their doubts, or consider positions that are disadvantageous. Fundamentally, both parties must demonstrate their willingness to show vulnerability. Each must be convinced that the other people don't want the war, or that enough of them don't want the war. The person wronged or who feels wronged must be willing to forego the pleasure of saying "Cry me a river" or "Nothing you can say can help." There must be a show of being open, a willingness to listen, an investment in trying to understand the other, not just in being understood. The unavoidable upshot is that whole-self rhetoric cannot be performed in all situations by all people. In the same way restorative justice does not always work, and cannot be relied upon for all people in all situations, whole-self rhetoric is not a panacea.

Rather, whole-self rhetoric is a goal and a neglected dimension of rhetorical skill and understanding. In this sense, my argument does not claim rhetorical vulnerability should be employed universally but rather that there are many situations in which whole-self rhetoric would be much more productive than courtroom rhetoric yet is not attempted because of the assumption that whole-self rhetoric is not even possible—and that assumption keeps everyone overly weaponized. Partly, we are weaponized because we overestimate the application of courtroom rhetoric and we dare not show our vulnerability—the default assumption is that our only option is to draw blood. This paper attempts to put the normalization of whole-self rhetoric on the table, which could eventually contribute to a world in which whole-self rhetoric becomes increasingly possible. The more the sharing of vulnerability becomes possible and talked about as a part of whole-self rhetoric, the more we can all consider the possibility that more communication, in more situations than we realize, can be deweaponized.

APPENDIX 5.A

As part of developing this chapter's conception of whole-self rhetoric in the composition classroom, I have incorporated a writing project into first-year writing classes called the "Doubt Paper," shared below. It is intended to teach students to harness their uncertainty, which they have in abundance, as a valuable resource in open inquiry and as an essential element of whole-self rhetoric. I have used the assignment as one-half of a "genre-switching" project in which students compose both a manifesto about an issue and a "Doubt Paper" on the same issue and then reflect on the potential afforded by each genre. I have also assigned the "Doubt Paper" as an exercise in the research process while gearing up for formulating a promising inquiry. The "Doubt Paper" mobilizes students' ambivalence as whole-self rhetoric at the same time it models open inquiry.

I have assigned the "Doubt Paper" in socially engaged writing classes, and in some cases the students did use the assignment to write about issues related to justice. In other cases, students chose to write about more personal concerns, such as their religious faith, conflicts with family, whether to kick toxic people out of their lives, belief in the golden rule, and the value of kindness. Many students emphatically communicated their preference for the "Doubt Paper" over other assignments because it tapped into authentically held questions. In my experience, even when students write about personal issues, the "Doubt Paper" scaffolds into more public questions, which were incorporated into follow-up assignments.

Because I conceive the "Doubt Paper" as something to build towards and not something to start the term with, it serves nicely as an informal assessment tool by which to judge whether students are able to fulfill the assignment at that point. Based on this assignment, peers can weigh in on whether or not "this person has made it real." In my classes, through anonymized peer review, students are encouraged to provide compassionate but honest feedback about whether the paper comes off like "nerf doubt" or like the author is grappling with sincere doubt. A teacher can likewise judge whether or not the writer has picked an issue they really care about, and whether they have written about doubts that are uncomfortable to face; if they have, the teacher can rightly think the students are getting somewhere in terms of whole-self rhetoric.

The "Doubt Paper" can also be understood as preparation for going to the table in a negotiation, even in situations of conflict. The assignment and its requirements are designed to make use of complexity or ambivalence on a given issue instead of asking students to wager a decisive claim and defend it in the name of persuasion. Its focus and strictures encourage the writer to face their whole self, including their doubts, on an issue that matters to the writer, precisely because it is counterintuitive to do so. Students may openly wonder, why would I make my case weaker? Why would it make sense to devitalize myself while trying to win an argument? The answers to these questions are related to why one might enter into a restorative-justice dialogue. The point is subversion of the war paradigm, disarming, and not approaching the table in a spirit of trying to win or to vanquish.

DOUBT PAPER: REQUIREMENTS AND HINTS

Vocabulary: Conviction—a firmly held belief or opinion

> *"A very popular error: having the courage of one's convictions—?*
> *Rather it is a matter of having the courage for an attack on one's*
> *convictions."*
>
> —Friedrich Nietzsche

Explanation of the Paper:

Title: Consider calling your paper "Here Are My Doubts."

Length: 500 words, typed

Audience: Yourself, me, anonymous peers, possibly the wider public

Goal: Your peers read your paper and think, "This person is deep!"

Purpose: To get real. To not front. Not to persuade. To open up an issue.

Format: I ask that the paper be typed and have coherently organized paragraphs with paragraph breaks.

Hints:

1. Pick a belief/conviction to write about that you actually care about. Not "I have my doubts about whether the lottery should be legal."

2. Pick something specific to write about. Not "I have my doubts about economics."

3. This paper is not *describing* your doubts about something.

4. This paper is not *listing* your doubts about something.

5. It's thinking them through carefully.

6. Provide a clear statement of your conviction as the basis for exploring doubt about it.

7. Remember not to make the whole paper about your conviction. (That's just the opening move! It might be just a sentence or a paragraph early on in the paper. The focus should be your doubts about that conviction.)

Required Structure

Paragraph 1: What's your conviction? What are your reasons for it? Get specific. Don't leave this vague.
   • Elaborate.

Give reasons.

Paragraph 2: Setting aside whether you're right, explain why you WANT #1 to be true. What are the unscientific reasons you believe the stuff in #1? (You're going to have to get kind of personal here.)

All remaining paragraphs: Thoughtfully considering your doubts:

- Maybe there is a story you can tell: a moment that made you pause.
- Maybe there is a conversation you can describe that made you worry.
- Maybe there's a news story that troubles your conviction in some ways.
- Maybe you can admit the limits of the evidence on this issue.
- Maybe you can admit the limits of your certainty on this issue.

NOTES

1. This analysis was also inspired by the scholarship of Candice Rai, whose 2017 and 2018 CCCC presentations explored the potential for a politics of vulnerability and ambivalence within argumentation pedagogy in the age of Trump.
2. In *The Philosophy of Literary Form* Kenneth Burke famously compares rhetoric to participating in a conversation already under way in a parlor, to which you arrive late. "You listen for a while, until you decide that you have caught the tenor of the argument; then you put in your oar" (1941, 110).

REFERENCES

Burke, Kenneth. 1941. *The Philosophy of Literary Form*. Berkeley: University of California Press.

Foss, Sonja, and Cindy Griffin. 1995. "Beyond Persuasion: A Proposal for Invitational Rhetoric." *Communication Monographs* 62 (1): 2–18.

Graff, Gerald, and Cathy Birkenstein. 2006. *They Say/I Say*. New York: Norton.

Johnstone, Gerry. 2011. *Restorative Justice: Ideas, Values, Debates*. New York: Routledge.

Knoblauch, A. Abby. 2011. "A Textbook Argument: Definitions of Argument in Leading Composition Textbooks." *College Composition and Communication* 63 (2): 244–68.

Lunsford, Andrea A., John J. Ruszkiewicz, and Keith Walters. 1998. *Everything's an Argument*. Boston: Bedford/St. Martin's.

Marback, Richard. "A Meditation on Vulnerability in Rhetoric." *Rhetoric Review* 29 (1): 1–13.

Rai, Candice. 2017. "Objects of (In)Justice in the Global University." Paper presented at the annual convention of the Conference on College Composition and Communication, Kansas City, MO, March 16.

Rai, Candice. 2018. "On Vulnerability, Persuasion, and Ethics and Persuasion." Paper presented at the annual convention of the Conference on College Composition and Communication, Kansas City, MO, March 17.

Ratcliffe, Krista. 2005. *Rhetorical Listening: Identification, Gender, Whiteness*. Carbondale: Southern Illinois University Press.

Southern Poverty Law Center. 2019. "Hate Groups Reach Record High." February 19. https://www.splcenter.org/news/2019/02/19/hate-groups-reach-record-high.

Sullivan, Dennis, and Larry Tifft. 2005. *Handbook of Restorative Justice: A Global Perspective*. New York: Routledge.

Western, Bruce. 2018. *Homeward: Life in the Year After Prison*. New York: Russell Sage Foundation.

Zehr, Howard. 2015. *Changing Lenses: Restorative Justice for Our Times*. Independence, MO: Herald Press.

6

REWRITING THE BIOLOGY OF DIFFERENCE
How a Writing-Centered, Case-Based Curricular Approach Can Reform Undergraduate Science

Megan Callow and Katherine Xue

The biological sciences play a crucial role in shaping discourse around categories of human difference. Deeply rooted understandings of difference have monumental implications for research agendas, biomedical practice, and stereotypes that arise from scientific uses of race (Duster 2003; Friedman and Lee 2013), gender (Maney 2016; Saini 2017), and other identities. However, recent work in science and technology studies (STS) has scrutinized the notion that there is a purely biological basis for difference among human groups. Yet the absence of this scrutiny in undergraduate science and science-writing classrooms directly influences how foundational knowledge is built. Currently, undergraduate science and science-writing education are often overlooked as potential sites for critiquing normative discourses about human difference (Brickhouse and Letts 1998; Howitt and Wilson 2014). Science education tends to disregard science as contested, instead teaching theory and method as unimpeachable paradigms and emphasizing form and convention in its texts. By putting into conversation some of the strands of STS, writing studies, and science-education scholarship, in this chapter we show how centering social contexts and epistemological controversies in the sciences and thinking rhetorically about scientific texts are essential for deepening students' understanding of social/biological difference and for helping them become more critical practitioners and communicators.

In this chapter we survey several key studies from STS, a multidisciplinary field that focuses "on how scientific practitioners organize their work activities; make claims about knowledge and strive to endow those claims with credibility; and defend, or extend, the boundaries of their practice" (Epstein 2007, 18–19). STS is interested in "philosophical

https://doi.org/10.7330/9781646421732.c006

bias"—the fundamental assumptions about ontology (ways of being), epistemology (ways of knowing), and subsequent normative methodologies (accepted ways of practicing) in the sciences (Anderson, Anjum, and Rocca 2019). This scholarship illuminates how scientific practices help construct categories of human difference, like race and gender.

In our exploration of several cases of race and gender, we first consider how long-held conceptions of human difference reinforce and are reinforced by the traditional modes of empiricism and how these modes underlie contemporary undergraduate science education (Stanley and Brickhouse 2001). Next, the chapter outlines how these ways of knowing are constituted linguistically. Writing-in-the-disciplines scholars explore the "integrative relationship between writing and knowing" (Carter 2007, 386) and argue that effective disciplinary writing instruction is grounded in the knowledge traditions of a given field. As we argue, writing-intensive, case-based instruction offers a meaningful way for students to critique traditional modes of thinking in the sciences. Finally, we propose a pedagogical approach that introduces these ideas to students, specifically emphasizing science communication as multimodal, contested, and personal.

We offer this chapter to writing-across-the-curriculum administrators, and to science and science-writing instructors, as an introduction to some of the ways scientific knowledge production is being contested, focusing on debates about human difference but touching more broadly on the socially situated nature of science. Our hope is that instructors will engage such debates in their classrooms. A critical pedagogical approach to scientific literacy (Brown, Reveles, and Kelly 2005; Priest 2013) can help students learn and communicate fundamental principles of the field; and, we would add, writing as a curricular intervention in science can help students deconstruct accepted categories of difference. Understanding that the "linguistic component of science requires analysis to the same extent as does laboratory work" (Condit 1996, 96) is essential for preparing students to be more attuned to and critical of normative practices, and as a result, better scientists.

DIFFERENCE AND ITS (NON)CONTROVERSIES IN SCIENCE

Debates about human difference have proliferated in recent years. On March 23, 2018, Harvard geneticist David Reich published an op-ed in the *New York Times*, "How Genetics Is Changing Our Understanding of 'Race,'" in which he argued it is "simply no longer possible to ignore average genetic differences among 'races.'" Distancing himself from scientific racism-rationalizing eugenics, Reich argues that research focused on understanding average genetic differences between human populations has clear therapeutic potential and thus global health implications.

The reaction to Reich's piece was swift and fierce, both for and against. In an open letter signed by sixty-seven scholars across the natural and social sciences, Reich was decried for harmfully mischaracterizing race by repeating the common error of conflating race with geographical origin or ancestry. One often-cited example is that sickle cell anemia is commonly named as a " 'black' disease" (Jonathan, Nelson, and Graves 2018). To claim a genetic relationship between the disease and a single racial category is not only a false correlation but also disregards the populations that do suffer from the disease but don't identify as Black. In fact, the gene variant that contributes to the disease is higher among descendants of regions with high rates of malaria—a covariate that has much greater explanatory power than race does (see Maney [2016] for more on covariation). Ian Holmes (2018), a UC Berkeley geneticist, pointed out that the distinctions between race (a social construction) and ancestry are actually "remarkably uncontroversial" among geneticists. The issue is one, rather, of "poor communication." Blurring "race" and "ancestry," categories that *can* help explain genetic patterns among human populations, not only displays fallacious logic but can also act as an ideological dog whistle (see Ann Morning's March 29, 2018, blog post "Race, Genetics, and the Lure of Forbidden Knowledge" for another rhetorical critique of Reich.)

We share this extended example for a number of reasons. First, it exemplifies a growing conversation that has been playing out at least since Thomas Kuhn's *The Structure of Scientific Revolutions* (1962) began troubling the universalist, essentialist narrative of Western science. Recently, the controversies have begun to center on issues related to human difference. Biological (i.e., genetic, neurochemical, and physiological) characteristics of racial difference are no longer taken for granted, and new questions are emerging about the relevance of race—and of other human categorizations like sex—to science. Consequently, Reich and his responders circulated important ontological and epistemological questions for the field.

Second, the Reich example demonstrates how these debates should be understood rhetorically. Understanding how scientific concepts get reified via linguistic practices reveals that scientists are, like anyone else, "holders of multiple interests and insights" (Condit 1996, 101). Linguistic precision matters, not just in communicating science but for its very practice—how humans are studied, how their classifications are quantified, and how they, as a result, are diagnosed and treated (medically and socially). For that reason, as this chapter argues, analyzing systems of science communication can better prepare novices to question conceptions of difference and to approach traditional methods more critically.

Finally, the Reich example is a case we believe to be of immense educational value; it, along with other cases we describe, provides content for a relevant and timely case-based curriculum. Given the preponderance of mainstream debates like these, it is surprising they remain largely absent from science classrooms, particularly large, undergraduate survey courses. Despite decades-long educational-reform efforts (American Association for the Advancement of Science 1993), the supremacy of Western mainstream science and its methods continues to be taught, with only rare inquiry into the discipline's uncertainties (Howitt and Wilson 2014). Of particular consequence is the concept of scientific difference: the ways organisms, species, and the types thereof are categorically distinct.

Difference has unique significance in the sciences. Scientific methods rely on the comparison of traits or behavior between groups, whether these groups are characterized by differences across species, differences in phenotypic traits within species, differences in medical treatment between groups, differences in genetic traits between groups . . . bases for comparison go on and on. Whatever the units of analysis, distinction between groups is an "ineliminable feature" (Epstein 2004, 198) of the production of scientific knowledge. Yet in *Sorting Things Out: Classification and its Consequences*, George Bowker and Susan Star (1999) ask, "What are these categories? Who makes them, and who may change them? When and why do they become visible? How do they spread?" (2–3). Even in the sciences, the principles underlying human categorization have political and moral qualities, which are often invisible, at least until social forces bring classificatory boundaries into contention. For example, it was only after intense lobbying efforts from gay-rights activists and allied mental-health workers that the American Psychological Association voted to drop homosexuality as a category of pathology from the *Diagnostic and Statistical Manual of Mental Disorders* (DSM) in 1973 (Drescher 2015). This instance shows that emerging scientific theories depathologizing homosexuality were not sufficient in and of themselves to dislodge the term from the DSM; a concurrent political mobilization was required as well. The example also shows the multidirectional relationships among scientific and social change: political action

demedicalized homosexuality, and demedicalization subsequently facilitated other social and legal changes, such as the repeal of sodomy laws,
the establishment of workplace protections for LGBTQ populations,
and marriage equality (Drescher 2015).

The science of human difference puts multiple understandings of
our species in tension: on the one hand, differing traits function as
testable variables that "confirm" essential differences; on the other
hand, as the homosexuality-DSM example illustrates, these traits have
histories long saturated with political motives and social hierarchies.
Consequently, categories give off an "aura of self-evident naturalness"
(Epstein 2007, 205), and thus stamped with scientific legitimacy, they
reify difference across educational, biomedical, public, legal, and policy
settings. Assumed truths about difference lead to unscientific and harmful stereotypes and can deprioritize other social interests. Ignoring the
histories of human difference in science education is consequently a
risk, as students become citizens, researchers, and policymakers in their
own right.

Sociologist of science Steven Epstein (2007) proposes an "inclusion-
and-difference paradigm" for thinking about how groups are included
in scientific research and how differences are measured within and across
those groups. Considering "the *making of identity and difference* (how the
human population is divided and what meaning is assigned to stratifying terms such as race and gender)" (author's emphasis) through this
framework reinforces how socially and politically infused "pure" scientific
categories can be (18). Epstein's model considers how human categorizations intersect with all kinds of social forces, both prior to and as
outcomes of research-study design. As the demedicalization of homosexuality shows us, how groups are systematically ("objectively," "neutrally")
distinguished is ideological, and reexamining those characterizations
can sometimes require an enormous political effort. We hope that effort
will be pedagogical too. Through rhetorical analysis of scientific texts
and through writing to learn, students will be able to subject those categories, and the practices that secured them, to greater scrutiny.

EXAMPLE CASES: THE SCIENTIFIC
CONSTRUCTIONS OF RACE AND SEX

Before exploring implications for science education and the role of writing, we first outline two cases as they pertain to race and sex—categories
that have long served as independent variables in scientific research and
whose use in science has rationalized centuries of harm, ranging from

forced sterilization to contemporary race-based beliefs about pain toler-ance (Hoffman et al. 2016). These case topics help illustrate how schol-ars are lately dissecting difference and how essentialist ways of thinking reinforce seemingly impermeable boundaries. They also provide poten-tial curricular fodder for complicating (and enriching) foundational knowledge taught in undergraduate science courses. The works cited provide informational and intellectual grounding for instructors, and some of them may serve as helpful teaching texts as well.

DNA Testing and Race

The visibility of genome sequencing has increased dramatically since the completion of the Human Genome Project in 2003, and the explo-sion of direct-to-consumer (DTC) genetic testing has influenced both scientific and popular thinking about concepts of race, ancestry, and identity. According to the CDC (Bowen and Khoury 2018), more than seven million consumers have submitted their DNA to companies like 23andMe and Ancestry, which provide detailed estimates of ancestry "down to the 0.1%" (23andMe). Yet human geneticists have pointed out complexities associated with the tests. Individual ancestries are inferred based on differences in average frequencies of genetic markers among arbitrarily defined modern population groups. Statistical uncertainty can be substantial in these individual estimates, and conclusions depend heavily on the particular company's database. However, the influence of these tests is hard to deny. In *The Social Life of DNA: Race, Reparations, and Reconciliation after the Genome,* Alondra Nelson (2016) portrays the complex history of ancestry tests among African American communities. Public ancestry "reveals" on shows like PBS's *African American Lives* often feature celebrities like Oprah Winfrey and Whoopi Goldberg learning about their pre-Middle Passage roots, and these discoveries have helped descendants of the African diaspora reclaim histories and identities that were denied them. In one publicized example, based on ancestry test results, actor Isaiah Washington gained dual citizenship in Sierra Leone, where he was inducted as a chieftain and set up a $1 million aid foundation. As Nelson writes, "genealogy is as much about the needs and desires of the living" as it is about offering "portals to the past." Fulfillment (or disappointment) of these needs can have political as well as economic ramifications.

However, genetic testing as a means for (re)constructing identity can be problematic. In 2018, in response to persistent discussion of her ancestry, US Senator Elizabeth Warren released tests results ostensibly showing she likely had at least one Native American ancestor six to ten generations ago. Her use of genetic ancestry as a proxy for tribal belonging (and as a tool for political gain) provoked anger from tribal leaders and Indigenous scholars. Indigenous studies scholar Kim TallBear (2018) wrote in a public statement on Twitter, Warren "focuses on and actually privileges DNA company definitions in this debate, which are ultimately settler-colonial definitions of who is Indigenous. She and much of the US American public privilege the voices of (mostly white) genome scientists and implicitly cede to them the power to define Indigenous identity." Genetic testing prompts many new questions about what counts as group affiliation, as well as how the practice enables and, under the mantle of science, legitimizes, cultural appropriation.

DNA sequencing has important biomedical implications. The prevalence of genome sequencing in academic settings makes it more feasible to identify average genetic differences in disease risk among population groups, and the recent NIH Precision Medicine Initiative (National Institutes of Health 2020) aims to tailor medical treatment to individual genetic profiles. In clinical settings, however, genome testing is not yet routine, and coarse racial groupings can replace more precise genetic information. Sociologist of science Troy Duster (2003) writes, "When race is used as a stratifying practice . . . there is often a reciprocal interplay of biological outcomes that makes it impossible to disentangle the biological from the social" (262). He gives the example of blood-group antigens, whose prevalence varies among groups of different ancestries. Blood transfusions can cause potentially life-threatening reactions when these antigens are mismatched, but blood banks, which routinely test for only a subset of these antigens, often rely on race instead of complex biochemical assays to guide transfusions. Likewise, certain diseases can become associated with racial or ethnic groups—for instance, sickle cell anemia is commonly associated with people African descent, and cystic fibrosis with Caucasians—and these probabilistic associations can cause disease cases to be understudied or overlooked when they occur in other groups.

The issue is complicated, even among specialists. Recently, scientists and scientific societies have issued statements warning that "science and the categories it constructs do not operate in a political vacuum" (Kahn et al. 2018). Meanwhile, the NIH *requires* the use of racial categories in any human-subjects research it funds (National Institutes of Health 2017), and pharmaceutical companies market drugs toward specific racial groups based on unfounded assumptions that certain groups are more susceptible to a given disease (e.g., Kahn 2012). Duster argues that the concept of race has been "buried alive" and that the denigration of race as a "mere" social construct ignores some of the complex ways biological and social conceptions of race influence one another. Epstein (2007) also asks, "Who should determine the racial or ethnic identity of a patient or research subject—the clinician/researcher or the patient/participant?" (205). Posing such questions to students can be useful in portraying complexities surrounding race in science and can also stimulate inquiries into issues like the bioethics of technological advancement and the limitations and affordances of typological models (the principle by which organisms are separated into types) in biology.

Sex[1] and Experimental Research Design

Epstein (2007) points out that "differences across types of difference matter" and that to standardize all human differences can create false equivalencies (205). Consequently, whereas racial categories are fluid and overlapping, sex designates male and female as distinct categories. Around the turn of the twentieth century, the X and Y chromosomes helped reify the "sex as a biologically fixed and unalterable binary" (Richardson 2013, 2). Even as exceptions regularly emerged to throw the "rule" of chromosomal sex difference into question (e.g., males with one X "too many," females with one "too few"), traits ranging from hormones to anatomy to temperament and behavior have come to be seen as further reinforcement of essential sex difference.

However, statistically significant differences between sex-specific traits do not necessarily equate to "meaningful separation between the sexes" (Richardson 2013, 5). It would be more precise to say that "sex explains some small portion of the variance" between the two groups (5). Plotting data visually on a bell curve is a helpful way to clarify this point (figure 6.1).

Traits like height, brain volume, and brain-hemisphere activity are measured to test and affirm sex difference. In these images, *d* represents the effect size, or the standardized difference (standard deviation) between the means for each group, and the delta represents the percentage overlap. The percentage and the visual illustration of overlap prompt a more complex interpretation of the data: all of these effect sizes are statistically significant, but they range from large (e.g., height) to trivial (e.g., interhemispheric connectivity). For example, the connectivity (circuit-like connections among cells) between brain hemispheres in males and females overlaps by a whopping 88 percent. Yet the measures are taken as definitive confirmation of sex difference. Even the

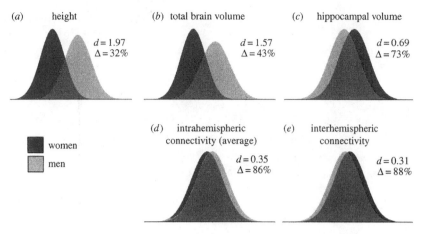

Figure 6.1. Graph depicting how frequently-cited sex differences often largely overlap. Maney (2016)

largest effect sizes—height and brain volume—are not very meaningful when we question the a priori assumption that there is essential difference between (only two) sexes.

Covariation can better explain difference than sex itself. In one study demonstrating a male advantage in multitasking, it was actually video-game-playing experience—not sex—that predicted multitasking ability (Maney 2016). While this example is amusing, the principle is relevant in more sobering contexts too, as Dorothy Roberts (2011) has shown with race, socioeconomic status, and health. Data affirming biological sex difference also support the myth that these differences are "hardwired" or "genetic," when in fact researchers are only just beginning to understand the entanglement of neuroanatomical traits and "sex-specific experience" (Maney 2016, 3). Sex is not monolithic but is rather a "choreography of genes, hormones, gonads, genitals, and secondary sex characters" (Richardson 2013, 8), including external factors such as gender-specific socialization and gene-environment interaction.

The biological basis for sex difference offers an excellent case for learning about experimental-research design. Experimental research is grounded in the logical positivist tradition, in which data are obtained through sensory observation (Crotty 1998). The problem, according to neurofeminist scholars and others, is not necessarily in the objects of analysis but in the assumptions underlying research questions, hypotheses, and rationales for selecting a given set of methodological tools. In her rhetorical critique of a set of brain sex studies, Celeste Condit (1996) writes that biased research design can lead to overall bad science.

Bad science may occur where hypotheses are drawn unreflectively from a hegemonic ideology and where resistance to alternate hypotheses is particularly strong. In the case of this brain sex research, hypotheses have been formulated such that difference is framed only as dimorphic, such that any minor locatable difference counts as substantive and important, and such that *averages* are taken as signifying *essential* differences. Each of those linguistic choices is insufficient and biased. (96)

Characterizing hypothesis construction as a linguistic choice, Condit claims that "bad science"—or the reification of problematic truths—can happen on the front end of research. Yet in the trajectory of a study, from initial design to publication of results, how the development of research questions and hypotheses can bake in biases is rarely scrutinized by students.

Exploring neurofeminist critiques of brain sex research would enrich curriculum on experimental-research design, which is typically part of introductory science curriculum. Such curriculum would be especially interesting against the backdrop of the National Institutes of Health Revitalization Act of 1993, which stipulates that all NIH-funded clinical research be conducted and reported in such a way as to "elicit information about individuals of both sexes/genders and diverse racial and ethnic groups" (National Institutes of Health 2017). State-mandated inclusion of information about difference among groups, though established with the intention of protecting marginalized populations, also *presupposes* the nature of such categories. Such biases, especially when they lead to conclusions about differences of inherent ability or intelligence between sexes, can lead to scientific reification of sexist views.

GRAPPLING WITH DIFFERENCE THROUGH LANGUAGE

Introductory science education helps novice scientists develop professional skills and identities (Poe et al. 2010) and prepares "citizens for life in a society where science impinges upon private and civic decisions" (Feinstein 2015, 149). However, we observe that college writers and novice scientists not only have infrequent opportunities to contemplate social contexts undergirding the biological phenomena they study but that they are also given to understand other knowledge frameworks as negligible or specious. The support for a universalist (empiricist, logical positivist) approach to teaching science remains widespread (Stanley and Brickhouse 2001). Science-education theorist Michael Matthews is not alone in arguing that "the character of the natural world is unrelated to human interests" (cited in Stanley and Brickhouse 2001,

37), and according to one study, about 40 percent of biology faculty interviewed conceived of race as an essentially biological phenomenon (Morning 2011).

Students must examine social contexts of science not just as adjuncts or alternatives to but as *means to* foundational scientific principles, which involves the study of language and communication. One definition of "scientific literacy" entails both participation "in the social structures that guide scientific enterprise" and engagement in "specific literate practices that underscore scientific endeavors" (Brown, Reveles, and Kelly 2005, 780). An appropriate vision of scientific literacy is one that presents science as historical, local, value laden, and, critically, *conducted* (not just communicated) through language. To study science as social practice is to study language in practice, and vice versa. A writing-intensive curriculum, then, foregrounds scientific literacy at the same time it prompts critical inquiry about the nature of science.

Existing studies of writing in undergraduate science courses tend to present writing as successful to the extent that it prepares students to participate in professional discourses (Freedman and Adam 1996; Szymanski 2014). While that effort is laudable, instructors' reliance on what Carter (2007) calls "academic genres" such as short-answer essay questions and their attention to surface errors is insufficient for teaching critical knowledge of scientific discourses. Writing is also often viewed as a tool for transmitting information rather than a vehicle for knowledge production and *re*production of ideologies. Framing writing as a skill, as Mike Rose (1985) explains in his classic article "The Language of Exclusion," means it will only ever be valued "as the ability to multiply or titrate a solution or use an index or draw a map is valuable. It is absolutely necessary but remains second-class" (347). The more sophisticated the student's understanding of the roles of writing in science, that is, when it is taught as a means for deepening disciplinary knowledge or for grappling with the rhetorical nature of scientific texts, the greater their achievement in undergraduate science courses (see also Ellis, Taylor, and Drury 2005, 2006; Poe et al. 2010)

We also note that writing toward a more social, contextual conception of science shapes individual students' affective experiences in the field. Poe (2013) writes that "learning to write in a discipline is a deeply personal and social activity, not merely a set of textual practices, and . . . we ignore the social dimensions of disciplinary communication at the peril of helping students become better writers" (172). Additionally, asking students to uncritically reproduce traditional discourses in the sciences can create "cultural conflict" for marginalized students (Brown 2004).

As we ask students to consider, through analysis and production of texts, how human differences are constructed, we must be mindful how language practices have perpetuated hegemonic traditions that alienate people from science. We encourage a social and rhetorical reframing of science curriculum, then, not just to critique scientific epistemologies but also to encourage more bodies and cultures spanning the range of human difference to enter—and stay—in the disciplines of science.

SUGGESTIONS FOR MEANINGFULLY INCLUDING WRITING IN UNDERGRADUATE SCIENCE COURSES

Here we offer some suggestions to science and science-writing instructors for teaching old conceptions and new debates about difference in the sciences and for prompting inquiry through writing. First we suggest a flipped model in which foundational scientific knowledge is introduced *via* case topics, such as the ones we offer above, as opposed to teaching foundational knowledge in the abstract and offering the occasional, limited example. A unit on current brain sex research, for example, could be a powerful avenue for exploring both the biological and sociopolitical factors informing definitions of sex difference while simultaneously teaching principles of experimental-research design (question and hypothesis development, independent and dependent variables, appropriate methods, statistical tests, etc.). Case-based teaching in science has been found to deepen students' critical thinking (Murray-Nseula 2011), to effectively teach foundational knowledge while also exposing students to current topics and debates (Cornely 2003), and to better replicate the actual professional practice of science than the traditional lecture-exam approach (DiCarlo 2006). A writing-centered case-based pedagogy offers greater potential for critical inquiry into the nature of scientific difference than a lecture-exam approach in a survey science course is likely to do, and it makes way for meaningful writing opportunities in a science-writing course.

To that end, we suggest three writing assignments, each featuring a characteristic of scientific knowledge and/or communication essential to a reformed science curriculum and to a more complex understanding of human difference. These characteristics, which we touch on to varying degrees in this chapter, are that science and its texts are multilayered/multimodal, contested, and personal. These assignments are adaptable and could be used in sequence in a science-writing curriculum, or they could be appropriated as stand-alone assignments in a survey science course. Versions of these assignments form the basis of a course the first author has developed, Critical Literacy in the Natural Sciences, which intentionally evokes "scientific literacy" as it is defined earlier in the chapter (Brown, Reveles, and Kelly 2005), while also making reference to "critical literacy," which uses the "technologies of print and other media of communication to analyze, critique, and transform the norms, rule systems, and everyday practices governing the social fields" of, in this case, the sciences (Luke 2012, 5). As a "rhetoric driven science writing course" (as opposed to a content-driven one) (Gigante 2014, 79), the course asks students to explore, through reading and writing, the cultural and sociolinguistic dimensions of bodies of knowledge traditionally viewed as pure, rhetoric free.

Multilayered/Multimodal

In her classic article "Accommodating Science," Jeanne Fahnestock (1986) traces the "fate of scientific observations" as they are translated from specialized research articles into mainstream journalistic accounts (275). Gigante (2014) urges science-writing instructors to take up Fahnestock's work and deploy "rhetorical training" that will heighten students' awareness of moral and political issues emergent in scientific texts and contexts. This assignment is an effort in that direction.

Because scientific findings are reproduced in a progression of genres, Fahnestock observes that different rhetorical appeals are employed depending on the audience and that "facts" take on shifting degrees of certainty and status. Donna Maney (2016) has also noted that distortions can occur as the findings of a particular study are translated for a public audience, particularly at the point that university press offices issue press releases. Howitt and Wilson (2014) are concerned that teaching science exclusively through textbooks and research articles can "sanitize" a process constantly marked by "failure, serendipity, and unexpected results" (481). They juxtapose James Watson and Francis Crick's famous *Nature* article (1953) reporting the discovery of the double helical structure of DNA with Watson's memoir, *The Double Helix* (2001). While the article was celebrated for its elegant concision, Watson's memoir demonstrates that this discovery, like many others, "was anything but straightforward" (Howitt and Wilson 2014, 781).

Students might similarly trace the rhetorical progression of a scientific "fact" by selecting an area of research that has ramifications for human difference and observe the platforms through which that research is communicated. These platforms could include any combination of genres such as grant proposals, conference presentations, research articles, posters, university press releases, scientists' memoirs, mainstream journalism, Tweets, or Op-Eds. Students might consider modalities like medium (e.g., institution website, print article, or social media platform) or visual or graphical representations of data, and they might also consider motives of different entities as they take up and reproduce information. Such an assignment would encourage students to move among dominant and nondominant forms of discourse and to consider how and why different forms gain credibility.

A rhetorical analysis like this cultivates genre knowledge related to scientific research and illuminates the ways scientific certainty about human difference is constituted linguistically, as well as visually, mathematically, and otherwise. The assignment could be an informal part of an effort to give students practice reading scientific research articles—a skill that is universally difficult, especially among novices, yet is key to socialization within the field. It can also work within a unit dedicated to the study of research design, externalizing relationships between linguistic framing of study components (like hypotheses, or criteria for inclusion/exclusion of research-subject categories) and the study's conclusions. The project works well in a multimodal format, and we recommend the free online design app Adobe Spark, which enables students to integrate visuals and text in a visually appealing online presentation.

Contested

Nancy Brickhouse and Will Letts (1998) have argued that science tends to be taught "dogmatically," focusing on the "theories and facts of science" to the exclusion of the "methodologies and social practices of science" (221). The theory of evolution by natural selection, for example, was developed "within a particular historical context"—when religious, cultural, and political values all had a shaping influence on the theory, including Victorian morality, which has informed traditional gender roles such as the "active male" and the "passive female" (224) that carry forward to this day. Instead of teaching scientific concepts as if they were definitively settled, we echo the suggestion that scientific controversies be made explicit in science curriculum. Familiarity with debates helps students see that the reification of scientific concepts is punctuated, unavoidably, by methodological limitations and human bias. Reified human categories, under such scrutiny, become more tenuous.

One way toward an exploration of scientific debate is to ask students to consider the research question, exploring how human difference is shaped by traditional linguistic structures inherent in the scientific method. Students might read and discuss a text such as Robin Kimmerer's *Braiding Sweetgrass (2013)*, in which the author, a Potawatomi botanist, describes her experience entering the academy and being discouraged from asking "unscientific" questions like "Why are golden-rod and aster so beautiful together?" Kimmerer shows the question is indeed testable and leads to some significant findings about the nature of optics and bee pollination. She explains poetically the ways her various identities, as a Western-trained scientist, as an Indigenous person, as a mother, and as a lover of plants, all combine to form a fuller, richer scientific worldview—a view that makes her a better scientist but that is still regarded skeptically by Western science.

Students can develop their own questions about the natural world; then, in an essay supported by both exploration of personal identity and peer-reviewed research, they could determine what kinds of cultural and political assumptions are embedded in their questions, whether they are "testable," and how or whether the framing of their questions might need to change in different settings. A follow-up on this exercise might include a research proposal. How can an imagined study answer the question they have developed? How does their proposed methodology explicitly reflect or control for cultural and ethical dimensions? How does the language shift from their essay to the formal proposal? In this project, students can apply and expand their technical knowledge while also considering how their own identity categories shape their work, as well as how difference is theorized and defined. Our own students report satisfaction in learning to write a genre that will be required knowledge in many scientific careers.

Personal

All scientists have intellectual, cultural, and linguistic histories. For the sake of neutrality and objectivity, apprentices are expected to divorce themselves from these histories, especially when they are doing and communicating research. Such training can be alienating and contributes in no small way to the notorious "pipeline" issue in STEM fields, where women, people of color, and other historically marginalized groups drop out of undergraduate, graduate, and postdoctoral programs in much greater numbers than their counterparts with normative identities. Such attrition leads to a community of persistently homogenous practicing scientists.

Given that a "person's sense of connection to a community" predicts whether or not they will stay in that community (Brown et al. 2016,

171), this assignment asks students to compose a narrative about their relationship to science. Students might read and compare examples of scientists' memoirs, such as Hope Jahren's *Lab Girl* (2016), in which the author describes her development as a lab researcher mediated by her experience as a woman with bipolar disorder; or Nobel Prize winner Youyou Tu's (2011) narrative about how her cultural grounding in traditional Chinese medicine enabled her to develop the antimalaria drug that has saved millions of lives. In their own narratives, students explore how their identities, investments, and intellectual interests have shaped their training; they do what Juan Guerra has done in this volume, which is to explore how intellectual concepts and "lived experience" have "entangled histories" (chapter 1). Consequently students' professionalization is enriched by their reflection on the ways human difference gets (re)produced through the lenses of their own and other scientists' identities and ideologies.

Such a project lends itself to a multimodal form, such as digital storytelling, which serves as a form of reflection, a potential professional networking tool, and also may provide students an orientation to and grounding within the scientific fields they are working to enter. We have also had success letting students select the genre most appropriate for their narratives and have received a variety of forms, including websites/blogs, podcasts, application statements (e.g., for medical school), and intricately rendered comics.

CONCLUSION

Many, if not most, of our daily behaviors and decisions are directly informed by science (Priest 2013). A healthy, functional, and fair scientific collective is therefore a fundamental prerequisite to a healthy, moral, and just society. In pursuit of these interests, STS scholars and rhetoricians have drawn attention to the sociopolitical dimensions of science, and they continue to raise important questions about the nature of scientific knowledge previously considered settled. While these debates grow across public spheres, science (and science writing) educators rightly argue there is much work to do in the classroom so the issues may be contemplated by scientists-in-training, as well as by young citizens whose lives will be daily touched by science in the media, by healthcare, and by science-informed social policy. We join that movement and in this chapter argue, first, that difference is significant to any discussion about the nature of science and that equality and health are at stake for all people; second, that the complexities of human difference can be taught by embedding more critical literacy practice into science and science-writing curriculums.

Rhetorician of science Leah Ceccarelli (2013) has written that her colleagues tend to neglect their "obligation to reach out to the very audiences who are empowered to make the alterations to practice that our critical findings recommend." Gigante (2014) echoes Ceccarelli's admonition with the hope that "more faculty collaboration and publication of pedagogical approaches" can lead to more tangible gains in learning in science and science communication classrooms (84). This chapter endeavors to contribute to that effort. As practitioners—of science-writing instruction, and of science, respectively—we have used this chapter to wade into some of the ways difference is constructed and contested in science, partly to synthesize disparate threads of scholarship but mainly to bring this work into the realms of pedagogical and scientific practice. As we ourselves learn how to teach, write, and research across difference, we hope our readers will experiment and share their efforts in return.

NOTE

1.   We use the term *sex* as opposed to *gender* in this chapter. This is partly for economy of language and partly because *gender* more strongly connotes an identity that is socially constructed and self-determined, whereas *sex* signals a collection of physiological and anatomical traits. However, as we indicate in this section, *sex* is perhaps problematic in its false clarity. Others use *sex/gender* because the combination signals the "entanglements" of physical and social/cultural elements (Schmitz and Höppner 2014) and because public officials tend to use the terms interchangeably (Epstein 2004).

REFERENCES

American Association for the Advancement of Science. 1993. "Benchmarks for Science Literacy." Oxford: Oxford University Press. http://www.project2061.org/publications/bsl/online/index.php?home=true.

Anderson, Frederik, Rani Lill Anjum, and Elena Rocca. 2019. "Philosophical Bias Is the One Bias That Science Cannot Avoid." *eLife* 8: 1–5. https://doi.org/10.7554/eLife.44929.

Bowen, Scott, and Muin J. Khoury. 2018. "Consumer Genetic Testing Is Booming: But What Are the Benefits and Harms to Individuals and Populations?" https://blogs.cdc.gov/genomics/2018/06/12/consumer-genetic-testing/.

Bowker, George C., and Susan Leigh Star. 1999. *Sorting Things Out: Classification and Its Consequences.* Cambridge: MIT Press.

Brickhouse, Nancy W., and Will J. Letts. 1998. "The Problem of Dogmatism in Science Education." In *Curriculum, Religion, and Public Education: Conversations for an Enlarging Public Square,* edited by James T. Sears and James C. Carper, 221–30. New York: Teachers College Press.

Brown, Bryan A. 2004. "Discursive Identity: Assimilation into the Culture of Science and Its Implications for Minority Students." *Journal of Research in Science Teaching* 41 (8): 810–34. http://doi.org/10.1002/tea.20228.

Brown, Bryan A., John M. Reveles, and Gregory J. Kelly. 2005. "Scientific Literacy and Discursive Identity: A Theoretical Framework for Understanding Science Learning." *Science Education* 89 (5): 779–802. https://doi.org/10.1002/sce.20069.

Brown, Bryan A., J. Bryan Henderson, Salina Gray, Brian Donovan, Shayna Sullivan, Alexis Patterson, and William Waggstaff. 2015. "From Description to Explanation: An Empirical Exploration of the African-American Pipeline Problem in STEM." *Journal of Research in Science Teaching* 53 (1): 146–77. https://doi.org/10.1002/tea.21249.

Carter, Michael. 2007. "Ways of Knowing, Doing, and Writing in the Disciplines." *College Composition and Communication* 58 (3): 385–418.

Ceccarelli, Leah. 2013. "To Whom Do We Speak? The Audiences for Scholarship on the Rhetoric of Science and Technology." *Poroi* 9 (1). https://doi.org/10.13008/2151-2957 .1151.

Condit, Celeste. 1996. "How Bad Science Stays That Way: Brain Sex, Demarcation, and the Status of Truth in the Rhetoric of Science." *Rhetoric Society Quarterly* 26 (4): 83–109.

Crotty, Michael. 1998. "Positivism: The March of Science." In *The Foundations of Social Research*, 18–41. Thousand Oaks, CA: SAGE.

Cornely, Kathleen. 2003. "Content and Conflict: The Use of Current Events to Teach Content in a Biochemistry Course." *Biochemistry and Molecular Biology Education* 31 (3): 173–76.

DiCarlo, Stephen E. 2006. "Cell Biology Should Be Taught as Science Is Practiced." *Nature Reviews Molecular Cell Biology* 7: 290–96.

Drescher, Jack. 2015. "Out of DSM: Depathologizing Homosexuality." *Behavioral Sciences* 5 (4): 565–75.

Duster, Troy. 2003. "Buried Alive: The Concept of Race in Science." In *Genetic Nature/Culture: Anthropology and Science beyond the Two-Culture Divide*, edited by Alan H. Goodman, Deborah Heath, and M. Susan Lindee, 258–77. Oakland: University of California Press.

Ellis, Robert A., Charlotte E. Taylor, and Helen Drury. 2005. "Evaluating Writing Instruction through an Investigation of Students' Experiences of Learning through Writing." *Instructional Science* 33 (1): 49–71. http://doi.org/10.1007/s11251-004-7686-y.

Ellis, Robert A, Charlotte E. Taylor, and Helen Drury. 2006. "University Student Conceptions of Learning Science through Writing." *Australian Journal of Education* 50 (1): 6–29.

Epstein, Steven. 2004. "Bodily Differences and Collective Identities: The Politics of Gender and Race in Biomedical Research in the United States." *Body & Society* 10 (2–3): 183–203. http://doi.org/10.1177/1357034x04042942.

Epstein, Steven. 2007. *Inclusion: The Politics of Difference in Medical Research*. Chicago, IL: University of Chicago Press.

Fahnestock, Jeanne. 1986. "Accommodating Science: The Rhetorical Life of Scientific Facts." *Written Communication* 3 (3): 275–96. https://doi.org/10.1177/07410883860030 03001.

Feinstein, Noah W. 2015. "Education, Communication, and Science in the Public Sphere." *Journal of Research in Science Teaching* 52 (2): 145–63. http://doi.org/10.1002/tea.21192.

Freedman, Aviva, and Christine Adam. 1996. "Learning to Write Professionally: 'Situated Learning' and the Transition from University to Professional Discourse." *Journal of Business and Technical Communication* 10 (4): 395–427.

Friedman, Asia, and Catherine Lee. 2013. "Producing Knowledge about Racial Differences: Tracing Scientists' Use of 'Race' and 'Ethnicity' from Grants to Articles." *Journal of Law, Medicine and Ethics* 41 (3): 720–32. http://doi.org/10.1111/jlme.12082.

Gigante, Maria E. 2014. "Critical Science Literacy for Science Majors: Introducing Future Scientists to the Communicative Arts." *Bulletin of Science, Technology & Society* 34 (3–4): 77–86. https://doi.org/10.1177/0270467614556090.

Hoffman, Kelly M., Sophie Trawalter, Jordan R. Axt, and M. Norman Oliver. 2016. "Racial Bias in Pain Assessment and Treatment Recommendations, and False Beliefs about Biological Differences between Blacks and Whites." *Proceedings of the National Academy of Sciences of the United States of America* 113 (16): 4296–4301. https://doi.org/10.1073/pnas.1516047113.

Holmes, Ian. 2018. "What Happens When Geneticists Talk Sloppily about Race." *Atlantic*, April 25. https://www.theatlantic.com/science/archive/2018/04/reich-genetics-racism/558818/.

Howitt, Susan M., and Anna N. Wilson. 2014. "Revisiting 'Is the Scientific Paper a Fraud?'" *EMBO Reports* 15 (5): 481–84.

Jahren, Hope. 2016. *Lab Girl.* New York: Knopf.

Kahn, Jonathan. 2012. *Race in a Bottle: The Story of BiDil and Racialized Medicine in a Post-Genomic Age.* New York: Columbia University Press.

Kahn, Jonathan, Alondra Nelson, Joseph L. Graves, Sarah Abel, Ruha Benjamin, Sarah Blacker, and Catherine Bliss. 2018. "How Not to Talk about Race and Genetics." *Buzzfeed* News, March 30. https://www.buzzfeednews.com/article/bfopinion/race-genetics-david-reich.

Kimmerer, Robin Wall. 2013. *Braiding Sweetgrass: Indigenous Wisdom, Scientific Knowledge, and the Teachings of Plants.* Minneapolis, MN: Milkweed Books.

Kuhn, Thomas. 1962. *The Structure of Scientific Revolutions.* Chicago: University of Chicago Press.

Luke, Allan. 2012. "Critical Literacy: Foundational Notes." *Theory into Practice* 51 (1): 4–11. https://doi.org/10.1080/00405841.2012.636324.

Maney, Donna L. 2016. "Perils and Pitfalls of Reporting Sex Differences." *Philosophical Transactions of the Royal Society of London. B* 371 (1688): 20150119.

Morning, Ann. 2011. *The Nature of Race: How Scientists Think and Teach about Human Difference.* Oakland: University of California Press.

Murray-Nseula, Marlene. 2011. "Incorporating Case Studies into an Undergraduate Genetics Course." *Journal of the Scholarship of Teaching and Learning* 11 (3): 75–85.

National Institutes of Health. 2020. "What Is the Precision Medicine Initiative?" Last updated February 12, 2020. https://www.nih.gov/about-nih/what-we-do/nih-turning-discovery-into-health/promise-precision-medicine.

National Institutes of Health. 2017. "NIH Policy and Guideline on the Inclusion of Women and Minorities as Subjects in Clinical Research." Last updated December 6, 2017. https://grants.nih.gov/policy/inclusion/women-and-minorities/guidelines.htm.

Nelson, Alondra. 2016. *The Social Life of DNA: Race, Reparations, and Reconciliation after the Genome.* Boston: Beacon.

Poe, Mya, Neal Lerner, Jennifer Craig, and James Paradis. 2010. "First Steps in Writing a Scientific Identity." In *Learning to Communicate in Science and Engineering: Case Studies from MIT,* 19–50. Cambridge: MIT Press.

Poe, Mya. 2013. "Re-Framing Race in Teaching Writing Across the Curriculum." *Across the Disciplines* 10 (3): 87–105. http://wac.colostate.edu/atd/race/poe.cfm.

Priest, Susanna. 2014. "Critical Science Literacy: What Citizens and Journalists Need to Know to Make Sense of Science." *Bulletin of Science, Technology & Society* 33 (5–6): 138–45. https://doi.org/10.1177/0270467614529707.

Richardson, Sarah S. 2013. *Sex Itself: The Search for Male and Female in the Human Genome.* Chicago: University of Chicago Press.

Roberts, Dorothy. 2011. *Fatal Invention: How Science, Politics, and Big Business Re-create Race in the Twenty-First Century.* New York: New Press.

Rose, Mike. 1985. "The Language of Exclusion: Writing Instruction at the University." *College English* 47 (4): 341–59.

Saini, Angela. 2017. *Inferior: How Science Got Women Wrong and the New Research That's Rewriting the Story.* Boston: Beacon.

Schmitz, Sigrid, and Grit Höppner. 2014. "Neurofeminism and Feminist Neurosciences: A Critical Review of Contemporary Brain Research." *Frontiers in Human Neuroscience* 8: 546. https://www.frontiersin.org/article/10.3389/fnhum.2014.00546.

Stanley, William B., and Nancy W. Brickhouse. 2001. "Teaching Sciences: The Multicultural Question Revisited." *Science Education* 85 (1): 35–49.

Szymanski, Erika A. 2014. "Instructor Feedback in Upper-Division Biology Courses: Moving from Spelling and Syntax to Scientific Discourse." *Across the Disciplines* 11 (2): 1–14.

TallBear, Kim. 2018. "After Too Many Media Inquiries Here Is My Statement on the #Elizabeth Warren DNA Testing Story." October 15. https://twitter.com/kimtallbear/status /1051906470923493377?lang=en.

Tu, Youyou. 2011. "The Discovery of Artemisinin (Qinghaosu) and Gifts from Chinese Medicine." *Nature Medicine* 17 (10): 1217–20. http://doi.org/10.1038/nm.2471.

23andMe. n.d. "What Health-Related Information Can I Learn from 23andMe?" Accessed April 24, 2020. https://customercare.23andme.com/hc/en-us/articles/115013843028 -What-health-related-information-can-I-learn-from-23andMe-.

Watson, James D. 2001. *The Double Helix: A Personal Account of the Discovery of the Structure of DNA.* New York: Simon & Schuster.

Watson, James D., and Francis H. C. Crick. 1953. "Molecular Structure of Nucleic Acids: A Structure for Deoxyribose Nucleic Acid." *Nature* 171 (4356): 737–38. https://doi.org /10.1038/171737a0.

7

DISABILITY IDENTITY AND INSTITUTIONAL RHETORICS OF DIFFERENCE

Neil F. Simpkins

When Ana and I discussed her negotiations around disability with instructors, I asked why she didn't have institutional accommodations. Ana paused and responded, "Mostly I haven't identified with the label of disabled. That's possibly changing for political reasons." I was surprised by this statement, as Ana discussed other parts of her identity in the interview and described the perspectives she gained about writing with diabetes and depression. Ana's interview was my second in my longer project examining how disabled students experience college writing. While I had designed my study to invite people with many different relationships to disability, I had naïvely assumed most of my participants would openly identify as disabled. Here in my second interview emerged a tricky problem for me, a finding I wasn't expecting and didn't quite understand.

Identifying as disabled is a complicated personal decision, and many people who use their experience with disability rhetorically don't use *disabled* as a label. Disability's social construction impacts how people embrace or resist disability as an identity. Dustin Galer (2012) notes how disabled people "share the mainstream ethos that participation in the competitive workforce is a primary feature of their identity," which can create "sometimes conflicting dynamics of individual and collective identity formation in the disability community" due to the relationship between disability and autonomy in our capitalist society. Disability often complicates how and whether disabled people are seen as rhetors with agency; being labeled *disabled* can deeply impact how one's communication is understood. Disability can create conflicts with one's other identities; as I interrogate in depth in this chapter, disability's intersecting relationship to a person's other identities can exacerbate negative experiences of disability or cause a person to feel more at home in their other identities.

https://doi.org/10.7330/9781646421732.c007

This moment with Ana crystallized how identities jockey as we move through our lives and form the stories we tell about ourselves. For me, coming into a disability identity was complicated; growing up in a white Southern family, my mental illness was accepted with relative ease but my queer and trans identity rejected. I had forgotten how writing in college and working in my writing center both intensified my mental illness and provided me a way to express mental illness as an identity. Ana's statement was a reminder that disability identity is contextual, political, relational, and all in ways that make it distinct from other categories of identity. Theories of difference helped me understand how my participants used their disability identity rhetorically and explained some ways disability identity moved through my data.

Difference can help us understand how disability identity functions and can assist us as we consider best access practices for writing classrooms. I start with a review of theories of difference and disability identity, particularly how they are treated in composition and rhetoric. I then consider stories of two participants who grappled with difference around disability in classroom contexts. I examine how diagnosis and accessing accommodations enact disability difference, shaping how disabled students experience disability identity. I conclude with theoretical and practical suggestions for thinking about difference and disability identity. I suggest that instructors consider how disability difference is framed as a deficit and avoid mounting roadblocks that mirror deficit approaches to access mounted by institutions. I also offer that instructors should honor choices students make around disability disclosure and adopt an open stance towards access practices because of the dynamic nature of disability difference.

LITERATURE REVIEW

In composition and rhetoric, difference is one way to understand how identities come into contact with one another through rhetorical and discursive practices. Stephanie Kerschbaum's book *Towards a New Rhetoric of Difference* (2014) and article "Avoiding the Difference Fixation" (2012) provide a roadmap for how difference can be used. Kerschbaum defines difference as "dynamic, relational, and emergent," rooted in a Bakhtinian frame that understands difference as "a relation between two individuals that is predicated upon their separateness from one another" (Kerschbaum 2014, 57, 67). Markers of difference help us see how we are distinct from others; at the same time, markers can encourage division and marginalization. Drawing upon Sara Ahmed's (2012) work about the disingenuous rhetorics of diversity that abound in higher education, Kerschbaum argues that we must attend to how difference is commodified by institutions without real movement toward institution-wide cultural change. Zhaozhe Wang (2019) continues this conversation about difference by calling for an understanding of how difference is "textually materialized and shapes and reshapes the relations between the writer/reader and the text, rather than merely shaping and reshaping the relations between two individuals" (386). Wang's consideration helps us see how diagnosis and the bureaucracy of institutional accommodations, which are mediated through personal and technical documents, impact how students negotiate difference based in disability.

Difference is also a useful concept for bridging conversations about identity in disability studies. Difference calls attention to interactions that label people as disabled and gives us a precise way to think about disability identity. Difference can help us understand how embodied impairment marks disabled people's bodies and minds. Earlier efforts in disability studies sought to separate disability from a medical model (disability as rooted in a medical condition) and move it towards a social model (disability as a social construction). Difference nuances these lines of thought by giving us a vocabulary for thinking about how disability is both social and embodied, as well as impacted by other markers of difference we carry in interpersonal interactions.

Recent conversations in disability studies and beyond have called for a deeper interrogation of difference in relation to disability identity. Within the social model, disability studies scholars grapple with how disability identity is deployed in the broader social context. Tom Shakespeare (1996), for instance, details how impairment as the framework through which disability is understood socially creates the experience of disability as a negative identity. Margaret Murugami (2009) finds that uncoupling disability identity from impairment, "accepting impairment as a reality that [a person] lives with without losing a sense of self," is crucial for developing a positive personal relationship to disability. Difference as an interactional identity model can help us understand how concepts that frame painful or othering experiences of embodiment (i.e., impairment and discrimination) relate to and complicate taking on disability identity. Using myself as an example, seeing my difference interactionally helps me understand both how my depression and anxiety work as impairment (e.g., unrealistic expectations of productivity in academic work) and also a personal disability identity (e.g., a shared understanding between me and others about the need for flexibility around timing and deadlines).

Understanding disability identity as interactional and rooted in difference is necessary because disability negatively impacts different populations with differing force. The enactment of disability difference by states and institutions tends towards the use of difference as a means of disenfranchisement and social control. Indeed, the biggest elephant in the room with regards to disability studies is how its frameworks often fail to address how impairment and disability are used to control and monitor unruly subjects. Jasbir Puar (2017) argues that disability studies has yet to adequately address the unquestioned whiteness and Euro- and US-centric focus of disability studies (as well as transgender studies). In *The Right to Maim*, Puar examines how states produce disability in the form of debility, or bodily harm and deliberate social exclusion. In her view, disability as an identity and thus a touchstone of political activism avoids engaging with how states create and maintain debility through capitalism in an effort to obtain legal rights. Debility as a measure of state control is not encountered or enacted as a reclaimable form of difference on which one can ground disability identity. In *Crip Times*, Robert McRuer (2018) describes how states single out their disabled populace as too expensive to support, which often results in early death. In the context of both K–12 and higher education, Nirmala Erevelles (2014) describes how disability difference becomes a framework to move youth of color through the school-to-prison pipeline, where difference coded as disability becomes "the animating logic of dis-location that hustles racialized youth along the dreadful trajectory of the school-to-prison pipeline via the everyday normative practices of schooling" (81). These theories provide needed critique of the mechanisms states and institutions use to create difference related to disability and impairment—often causing disability and impairment in their own populations and beyond. With this in mind, we need a model that can address disability's impact in different scales (the institution or state versus the interpersonal) in order to make sense of disability identity.

What do these broader understandings of disability identity and difference offer those of us who are thinking about how to teach writing and rhetoric? They impact how many disabled students experience higher education and the contexts of college writing. Disabled students experience both institutional and interpersonal dynamics of disability through difference. Writing is tied to identity, and part of developing as a writer in college involves understanding how one relates to writing in relation to other parts of one's identity. Lee Ann Carroll (2002) details how writers choose or are urged to take on the role of writer in different classroom contexts that impact their sense of writerly identity. Roz Ivanič

(1998) explains how writing and identity interact; part of the challenge of learning how to write involves negotiating the self directly or indirectly represented in writing. These identity challenges are impacted by disability, in part because of disability's complicated relationship to difference. As Tara Wood (2011) notes, the genre of the personal essay, a familiar assignment in many first-year composition classrooms, can pressure disabled students to present their disability difference in a narrative about overcoming disability. Without a critical framework around disability, the personal essay "can cause reproduction of a rhetoric of overcoming, one in which students feel both invited to entangle disability with trauma (problematic) and compelled to write about trauma in a way that reenforces the 'normal' body" (38). Amy Vidali (2007) describes the difficulty writers experience when thinking about how or whether to represent their disability in personal narrative. In short, disabled students negotiate both how disability functions through difference and how that difference impacts their relationship to writing.

METHODS

Before moving into the two cases I present here, I describe my research methods and their impacts. As I mention earlier, the interview data for this chapter come from a larger project in which I sought to describe how disabled students experience college writing. This larger project consists of twenty student interviews collected at a large midwestern university over a period of two and a half years starting in 2015. I sought a wide range of participants for my project to collect as many perspectives as I could and to see what might be generalizable across such a broad range of experience. This choice was important to me for two main reasons; first, like the story I mention in the introduction, I wanted to hear from many people so I could "get out of my own head" with regards to my own experience with disability. While my own experiences with disability in higher education led me to my larger project, it was crucial that I understand others' experiences to learn what common rhetorical tactics and shared experiences occurred across different experiences with disability in higher education. Second, I felt it was important to deepen shared experiences disabled people have across different physical and mental manifestations of disability. Disability studies, particularly in composition and rhetoric, tends to focus on specific types of disability rather than theorize across multiple experiences of disabled embodiment. While it is important that we build theories that describe specific experiences with disability (e.g., mental illness, autism, or D/deafness), a difference-based approach also helps us see where there are shared experiences of difference that allow for cross-disability coalition. I tried to collect interviews and theorize across them to learn through difference and develop a wider model.

Through snowballing and a recruitment email forwarded by the campus disability services, I was lucky to collect narratives from a wide range of majors and experiences (from first-year undergraduates to graduate students writing dissertations). I allowed my participants to select their own pseudonyms, many of which reflected how they wanted my audience to perceive their stories. For example, one participant whose story I delve into here chose Ozymandias based on his ironic identification with the hubris of those who seek power and prestige in academia. While the majority of my participants were white, my participants of color provided critical counternarratives that challenged how whiteness is the unspoken center of disability discourse. A large number of my participants were queer and trans identified, which shaped other useful comparisons across the data. I was able to hear stories across a wide range of experiences with disability and also varied experiences within specific categories (e.g., vision loss). In short, partly through design, partly through luck, and mostly through the generosity of my participants, I was able to work with a data set in which I could see difference itself in play even as I tried to suss out commonalities.

Many studies of difference employ an interactional method that captures relationships between parties and their environment, such as ethnographic methods or interview strategies that capture conversational dynamics. A limit to my conclusions in this chapter is that my data only offer the perspective of the student, as I captured single-subject interviews. One first-round coding method I used allowed me to plumb interactions between my participants and their recollected interlocutors—versus coding. A coding method that aids in finding tension and conflict in data, versus coding helped me unpack some of the interactional dynamics in my subjects' stories by helping me ground the trajectories of their conflicts (Saldaña 2015, 98–102).

I selected cases for this chapter that emphasize interactional moments in which difference came to the fore for my participants. Ozymandias's and Roz's stories both reveal how the negotiation of difference challenges and constructs disability identity. Since the aim of this piece is to consider pedagogy and difference together, I also highlight cases in which educational context and interactions with teachers play a large role. We dive into two categories in which disability difference impacted Ozymandias's and Roz's experiences with writing in higher education: diagnosis and accessing institutional accommodations. At moments of receiving or describing a diagnosis or asking for accommodations, many participants experienced how difference influenced their understanding of disability as an identity. For students with intersecting marginalized identities, interactions with diagnosis and institutional accommodations further highlighted how difference spreads across multiple categories of identity.

DIAGNOSIS

Diagnosis is an important rhetorical artifact many disabled students use as they negotiate their relationship to disability and difference. Diagnosis functions as a technical language framed by the medical industry, but its influence extends into social and educational systems. For disabled students, diagnosis itself becomes an important marker of difference that changes their relationship to disability. Drew Holladay (2017) frames how diagnosis works as a "tactical technical communication" disabled people use to navigate both their personal experiences and experiences with institutions. Describing how writers in online spaces use the language of diagnosis, he argues,

> Writers in online mental health discussion forums take up and transform the clinical, descriptive language of medical documents to more accurately reflect their own experiences of difference. . . . These tactical technical communicators reveal the ways in which the biomedical language of mainstream psychiatry inflects individuals' descriptions of mental and social experience. (6)

Students used their relationship to diagnosis across different experiences of disability to understand disability as an identity and how disability relates to higher education. Diagnosis provided a vocabulary students could use to comprehend the experience of their bodies and minds to share that experience with instructors. However, the successful use of diagnosis to understand and explain their disability identity relied on diagnosis being understood by the student and their audience. Since diagnosis can be a key marker of difference, one that could be both hidden and revealed by students, an audience's stance towards difference impacted how successful it could be used rhetorically.

Disability identity's relationship to diagnosis is culturally and historically contextual, impacted by other markers of difference. Diagnoses may be perceived differently by others based on a sense of "seriousness" or the cultural legibility of a diagnosis. Ozymandias, a second-generation South Asian graduate student, experienced disability difference when his mental illness began to emerge in his childhood. Before college,

Ozymandias began to recognize his disability difference but was unable to describe it to teachers, friends, and family without the vocabulary for it. As he described,

> I've always felt weird, like something was wrong with me. I always felt that, and people always told me it. So I've always been told that I was weird my whole life. I always felt weird and out of place. I was also one of the few people of color in a primarily white school . . . I was also weird. I am just weird, I'm just not right . . . I was always considered smart. But then [people] always mention that I was kind of strange and weird. Had a weird sense of humor. I think I started getting really depressed by the end [of high school]. I don't know . . . I didn't really understand it then. There was nothing for me to talk about with really anyone. I couldn't talk about it with my father.

Here, we see how Ozymandias struggled to communicate his difference rooted in disability and impacted by race as a child and young adult. Feeling "weird" (which he mentions over six times) and "just not right," he felt cut off from support. Without a vocabulary to talk about his disability difference, having "nothing for [him] to talk about with really anyone," he couldn't place what exactly made him different from others besides more visible and contextual forms of difference, particularly race.

When Ozymandias was younger, his parents struggled to understand his depression symptoms, and he thus did not see disability as part of his identity. Ozymandias noted how his parents' background shaped how they understood his emergent mental illness.

> My parents grew up upper-middle-class Indian, but upper-middle-class Indian and the 1960s was like utter poverty here. . . . My dad grew up wealthy-ish for India at the time. My mom came from a wealthy background but she didn't grow up wealthy. . . . But yeah, so what was I thinking, he didn't understand depression, you know? Because what's happiness? The idea of happiness wasn't something that existed in their mind. You're supposed to do A, B, and C.

Ozymandias's description of his family's cultural context is complex; it shows how disability is contextual to one's class and racial privilege, as well as relational to cultural norms. Ozymandias felt his mental illness was changing the path of his life, causing him to deviate from the directional force of doing "A, B, and C." Because his depression was undiagnosed in his youth, he and his family struggled to communicate without a vocabulary that helped them understand his markers of difference.

Ozymandias's relationship to his family changed as he met with psychiatrists in college who diagnosed his mental illness. Certain diagnoses hold stronger rhetorical force and can change how one identifies with or against disability, as well as how others identify one as disabled. They can have stronger impacts as students negotiate their experiences with family members, teachers, and classmates. Early in college, Ozymandias sought treatment for his depression and did not tell his parents. However, a later diagnosis of bipolar disorder changed how he related to disability and how his parents understood his mental illness. A diagnosis of bipolar disorder instead of depression became a way for Ozymandias's parents to see him as disabled and become more involved in his care and treatment.

> So my parents, for depression my dad didn't understand, and I never told him about the antidepressants. But when I got diagnosed as bipolar it was like a 180-degree flip. My dad researched . . . he knew that that was something that was not right, you know. . . . My parents were very support-ive . . . they take a lot of, they take care of me emotionally and financially in many ways.

In this moment, we see how one diagnosis over another caused Ozy-mandias's father to have a "180-degree flip" around how he understood Ozymandias as disabled. Because there was a more legible marker of dif-ference than his behavior, Ozymandias's family learned more about the experience of bipolar disorder. Rooted in caring for Ozymandias, they participated more directly in helping him manage his mental health, in part because they were impacted by the rhetorical weight of his diagnosis.

While diagnosis offered Ozymandias a partial vocabulary to help describe his difference, his experience with it grew more complicated as he moved through different educational and medical contexts. Starting graduate school at a school in New York City, he met with different cam-pus doctors who diagnosed him with many different kinds of mental illness. When markers of difference proliferate, negotiating them can be even more difficult. Diagnoses can cloud rather than clarify an under-standing of what is going on with one's body and mind. As Ozymandias grew older, he gathered more and more diagnoses, to the point that he found them comical.

> I've been diagnosed with everything. Let's see if I have to go in order, it started off with depression, then bipolar, then schizoaffective, then schizo-phrenia, anxiety . . . and I'm not even sure what that is . . . and ADHD, ADD. It's one of those things where I think that I'm like, I'm kind of like a New York mural. People put graffiti on me, each psychiatrist. Because I've never had a psychiatrist for more than a year, each person likes to put their own tag on me. So it's hard for me to describe what I am, because I can't be all of these things!

Here, Ozymandias points to how each doctor wants to "put their own tag" on the "New York mural" of his medical records and also his iden-tity. Many of these diagnoses are contradictory, which makes it hard for

Ozymandias to "claim" one specific diagnosis as a form of identity—he "can't be all of these things!" The struggle to find a diagnosis that "fits" can complicate using diagnosis as a way to build a disability identity.

When talking about his disability with professors, having multiple diagnoses functioned as a marker of difference that caused him to want to conceal his disability. After an experience with involuntary inpatient care, Ozymandias changed how he used diagnosis when he talked with instructors about his mental health.

> I usually describe what I'm diagnosed as. Before I used to just say, "My most recent one was schizoaffective." But like after looking through my medical records, it's just like, I'm . . . no wonder they locked me up! I'm diagnosed with everything! [laughs] . . . I don't know what I am. . . . And maybe I am some aspects depending on the stress level or situation, and I'm not like that now, excluding for the ADD which I can't help unless I take my Adderall, you know, I'm not like that now. So it's like, "Oh I'm not schizoaffective" or this kind of stuff.

Here, we see the double edge of diagnosis, particularly considering communication with professors. As Ozymandias's diagnoses proliferate, becoming less functional as a communication tool and also marking him as disabled, he rejects them as a useful way to talk with others about his disability. Ozymandias also describes here the risk of discussing diagnosis with faculty, which is exemplified in an encounter he had with a professor when he disclosed having a mental illness.

> I think people who are emotionally or intellectually disabled, they're already kind of in a guarded position because we're very vulnerable. Like even one of my professors, when I flat out said, I talked about being, you know, having a disability, she was like I wonder what it would be like to be an academic world and being open about being disabled. You know, when you're publishing papers, when you're putting out things, you know. That people can question you based on your mental illness or whatever. That your reality is compromised. That your word doesn't mean as much. That, you know, we're vulnerable because we can't speak up for ourselves.

In this moment, Ozymandias casts his professor as asking him an "I wonder" question that leads Oz down a string of rhetorical consequences. By asking what it would be like to be "open about being disabled" as an academic, Oz's professor reveals and reinforces the challenges of embodying a disability as an academic writer. Ozymandias describes here several of the rhetorical challenges disability, particularly mental illness, brings upon a rhetor. In this interaction, his professor could have listened to his experiences, if he desired to share, and oriented towards him in a way that would help him strategize his needs.

In Ozymandias's experience with diagnosis, we see how markers of difference shape interpersonal encounters around disability and impact identifying both as a scholar and a disabled person. Diagnosis proves a complicated textual tool that shapes the legibility of one's disability difference. As a brokered language filtered through medical interactions, diagnoses provide unreliable and inaccurate vocabularies to describe the experience of disability difference; however, the language of diagnosis is also powerfully legible and, as we see in the next example, sometimes the only language for getting what you need from an institution.

INSTITUTIONAL ACCOMMODATIONS

In university settings, disabled writers often encounter difference when they ask for what they need from instructors. Disability accommodations, and the systems of disability accommodation in higher education, shape this communication task. As I have written elsewhere, the process of learning the rhetorical skills for asking for what you need around writing is a challenging, recursive task marked by trial and error. The experience of difference in encounters with instructors is impacted by how accommodations are structured in higher education. In the United States, getting disability accommodations is a bureaucratic process of demonstrating that one's disability *causes* difference in academic settings. Accommodations provided by the university exist in a bureaucratic framework that sorts students based on a perception of how strongly their experience with disability affects their performance as a student. United States federal law requires that colleges and universities "take actions that can be characterized as reasonable accommodations," but "they are not required to take affirmative action, make fundamental alternations in the nature of programs, or experience undue financial and administrative burden" (Lynch and Gussel 1996). For a student to be guaranteed accommodations, they must work with the disability services office, as the university is not required to accommodate a student outside this process (Lynch and Gussel 1996). Many students choose to intervene in their own education without using disability services; however, they cannot be assured they will receive a necessary accommodation without moving through the interface of disability services. Thus, the performance of difference by a disabled student and the recognizability of their difference in relation to bureaucratic institutional norms mark many encounters disabled students have with instructors and fellow students.

At the institution Ozymandias and Roz attended, disabled students who wish to gain formal accommodations from the university must submit to a lengthy, bureaucratic process in which their academic performance is evaluated in relation to their disability. Students go through a multistep process, starting with applying through an online portal to schedule an intake appointment with staff at the disability resource center (DRC). At the appointment, students bring documents for the DRC to assess. Depending on the students' diagnosis and desired accommodations, differing forms of documentation are required in a rather complex combination. For instance, a student with a learning disability is asked to bring a psychoeducational evaluation, preferably from the last three to five years, and an individual education plan (IEP). Requiring an IEP lengthens a paperwork chain that marks a disabled student's difference. A student with low vision is required to bring a "general disability assessment form," a questionnaire filled out by a medical practitioner that details how a student's diagnosis affects their academic performance. These interactions require students to visit doctors to gain access to institutional accommodations, which costs time and money. The DRC does not guarantee accommodations if the student goes through this process; there must be a demonstrable gap between their "potential" academic performance with and without accommodations. Such a gap is compelling to think through in terms of its relationship to difference and diagnosis; receiving institutional accommodations shows how difference in one context (diagnosis) is taken up or ignored in other contexts (disability accommodations). This model is fairly similar to how most institutions of higher education in the United States perform disability services, though of course this pattern varies at every institution.

In terms of theories of difference, this process creates a rhetorical dynamic that marks disability as *the difference between one's academic success with and without accommodations,* and requires students to perform that difference in a paperwork-filled setting involving multiple powerful parties. This use of difference frames access needs as a deficit, scripting performances of difference by disabled students as both necessary to gain access to classrooms and negative with regards to their identities as students. As Jay Dolmage (2017) explains, this system functions as a "retrofit" to the inaccessibility of higher education that highlights how disability difference continues to constitute the exclusiveness higher education demands. As we see with Roz's story below, difference in this formulation encourages instructors to perform scripts around students' differences rather than connect with them and learn from their needs.

At the time of our interview, Roz was a white, queer-identified junior majoring in women's studies. Roz had institutional accommodations for depression and anxiety, which had emerged in college. Before Roz went through the process of getting accommodations, they encountered an instructor invested in the bureaucracy around disability accommodations at the institution. Anxious about Roz's accommodations requests, the instructor's response to Roz's disability difference encouraged distrust, forced Roz to "prove" their disability, and mounted paperwork as a barrier to accommodation.

Near the middle of the semester, Roz realized they had misinterpreted the absence requirements, and they had missed several classes because of anxiety and depression while maintaining the daily work of the class. The professor had no specific disability policies in her syllabus, and it was unclear to Roz whether she would be flexible about attendance. As Roz said, "I didn't realize that if you miss over the amount of excused absences it's not only that your absence grade goes down, it's that your entire grade in the class goes down a full letter grade." Roz had an emotional exchange with the professor, admitting they had "been really depressed and having a hard time coming to class." Roz felt compelled to frame their needs as a difference-based deficit, in part because they were learning how to ask for what they needed around their disability access needs.

Roz's professor was willing to accommodate them—but only if they created a paper trail to stand in for formal accommodations. Roz said,

> She was like, okay, well I need a note from your doctor. I was like, okay, I can do that. And she was like, but I don't want this to be a personal thing, I don't want to seem like I'm giving you a personal favor. So what I need you to do is have your doctor send it to a dean, and have the dean send it to me . . . this is not anywhere a rule that you need to have the dean send it to you and then it's more official.

Roz's professor thwarted Roz's access request by creating more paperwork roadblocks meant to emphasize Roz's difference required bureaucratic intervention to be taken seriously. Even though Roz's professor had no disability policy on her syllabus, she relied on institutional bureaucratic structures to approach difference, in part because of broader pressures to do so from the rigid institutional structure of disability accommodation. These roadblocks mirrored the process Roz would need to take to get formal accommodations from the university's DRC: getting a diagnosis from a doctor proving there would be a difference between Roz's performance in the course with and without intervention, then having a university official "approve" the paperwork and authorize accommodations. To avoid giving Roz a "personal favor" after being moved by Roz's rhetorical efforts, the professor relied on her position of power to create a false paperwork channel that mirrored the vetting process of disability services. Such a structure rendered Roz's disability difference in the exchange as a negative trait, perhaps even a marker of duplicity.

With Roz's and Ozymandias's stories, I examine how diagnosis and negotiating disability accommodations impact the disability identity of disabled students. Disability difference functions rhetorically to shape how Ozymandias and Roz are perceived by professors, friends, and family at the moment their experiences with disability in higher education are emergent. With Ozymandias's case, we see how difference can function as a means for creating support from his family, even if the process of getting diagnosed can have frustrating impacts on his understanding of his own mental health. Roz's case shows us how disability difference is framed as a deficit in institutions of higher education and how tightly it is tied to institutional accommodations. Both of these cases speak to relevant interventions writing teachers and writing program administrators should consider.

CONCLUSION

With Ozymandias's and Roz's stories in mind, I offer some practical suggestions for writing teachers and program administrators. First, we must consider how institutions of higher education frame disability difference as a deficit in interactions with disabled students. We also must respond carefully to disclosures of specific diagnoses and other knowledge shared by students, knowing how diagnosis impacts and shapes disability identity. Finally, we must examine course policies to see whether they reify disability difference as a deficit. With this last move in particular, writing teachers and administrators can put pressure on our institutions to shift the rhetorical dynamic of deficit.

Understanding how difference shapes disability identity reminds instructors to consider how institutions of higher education ask students to perform disability difference as a deficit. This performance can come at the expense of students developing positive associations with disability identity. Part of Roz's hesitancy to talk with their professor arose from how deficit models of disability difference shape instructor/student interactions. In a different portion of our interview, Roz described how they asked for what they needed from a different professor:

> Even though he had already been very understanding and this was my second class of him and I had built a relationship, I definitely felt weird about asking him. . . . At that point I lied, and I emailed him, and I was like . . . I have a really bad migraine and I had planned this amount of time to finish it, but it ate a day of my time. And what had actually happened was that I

> was really anxious and overwhelmed by all my classes. And he may or may
> not have known that my reasoning was a little bit bullshit, but he had had
> me as a student for a while, and he was like, yes, take an extra day, that's fine.

Roz's reluctance to describe their needs in relation to mental illness speaks to how a deficit model of disability difference impacts accommodation asks. Here, Roz felt compelled to use a different, seemingly more legible form of impairment to ask for what they needed. Knowing this, instructors can create classroom structures that push against how disability difference is framed as a deficit. One key way can be to invite students to speak to us about disability accommodations whether or not they have formal accommodations from the university. Moving out of the model of only offering interventions for students if they have the proper paperwork can push against the bureaucratic structure of university disability accommodations. Avoiding punitive policies of classroom management, such as attendance policies that lower grades for absences, can help instructors create classroom cultures that do not punish disability difference.

Since institutions often understand disability difference as deficit, we must be conscious of the institutional rhetorics we invoke in our syllabi, assignments, and other documents that lay out course policies. Roz's examples show that the lack of a disability policy on the syllabus encouraged the instructor to lean on bureaucratic frameworks of accommodations rather than creating a channel through which Roz could share their needs directly. Course policies are crucial for writing instructors to examine, for two key reasons. First, as Jay Dolmage, Melissa Helquist, and Tara Wood (2019) note, institutional accommodations often don't accommodate the way writing projects occur on longer timescales and in more flexible environments than, say, exams. Second, as Margaret Price (2011) details in *Mad at School: Rhetorics of Mental Disability and Academic Life*, many of the commonplaces of the writing classroom, such as attendance, participation, and deadlines create access problems for disabled students, as well as many other marginalized students. With course policies in mind, it is important to note that copying and pasting a disability statement only on a syllabus does not do much to serve disabled students; Dolmage (2017) notes, "Most often, the only time disability is spoken or written about in class is in the final line of the syllabus, when students are referred to Disability Services should they desire assistance. The message to students is that disability is a supplementary concern—and then that it is not the teacher's concern, not really a part of the course; it's at the back door of the syllabus" (78). Thus, taking a long view about the structure of a course and communicating intentions about course design clearly to students are crucial access practices.

Because diagnosis can be a loaded and inaccurate vocabulary that is nonetheless rhetorically powerful, instructors should consider how they respond to disclosures of specific diagnoses. Diagnoses are not only a technical vocabulary mediated between doctor and patient but are also a bureaucratic language used to broker accommodations for students seeking formal support from the university. They can also be a complicated interpersonal vocabulary impacting students as they negotiate their disability difference with family, classmates, instructors, and friends. Instructors should honor a student's disclosure of disability and understand the role diagnosis plays in such disclosures. We should never demand that students disclose diagnoses; similarly, we should avoid assigning "diagnoses" to students based on our perceptions of them. At the same time, we should treat disclosure of diagnoses with particular respect and understand how they are rooted in the process of developing disability identity.

The interactions of disability difference I discuss here remind us that as instructors we need both a broad framework for implementing disability access in our classes and the ability to adapt to the singularities of interactions with individual students. We should ask ourselves, "How am I creating structures of access in my classroom and how can I adapt to different accommodation needs requested by students from class to class?" These stances help us negotiate how difference is "not 'out there' waiting to be found and identified but is always coming-to-be through the here-and-now of interaction" (Kerschbaum 2012, 626). As an example, an instructor might use course-wide policies such as deadline windows, a practice described by Anne-Marie Womack (2017) in which students and instructors negotiate a rolling deadline for writing projects (516). At the same time, after talking with a student, the instructor might create a firmer deadline for a student who describes needing more structures as an access need. Since we cannot know how to best serve each student without negotiating difference on the scale of both the structural and interpersonal, an open stance towards course structures—even those created for access—is crucial.

Identifying as disabled can be a challenging process, one often negotiated by disabled students in higher education. Theories of difference help us understand both the flexible ways disability identity is deployed and the particular challenges that exist in identifying as disabled. As writing teachers, we can better serve disabled students in our classrooms if we understand how disability difference operates in higher education and the complex impacts it has upon our students.

BIBLIOGRAPHY

Ahmed, Sara. 2012. *On Being Included: Racism and Diversity in Institutional Life*. Durham, NC: Duke University Press.

Carroll, Lee Ann. 2002. *Rehearsing New Roles: How College Students Develop as Writers*. Carbondale: Southern Illinois University Press.

Dolmage, Jay. 2017. *Academic Ableism: Disability and Higher Education*. Ann Arbor: University of Michigan Press.

Dolmage, Jay, Melissa Helquist, and Tara Wood. 2020. "Connecting Writing Programs and Faculty with Disability Services." Kairos PraxisWiki. http://66.113.161.124/praxis/tiki-index.php?page=PraxisWiki:_:disability_praxis.

Erevelles, Nirmala. 2014. "Crippin' Jim Crow: Disability, Dis-Location, and the School-to-Prison Pipeline." In *Disability Incarcerated: Imprisonment and Disability in the United States and Canada*, edited by Liat Ben-Moshe, Chris Chapman, and Allison C. Carey, 81–100. New York: Palgrave Macmillan.

Galer, Dustin. 2012. "Disabled Capitalists: Exploring the Intersections of Disability and Identity Formation in the World of Work." *Disability Studies Quarterly* 32 (3). https://dsq-sds.org/article/view/3277/3122.

Holladay, Drew. 2017 "Classified Conversations: Psychiatry and Tactical Technical Communication in Online Spaces." *Technical Communication Quarterly* 26 (1): 8–24.

Ivanič, Roz. 1998. *Writing and Identity: The Discoursal Construction of Identity in Academic Writing*. Amsterdam: John Benjamins.

Kerschbaum, Stephanie L. 2012. "Avoiding the Difference Fixation: Identity Categories, Markers of Difference, and the Teaching of Writing." *College Composition and Communication* 63 (4): 616–44.

Kerschbaum, Stephanie L. 2014. *Toward a New Rhetoric of Difference*. Champaign, IL: NCTE.

Lynch, Ruth Torkelson, and Lori Gussel. 1996. "Disclosure and Self-Advocacy Regarding Disability-Related Needs: Strategies to Maximize Integration in Postsecondary Education." *Journal of Counseling and Development* 74 (4): 352–65.

McRuer, Robert. 2018. *Crip Times: Disability, Globalization, and Resistance*. New York: New York University Press.

Murugami, Margaret Wangui. "Disability and Identity." *Disability Studies Quarterly* 29 (4). https://dsq-sds.org/article/view/979/1173.

Price, Margaret. 2011. *Mad at School: Rhetorics of Mental Disability and Academic Life*. Ann Arbor: University of Michigan Press.

Puar, Jasbir K. 2017. *The Right to Maim: Debility, Capacity, Disability*. Durham, NC: Duke University Press.

Saldaña, Johnny. 2015. *The Coding Manual for Qualitative Researchers*. Newbury Park, CA: SAGE.

Shakespeare, Tom. 1996. "Disability, Identity and Difference." In *Exploring the Divide*, edited by Colin Barnes and Geoff Mercer, 94–113. Leeds: Disability Press.

Wang, Zhaozhe. 2019. "Relive Differences through a Material Flashback." *College Composition and Communication* 70 (3): 380–412.

Womack, Anne-Marie. 2017. "Teaching Is Accommodation: Universally Designing Composition Classrooms and Syllabi." *College Composition and Communication* 68 (3): 494–525.

Wood, Tara. 2011. "Overcoming Rhetoric: Forced Disclosure and the Colonizing Ethic of Evaluating Personal Essays." *Open Words* 5 (1): 38–53.

Vidali, Amy. 2007. "Performing the Rhetorical Freak Show: Disability, Student Writing, and College Admissions." *College English* 69 (6): 615–41.

8

INTERROGATING THE DEEP STORY
Storytelling and Narratives in the Rhetoric Classroom

Shui-yin Sharon Yam

During Donald Trump's rapid rise to political power before the 2016 presidential election, sociologist Arlie Hochschild set out to answer why working-class whites in the Deep South appeared to be voting against their own material interests: Had they been duped, or were there more complex sociocultural and affective reasons behind their political choices? What Hochschild found during her ethnographic study in Louisiana were not uninformed and bigoted individuals who shared no common ethical or material concerns with more liberal voters. Rather, Hochschild found that like her and the people in her social circle, her research subjects were often equally concerned about the welfare of their community and family and about maintaining equality in society. However, while the two groups might share similar values, the deep stories that inform how they see the world are completely different. As Hochschild (2016) defines it, "A deep story is a *feels-as-if* story—it's the story feelings tell, in the language of symbols. It removes judgment. It removes fact" (135). In their deep story, working-class whites have been struggling to achieve the American dream for generations, but they have been unfairly taken advantage of by people of color and immigrants, whom they see as cutting in line to receive the good life. The emotional power of the deep story trumps factual evidence, thus preventing this group from objectively evaluating their material interests during the election. Based on this finding, Hochschild suggests that if we want to cultivate coalition moments across difference, we ought to interrogate the deep stories communities and individuals subscribe to rather than engaging in arguments and persuasion that undermine the fundamental worldview of others.

Hochschild's (2016) theory of the deep story is particularly relevant in a public sphere rife with ad hominem attacks and dehumanization on both ends of the political spectrum. It is important to interrogate

https://doi.org/10.7330/9781646421732.c008

the different deep stories we and others hold because, as Hochschild points out, a knowledge of these stories "permits those on both sides of the political spectrum to stand back and explore the subjective prism through which the party on the other side sees the world" (135). By mutually inquiring as to how their views are influenced by the deep stories they hold, individuals from different positionalities are less likely to ridicule, dehumanize, and dismiss people whose worldviews are incongruent with theirs. Rather, they will be more inclined to reflect on the sociopolitical and affective causes of political beliefs, including their own. In this article, I make use of Hochschild's deep-story theory to argue that writing and rhetoric teachers should create opportunities for students to engage with different deep stories and reconsider their relationships with those whose views and lived experiences differ from theirs.

While a focus on argumentation dominates most conventional rhetoric textbooks, scholars have argued for the pedagogical and social value of mutual inquiry and nonpersuasion (Baker, Dieter, and Dobbins 2014; Elbow 1998; Gagarin 2001). Specifically, they emphasize that while students are often taught to persuade, they are not given many opportunities in the classroom to develop an openness to the idea that their views and relationships with their interlocutors might change because of this engagement. Recent work has been done on the importance of mutual inquiry in a rhetorical education. Drawing from Wayne C. Booth's legacy, composition scholars Marsha Lee Baker, Eric Dieter, and Zachary Dobbins (2014) suggest mutual inquiry helps students understand how they could *be* persuaded which, as the authors argue, is an important "critical and civic capacity" that promotes sustainable and nonviolent public communication (13). In addition, Susan Kirtley (2014) and Abby Knoblauch (2012) advocate for the pedagogical use of invitational rhetoric—a feminist model of rhetoric that emphasizes mutual respect and self-determination rather than persuasion—to promote collaboration in the classroom. Instead of attempting to actively change the students' minds, Knoblauch (2011) posits, writing teachers could ask how the students' experiences motivate their resistance and engage in an open dialogue with the students that does not prioritize persuasion. Along a similar vein, many writing scholars have examined how assigning nonpersuasive genres such as personal narratives and autoethnography allows students to critically consider, negotiate, and articulate their positionality in the academy and in the public sphere among those whose opinions and experiences differ from theirs (Hesford 1998; Juzwik et al. 2014; Schlib 1996; Young 2004).

I connect studies on personal narrative with research on mutual inquiry because together they are productive in informing a pedagogy that allows students to interrogate how seemingly personal deep stories have immense public and political impacts, and how the mutual inquiry of such stories could help eradicate toxic and dehumanizing rhetoric across political difference and positionality. I posit that the principles of invitational rhetoric give students the language and context to collaboratively compose an ethical protocol to engage with each other's deep stories and their effects on one's political opinions and relations with others. Specifically, I argue that the writing and sharing of personal narratives among students, when paired with the terms of engagement outlined in Sonja Foss and Cindy Griffin's essay (1995) on invitational rhetoric, could serve the following civic and ethical functions: (1) prompt students to cultivate self-reflexivity through the articulation of their own deep story; (2) encourage students to critically examine how their and others' beliefs are formed in relation to specific sociopolitical and cultural contexts; (3) provide a sound rhetorical situation for students to engage in mutual inquiry with peers from different positionalities; and finally, (4) offer room for marginalized students to tell their stories on their own terms at a time when their narratives are often undermined or distorted in dominant public discourse. In the following sections, I first elucidate the key principles of invitational rhetoric to illustrate how they serve as a set of guidelines that inform students about how they could enact mutual inquiry as they share and explore each other's deep stories. I then describe a series of pedagogical activities and assignments I designed based on such principles and analyze the texts my students produced to highlight the productiveness and limitations of such activities.

INVITATIONAL RHETORIC AS GROUNDING PRINCIPLES

In order to productively and ethically participate in public discourse across difference, students must first understand that political arguments and ideologies are intimately tied to one's positionality, lived experiences, and emotional responses to the world. A pedagogical model that considers rhetoric only as persuasion and emphasizes the use of argumentation devoid of emotions, material conditions, and lived experiences, therefore, is sorely inadequate in preparing students to engage in dialogues across difference, especially on polarizing and high-stakes public topics.

Feminist scholars have repeatedly argued we should take seriously emotions and personal experiences in relation to the way we form judgments, participate in public discourse, and engage with others who do not share our positionality (Koziak 2000; Lugones 1987; Narayan 1988). Hochschild's (2016) findings on deep stories highlight how one's self-narrative and emotional perceptions of the world are more salient to public discourse than traditional argumentation theory has given them credit for. As Baker, Dieter, and Dobbins (2014) argue, "Teaching students to observe *how*, instead of *what*, their classmates think" is essential to helping them develop the ethical capacity to relate to others not as enemies who must be proven wrong, but as equal interlocutors (17). The focus on the *how* encourages students to attune to the deep stories that inform their claims and to the affective power that undergirds an argument. The attunement towards their deep stories also requires students to never lose sight of the humanity of their interlocutors because while an argument could be depersonalized, a deep story is always saturated with feelings and experiences that are simultaneously personal, social, and public. By transcending the win/lose and right/wrong binaries to consider the contextual and emotional nuances that undergird each argument and belief, rhetoric as mutual inquiry allows students to be in relations with others via collaboration rather than antagonism.

I draw on the principles of invitational rhetoric to promote the mutual inquiry of deep stories because it clearly articulates the guiding principles and terms of engagement necessary to promote "ethical exchanges in difficult situations" (Bone, Griffin, and Scholz 2008, 434). Defined by Foss and Griffin (1995) as "an invitation to understanding as a means to create a relationship rooted in equality, immanent value, and self-determination" (4), invitational rhetoric seeks to challenge the primacy of persuasion in traditional rhetorical theories. Challenging an antagonistic model of communication that pits interlocutors against each other, invitational rhetoric decenters persuasion, or the attempt to change someone's mind. Rather, rhetors invite others to present their respective perspectives. As Foss and Griffin highlight, "The invitational rhetor does not judge or denigrate others' perspectives but is open to and tries to appreciate and validate those perspectives, even if they differ dramatically from the rhetor's own" (5). If the audience accepts the invitation, both parties must be open to the possibility that they may change their minds after the exchange—not because of persuasion but because of a deeper and more nuanced understanding of the issue that arises from the dialogue. By prompting interlocutors to engage with each other dialogically through their lived experiences, emotions, and rationales behind their specific worldviews, invitational rhetoric calls for rhetors to participate in the conversations in a fully embodied manner that reveals their humanity and vulnerability.

Because of the risk of vulnerability, invitational rhetoric and the practice of mutual inquiry hinge upon a trusting relationship between the interlocutors. This trust, however, is not easy to achieve both in and out of the classroom when structural power imbalance translates into interpersonal interactions and when rhetoric is often taught as a battle of argumentation. Reflecting on coalition building across difference, Uma Narayan (1988) posits that it is crucial to take interlocutors' feelings and emotional reactions towards an issue or interaction more seriously. This is particularly important for interlocutors who are structurally marginalized, as they possess epistemic privilege because of their conditions—"a more immediate, subtle and critical knowledge about the nature of their oppression than people who are non-members of the oppressed group" (35). When this knowledge and the emotions that accompany it are not properly acknowledged and incorporated into the dialogue, the exchange inevitably reproduces a structural power imbalance and distrust rather than promoting dialogic understanding and mutual inquiry on a given issue.

The principles of invitational rhetoric, while not a universal solution, provide guidance on creating a discursive environment that promotes the sense of safety and mutual respect. At the heart of invitational rhetoric is the "offering perspective": as Foss and Griffin (1995) explain, "In offering, rhetors tell what they currently know or understand; they present their vision of the world and show how it looks and works for them" (7). Rhetors offer their life stories not as support for specific arguments but to articulate their worldviews—that is, the deep story that informs how they make sense of the world. Interlocutors ask questions and make remarks that seek to cultivate deeper understanding of each other's perspectives and to offer different ways to approach and interpret the subject at hand rather than undermining how the other person sees the world.

In addition to the offering perspective, invitational rhetoric asks that interlocutors interact in ways that create the conditions of "safety, value, and freedom" (Foss and Griffin 1995, 10). In order to satisfy these three external conditions, interlocutors must aim to share their perspectives without any attempts to degrade, belittle, or humiliate others; this is akin to Krista Ratcliffe's (2005) proposal that a person should "stand under" worldviews and discourse that differ from their own and consciously acknowledge the fluidity of their viewpoints in relation to their positionality (28). Finally, to promote freedom and self-determination, interlocutors enacting invitational rhetoric must provide ample opportunities for others to develop different options and decide for themselves which ones they subscribe to. Rather than assuming there is one dominant and unchanging agenda the audience must move towards, invitational rhetoric prioritizes an interlocutor's freedom to choose from options that do not undermine their subjectivity. These three conditions, when produced by a specific protocol that holds interlocutors accountable to each other, are effective in protecting marginalized rhetors from being diminished or denigrated for not subscribing to the dominant worldview.

Invitational rhetoric, however, is not without its critics: while many find it unacceptable and unproductive that Foss and Griffin equate persuasion with violence (Dow 1995; Pollock et al. 1996), some criticize the authors for unrealistically advocating for invitational rhetoric in all contexts (Fulkerson 1996); others question whether invitational rhetoric perpetuates respectability politics that further polices marginalized rhetors (Dow 1995; Fulkerson 1996; Lozano-Reich and Cloud 2009; Pollock et al. 1996). I adapt the terms of engagement for invitational rhetoric despite such critiques for a few reasons. First, while I do not agree that persuasion is inherently violent, the turn away from antagonistic models of rhetoric is helpful in prompting students to inquire into, instead of immediately critiquing and attacking, deep stories that differ from theirs. Second, as Jennifer Emerling Bone, Cindy Griffin, and T. M. Linda Scholz (2008) point out, in Foss and Griffin's 1995 article, they are careful to posit that invitational rhetoric is not the only appropriate form of engagement: certain rhetorical situations and contexts call for a different rhetorical response. Likewise, I understand and present invitational rhetoric to students as an option rather than a panacea for all difficult exchanges. When understood only as an option rather than a mandate, invitational rhetoric does not preclude acts of resistance or disruption. As such, I see invitational rhetoric not as a mandate for marginalized rhetors to refrain from confrontation but as an additional rhetorical tactic for them to engage with those in a dominant position.

ENACTING MUTUAL INQUIRY IN THE CLASSROOM

In fall 2017, I incorporated invitational rhetoric as part of the curriculum for my intermediate Argument and Rhetoric course with twenty students. For the first half of the semester, students learned about and enacted classical rhetorical theories—such as stasis theory and the five canons of rhetoric—that characterize rhetoric primarily as a means of persuasion. Rhetoric, however, includes communicative acts not based on argumentation, and effective persuasion is not always the intended goal or outcome. After examining nonpersuasive rhetorical acts such as constitutive rhetoric and performative deliberation (Charland 1987; Lyon 2013), in conjunction with research in psychology that demonstrates the effectiveness of storytelling over argumentation in fostering productive engagement across difference (Haidt 2013; Mooney 2011; Shermer 2017), I introduced the class to invitational rhetoric, and below are descriptions of the writings and activities that were to be completed over the span of five class periods:

1. Students were asked to write a critical personal narrative based on a public issue (or a few interrelated ones) the student cared deeply about.[1] The goal of this assignment was for students to critically evaluate the ways their identities and cultural, socioeconomic, political, and geographical backgrounds influenced their opinions and feelings on that topic. This assignment also asked students to discuss how larger sociopolitical and cultural forces had influenced the way they engage—or choose not to engage—in conversations with those who disagree with them on the issue.

2. Based on the narrative abstracts submitted by students, I put them into groups comprised of individuals from different positionalities who held diverse opinions on the same or similar subject matter. Students were informed during the drafting process that their narratives would be read by their peers and me.

3. Students exchanged and read each other's narratives as a group. They then spent the rest of class time holding a conversation guided by the protocol we had developed collaboratively as a class based on invitational rhetoric.

4. After the dialogue, students wrote letters to their group members articulating what impact the conversation and their peers' personal narratives had on them: whether their views on the topic had changed or expanded and whether this exchange had shifted their perception of those whose positionality and worldview differed, or in some cases directly contradicted, theirs.

5. During the next class period, while remaining in groups, students read letters addressed to them. They then had another round of conversation with their group members to address and discuss any remaining issues.

6. At the end of the letter exchange, students responded to prompts that asked them to reflect on how they felt about this assignment series; what they found to be the most illuminating and challenging about the process; how their perception of rhetoric and the usage of rhetoric had shifted; and what they perceived to be the advantages and limitations of invitational rhetoric.

This series of assignments and activities (see appendices) were completed after students had discussed in detail Foss and Griffin's proposal (1995), together with Baker, Dieter, and Dobbins's (2014) "The

Art of Being Persuaded: Wayne Booth's Mutual Inquiry and the Trust to Listen." Discussions surrounding these articles prompted students to first interrogate the theoretical model of invitational rhetoric and mutual inquiry. These articles asked students to examine the ideological assumptions and ethical implications behind seeing rhetoric as solely a persuasive tool; they also jump-started discussions about the privileging of reason over emotions and the limitations of this binary view. Most important, the reading materials and discussions ensured students had a strong understanding of the central principles and ideologies of invitational rhetoric and mutual inquiry and could later draw on them to create a protocol to hold themselves and their peers accountable during the narrative exchange and dialogues.

Given the existing critiques of invitational rhetoric, during class discussions I asked students to use various thought experiments to consider the limitations of invitational rhetoric and situations in which interlocutors should resort to argumentation or other forms of confrontation. Based on these discussions, the class agreed rhetors had no responsibility to deploy invitational rhetoric when engaging with worldviews that dehumanize or purposefully undermine the value and well-being of others (e.g., neo-Nazism, white supremacism). This clause was added to the collective protocol to remind students of the terms of engagement they must adhere to during the narrative exchange. I incorporated writing instructions about the critical personal narrative assignment into our discussions of these readings as well.

In particular, I presented the following rubrics to ensure the narratives connected the personal to the public and the political so the narratives would be generative for upcoming conversations that interrogated how worldview is constructed. The assignment asked students to consider the following:

- connections between your personal communicative practice and larger social, economic, political, or cultural structures and influences;
- analysis of concrete examples from your lived experience, drawing particularly on exchanges you have had with those who disagree with your stance;
- connections between your personal experience and communicative practice with any course readings and discussions.

These guidelines required students to approach their own opinions, lived experiences, and feelings as objects of analysis. In fact, many students remarked that the narrative assignment alone had prompted them to reconsider their worldview because the rubric asked that they articulate the rationales behind beliefs so ingrained they had never questioned them before.

Before I put students into groups to exchange their narratives and hold the first round of conversation, the class engaged in a range of activities that helped ensure an environment of safety and respect. Since the enactment of invitational rhetoric renders interlocutors—particularly those who are structurally marginalized and have traditionally borne the burden of explanation—extremely vulnerable, it is crucial to first address in class how structural power imbalances and differential positionalities could impact engagement across difference. Narayan (1988) describes six ways interlocutors from the dominant group could undermine their marginalized counterparts. Collaboratively, students examined each of these cases and came up with a set of guidelines and protocol for the upcoming dialogue, detailing how they would—and would want their peers to—behave to ensure a respectful, ethical, and generative exchange. Despite the protocol and careful preparation beforehand, engaging in invitational rhetoric necessarily entails risks—the risk of encountering an interlocutor who fails to reciprocate the openness, or a partner who intentionally or unintentionally undermines one's life world. To ensure the emotional safety of students, particularly students from marginalized positionalities, I repeatedly made clear that students did not have to write about a topic they did not feel comfortable sharing and discussing with others. Students, in other words, had control over how much risk they were willing to take.

AN ANALYSIS OF HOW STUDENTS DEPLOY INVITATIONAL RHETORIC

At the end of the series, I collected from each group compiled personal narratives, letters, and reflections. Because I was circulating around the classroom while the two rounds of conversations took place, I was not privy to any complete sets of exchanges within the groups. Nevertheless, the letters and final reflections have allowed me to reconstruct parts of the discussions and evaluate the productiveness and effects of these exchanges. My analysis below is driven by the following questions: How do students deploy principles of invitational rhetoric in writing and in conversation with each other? What rhetorical decisions do students make when they are explicitly asked not to persuade? What are the impacts of this series of activities in promoting self-reflexivity and the mutual inquiry of deep stories across difference? In this section, I focus on the data I collected from two groups of students to highlight both the advantageous learning outcomes and limitations. These data demonstrate that this assignment series is effective in prompting students to critically reflect on the sociopolitical and cultural roots of their worldviews and to reexamine the relations they have with others and the way they communicate with those whose ideologies or positionalities differ from theirs.

Ed, Tom, Salu, and Lee

Ed, Tom, and Salu were assigned to the same group because they engaged with policies on the ethical status of the fetus in relation to women's right to their bodies: while Ed advocated for stem-cell research, Tom and Salu were respectively pro-life and pro-choice. Lee joined the group after her assigned partner missed class that day due to illness. Reflecting on her experience as a trans woman, Lee's narrative addresses her stance on the bathroom bill. While Lee's topic did not fit in seamlessly with the others', the group coalesced their overlapping reflections on gender and biopolitics.

Because Tom and Salu disagreed most explicitly with each other's ideology on abortion, they engaged each other immediately during the first round of conversation. As a white male who grew up in a religious and conservative household, Tom explains in his narrative that his view against abortion comes both from the teachings of his church on the immorality of the act and from his parents, who both "abhor the practice of abortion, especially so when they know their tax dollars are helping fund various aspects of Planned Parenthood." Tom's views, in other words, were influenced simultaneously by religious, moral, and economic discourse. While Tom does not waver from his anti-abortion stance throughout the narrative, he does repeatedly consider its limitations based on his positionality. For instance, after explaining why he believes the opinions of men on abortion should be taken as seriously as those of women, Tom engages with Narayan's framework of epistemic privilege to critique his own limited worldview: "To borrow from Uma Narayan, I am the ultimate 'outsider' on this subject—I have zero 'epistemic privilege' of what it is like to know that one day you may have to go into labor . . . the reality is that I have also never been a father. I must concede that I have never gone through a traumatic pregnancy either."

Attempting to make sense of his strong opinions against abortion despite these limitations, in his narrative Tom recounts a memory of a conversation in which his mother made it extremely clear that teen and unwanted pregnancy must be prevented at all costs in order to avoid the penultimate immoral act: abortion. In addition to his gender,

Tom is also reflective about how his whiteness influences and limits his view on abortion: growing up in a middle-class, predominately white neighborhood, Tom was taught that abortion is an irresponsible act only poor, black youths would commit. While Tom now understands that as a racist and unsound argument, the fear he has associated with abortion nevertheless continues to linger. At the end of the narrative, he recounts that he often avoids having any discussions related to abortion with his female friends, fearing they would be offended by him and being too self-conscious about his own limitations. Tom then expresses the hope that invitational rhetoric would allow him to begin engaging more actively in conversations about the topic.

As an Indian American woman who grew up in a white conservative neighborhood, Salu had a set of experiences and an ideological stance very different from Tom's. Growing up in a Sikh household, Salu was taught by her parents that she must question everything and arrive at her own answer. Salu's view in support of abortion was formed both by research she had conducted on secular pro-life arguments and on her experience being excluded in her predominately white high school as the "angry brown woman." Her own experience of marginalization resonated with the history of colonialism and white patriarchy, which she had learned about from a young age; Salu writes that because of such knowledge, her deep story has always been filled with skepticism and resentment towards the way the authority polices marginalized bodies. Because engaging in direct arguments with her peers had in the past resulted in further marginalization, Salu reflects that she has been practicing invitational rhetoric unknowingly since her senior year of high school. Unlike Tom, in other words, Salu had ample experience discussing abortion with people who hold different opinions. However, like Tom, Salu believed her worldview on the topic would likely remain unchanged. What enabled them to nevertheless have a productive conversation in the end was a mutual willingness to engage with each other's experiences and opinions when persuasion was off the table.

Salu's and Tom's letters to each other and their final reflections highlight the effectiveness of this activity in promoting open engagement across difference. After the first round of conversation, Salu and Tom wrote letters to each other. In his letter, Tom opens by thanking Salu for her receptiveness and engagement and admits the conversation he had with Salu was the longest he had ever had with someone who is pro-abortion rights. Tom then spends the next two pages engaging with the reasoning and ideologies Salu discussed during their first conversation and in her personal narrative. Tom does so in a way that encourages Salu to clarify and more explicitly articulate the grounding of her opinion. For example, while discussing the legality of abortion, Salu made an analogy between abortion and face-lift surgery: for her, the two procedures share the same moral value because neither harms any third parties. In his letter, Tom wonders whether likening the two procedures is a false equivalence because he believes that when left alone, the fetus will grow into a human form, while the face would not turn into a new life if left without the surgery. While Tom appears to be engaging in an argumentative act in his letter by identifying logical fallacies in Salu's judgment, he continues to acknowledge his intention and desire for mutual inquiry over persuasion. Many of his critiques are phrased as open-ended questions, and he explicitly explains that the questions are not meant "to be interrogative, but rather investigative." Because of the trust they had established during the first conversation, Salu did not approach Tom's letter with skepticism.

In her letter to Tom, Salu reciprocates his gratefulness for the exchange and highlights that her discussion with Tom has reminded her that "certain beliefs, like being pro-life, is not necessarily something that is always rooted in hard-lined rationality." Because she often forgot worldviews and moral values are emotional, conversations she had had with those who are pro-life often turned into hostile, unproductive debates. Echoing Tom's appreciation of the exchange, Salu writes that, "I forget that I am hypocritical when I say that being pro-life is inherently wrong, because obtaining an abortion is a personal and hard decision. Your narrative made me remember that your belief, then, is a personal and hard decision." Instead of further questioning Tom's belief, Salu is very reflective in her letter about how, despite the fact that she maintains her existing view on abortion, her view on those who are pro-life has shifted: "From this exchange, I definitely internalized the notion that I should not judge someone solely based on their opinion on abortion. I do this literally all of the time, and our conversation actually made me reverse this mentality." Salu then recounts how after her discussion with Tom, she was able to finally have a conversation with her Christian roommate about religion and abortion without turning the dialogue into a fight like before. The highly structured and scaffolded classroom activities, in other words, are transportable to other contexts. The emphasis on mutual inquiry and reciprocal exchange, in other words, is more conducive to productive civil discourse outside class than the conventional focus on persuasion.

While abortion was not the focus of their narratives, the other two students in the group, Ed and Lee, also identified as pro-choice. Their letters to Tom further demonstrate the way invitational rhetoric allows students to examine the rationale behind their own political stance and helps undo the fear of difference that often prevents mutual inquiry of different worldviews. In his letter to Tom, Ed establishes that Tom's discussion of his religious upbringing initially triggered his fear but that Tom's narrative ultimately helped him better articulate his own reasoning and understand how others arrive at worldviews different from his. Ed further writes, "Your piece has provoked me to question my own beliefs and ultimately strengthen them. . . . Up to this point, I have never really explored in depth the influences that support and shape the specific views of those opposite to mine. . . . As I see how your experiences have influenced you, I now understand my own opinions better." Ed's reflection highlights that effective rhetorical education need not focus only on persuasion. In fact, when we decenter persuasion, students are free to engage in collaborative inquiry across difference that prompts them to examine the ideologies and deep stories that undergird their respective worldviews. Such self-reflexivity is crucial in any deliberative process, as it demonstrates the rhetor's acute understanding that people do not "reason together in a logos-centric vacuum" and that it is unethical to assume one's worldview is inherently more correct than someone else's (Baker, Dieter, and Dobbins 2014, 21). The principles of invitational rhetoric are helpful in cultivating students' willingness to listen without immediately mounting counterarguments. The exchange between Lee and Ed on the transgender bathroom bill highlights how the practice of listening as part of mutual inquiry helps develop students' capacity to critically consider subject matter that challenge the social norms they adhere to.

While respectively about stem-cell research and the bathroom bill, Ed's and Lee's topics did not cohere with one another's the way Tom's and Salu's did; the four nevertheless still benefitted from engaging in an equal, open, and reciprocal exchange with one another. Reflecting on her experience transitioning and the anxiety she frequently experiences in public bathrooms, Lee discusses in her narrative that she often avoids having any discussions related to the topic and would "try desperately to ignore [her] personal stake in the issue almost completely" for fear such exchanges would influence how people view her as a person. In a marginalized nonnormative body that has been repeatedly demeaned in dominant public discourse, Lee takes on a huge risk every time she discusses her lived experiences with cis people: she may, as Narayan (1988) points out, experience disparaging and condescending remarks from outsiders and feel her personhood is being undermined. This risk exists in the classroom space despite the extensive scaffolding that prepares students to engage in invitational rhetoric and mutual inquiry. Students may not always be able to critically examine and set aside their emotional reactions towards nonnormative bodies and gender. By sharing her experience and deep story, Lee was rendering herself vulnerable.

Lee's narrative resonated a lot with Ed, a white, cis, straight male. While Ed's and Lee's topics and respective positionality differed from each other's, they were able to utilize invitational rhetoric to advance not only their understanding of each topic but also the way they conceptualize civil discourse. In his letter to Lee, Ed writes,

> I never really understood what being transgender is. I had not known anyone who has experienced the same thing that you have experienced. I had almost no knowledge about the topic of transgenderism. To be honest, I had no real interest learning about transgenderism as it made me uncomfortable to talk about. Your narrative is the first real personal piece I have read that talks about being transgender.

Referencing Lee's discussion on her difficult experience coming out to her family, Ed explains why Lee's narrative has had such a profound impact on him:

> My whole life revolves around my family and my friends, who I consider an extension of my family. I have never really put much thought into how a transgender person can feel uncomfortable in a setting with their family. This reality resonates with me on a very personal level. I cannot imagine not feeling comfortable or accepted among my own family.

While here Ed engages with empathy in a way that centers his own feelings, Lee's narrative is so deeply contextualized Ed never assumes he could completely stand in Lee's shoes. As rhetoric scholars have previously argued, while personal narratives often promote an empathetic response, they can risk subsuming difference if the members of the audience believe they identify perfectly well with the marginalized narrator (Lynch 1998; Rothfelder and Thornton 2017). Because asking students to highlight in their narratives how their lived experience is related to and influenced by larger sociopolitical and cultural forces, the resulting papers are more conducive to the examination of respective deep stories—stories that bridge the personal and affective with the public and political.

Addressing the debate on public bathrooms, Ed first acknowledges Lee's anxiety whenever she must enter a public restroom before attempting to reconcile his discomfort with nonnormative bodies with the value of inclusion:

> For me, I honestly think that I would be uncomfortable if a trans person were to walk into the men's restroom while I was in there. Not because I am against transgenderism or that person's beliefs; I would feel this way

because it is something that is new to me and hard to understand at times. Ultimately, I think that transgender people should be able to use the bathroom that corresponds to the gender that they most comfortable as. . . . Your narrative is a very powerful piece. Reading about your personal experiences allows me to be more comfortable and understanding when it comes to the acceptance of trans people.

Ed's letter highlights how public anxiety surrounding nonnormative bodies often forestalls civil discourse and coalition between marginalized and dominant communities. If we seek to cultivate students' civic capacity to productively and ethically engage with difference, it is crucial to give them the opportunity to practice self-inquiry, interrogate why they feel fearful or uncomfortable about certain topics, and examine how the opinions they form affect others. Ed's letter makes clear that he continues to grapple with his discomfort. Lee's narrative and her conversation with Ed, in other words, have not changed his view entirely, but they nevertheless prompt Ed to see the public and personal stakes in this issue and to confront his emotional biases.

The students' final reflections further highlight the productiveness of invitational rhetoric in fostering dialogic engagement across difference. The emphasis on mutual inquiry renders the exchange an ongoing process rather than a contained battle in which one side wins and the other loses. Tom writes about his experience with the series of exchanges,

After reading Salu's narrative and getting to talk to her one-on-one, I had time to go home and think about the encounter. The next day, the encounter was still on my mind. The next time we had class, I was much more prepared and excited to carry on the conversation that was started the class period prior. And I guess this is the ultimate draw to invitational rhetoric: it does not emotionally drain or fatigue the interlocutors with conflict.

Comparing this activity with the traditional debate we had earlier in the semester, Tom reflects,

I remember after the debate, even though I enjoyed the process, I was spent. I was glad it was over with and I didn't have to reintroduce the conflict in the next class. With invitational rhetoric, I felt that the conversation was able to ruminate between the two of us, and the next time we were even more prepared to constructively talk about our experiences.

Tom's reflection illustrates how invitational rhetoric is conducive to more sustainable and ongoing conversations across difference, as interlocutors no longer feel the burden to win the battle or risk having their self-worth and worldview undermined. This series of activities, in other words, promotes ongoing mutual inquiry by reframing the relationship between interlocutors as collaboration rather than competition.

In addition, by decentering logocentric arguments, invitational rhetoric also prompts students to see their interlocutors as fellow humans with unique backstories that deserve consideration and respect rather than as proxies of ideologies that offend them. Salu's reflection highlights how this shift in perspective has prompted sustainable changes in the way she sees and engages with others:

> This activity changed my view on people in general. I am guilty of attributing someone's views on one topic to aspects about their character. I then attempt to judge people based on that one view, even if I only spoke to them once. . . . This is not a healthy practice, nor is it productive. This activity changed the way I engage with people, and I think I've become a more empathetic person.

As Salu explains in her narrative, as a queer woman of color, she tends to form judgments of others quickly in order to protect herself from microaggressive and sometimes outright aggressive acts of racism and sexism. While unfortunate, such defensiveness is often crucial for the survival of marginalized people. By participating in an exchange guided by the principles of invitational rhetoric, Salu understands that given the appropriate context, she could suspend her defensiveness and learn to inquire in a way that does not instantly dismiss her dominant peers' views on how and why they see the world.

Previously skeptical of invitational rhetoric, Ed similarly reflects that this series of exchanges prompted him to think otherwise:

> At first, I used to think invitational rhetoric was bullshit. I saw it as a way to manipulate people, by using stories (true or false) to gain an advantage over someone and their beliefs. Now, I see that it is not that. Invitational rhetoric is an open invitation into the emotional aspect of someone's life. I see that this kind of rhetoric allows for more genuine conversations. We are no longer attacking a belief; we are stepping in someone else's shoes.

Salu's and Ed's reflections illuminate the rhetorical impact of tracing how individuals develop specific worldviews due to their experiences and positionalities within intersecting sociopolitical and cultural contexts. By asking students to take into account how emotions and lived experiences inform opinions on public issues, this series of activities allows students to see civil discourse as an embodied practice in which opinions, emotions, and experiences are all intimately connected.

Aaliyah and Megan

While Ed's, Salu's, and Tom's examples demonstrate the effectiveness of this activity in prompting students to reexamine their deep stories and their relations with others across power differentials, it does not completely address whether marginalized students are benefitting from it as much as their dominant counterparts. In her personal narrative, Aaliyah, an Afro-Latinx student, describes her childhood experience with racism and how police brutality led to the death of one of her friends. She then explains how such encounters form the basis of her deep story, prompting her to fervently support Black Lives Matter (BLM) despite the critiques the movement has received from across the political spectrum.

Aaliyah's two white peers, both focusing on race in their respective papers, found her narrative illuminating. Megan, a white student who previously opposed the demolition of public Confederate statues, writes in her letter that Aaliyah's essay has made a strong and lasting impact on the way she understands racism and BLM. Megan notes that prior to reading Aaliyah's narrative and conversing with her, she had never considered the everyday trauma and oppression Black people experience. She had previously thought BLM only concerned the rare instances of police brutality rather than the systematic problem of antiblack racism. Megan ends her letter by reiterating her gratitude for Aaliyah and by positing the political significance of Aaliyah's narrative:

> You have made me want to read more into this topic, and you have really proved how Black Lives Matter shouldn't be as controversial as it is. . . . I feel as though if more people were honestly educated on that then there could really be a difference made. You gave me a new insight and better understanding over a topic that I had previously not known much about, other than what I have heard and seen from news stories.

The exchange with Aaliyah allowed Megan to see racial politics through a different prism—a prism often discredited by dominant mainstream media. This activity, in other words, expanded Megan's worldview and prompted her to more critically examine public discourse on racial justice and social movements.

Aaliyah, on the other hand, did not receive the same intellectual benefit. She writes in her reflection that she did not find this series of activities particularly generative for her own thinking. Because Aaliyah did not elaborate on that further, I could only speculate that unlike their white peers whose deep story is rarely challenged in dominant discourse and practices, black students are socialized to be attuned to the worldviews of white people—sometimes failing to do so could be fatal (Lebron, *New York Times*, June 22, 2017). This distinction applies not only to students of color but also to students who occupy structurally marginalized positions who before this activity are already knowledgeable about the deep stories of their dominant peers.

Marginalized students, however, could still benefit from this exchange. Salu's reflection in the previous section demonstrates that the collaborative and respectful atmosphere of these mutual inquiries opens up the possibility for marginalized students to engage in open dialogues with their more dominant peers without feeling the immediate need to defend themselves. While such defensiveness is often necessary for nonnormative subjects to protect themselves from different forms of violence and oppression in their everyday lives, it is both physically and emotionally taxing (Zhang 2016). Making room for marginalized students to share their lived experiences in a relatively safe environment not only offers temporary reprieve but also gives them an alternative experience of engaging with interlocutors across power difference.

In addition, turning their experiences into stories shared with others could be an empowering experience for marginalized students. As anthropologist Michael Jackson (2014) points out, "A story enables us to fuse the world within and the world without. In this way we gain some purchase over events that confounded us, humbled us, and left us helpless. In telling a story we renew our faith that the world is within our grasp" (240). Articulating their deep stories, in other words, allows marginalized students to regain control of how they want to make sense of their reality and present it to others. Their narratives constitute what Aja Martinez (2014) calls "counterstories," stories that "expose, analyze, and challenge stock stories of racial privilege and can help to strengthen traditions of social, political, and cultural survival and resistance" (38). In other words, rather than promoting respectability politics, activities guided by invitational rhetoric help make room for alternative worldviews and discourses by allowing marginalized students to share their counterstories with their more dominant peers, prompting a more critical examination of the existing power hierarchy.

Indeed, the exchange with her white peers was not completely unproductive for Aaliyah. While she notes in her reflection that she did not gain any new social knowledge, she was profoundly moved by Megan's reaction to her narrative. After repeatedly commending Megan for her openness and willingness to reexamine her own view, Aaliyah notes, "If I can get through one person then that is enough for me."

CONCLUSION

The current political and discursive climate has rendered productive and generous civil dialogues across difference pressing and crucial. Building upon Hochschild's (2016) emphasis on deep stories, I argue that as writing and rhetoric teachers, we ought to help students foster self-reflexivity and reciprocal, open, and critical engagements with different worldviews. By foregrounding mutual inquiry and the affective and social importance of one's deep story and lived experiences, a rhetorical education based on invitational rhetoric could prompt students from dominant positionalities to reexamine how their worldviews are formed and how such views impact others relationally, politically, and emotionally. The activity outlined in this article provides the opportunity for marginalized students to engage in conversations about high-stakes public issues without being constantly undermined; it also makes room for them to articulate their deep stories against the grain to critique dominant discourses that erase their experiences. While mutual inquiry grounded in invitational rhetoric is not a panacea, it turns the classroom into an experimental place of collaboration where we can engage in conversations and relationships that simultaneously take into account our respective feelings, lived experiences, and the structural forces that contribute to them.

NOTE

1. While this assignment is akin to an autoethnography, I refrained from calling it such for pedagogical and theoretical reasons. Since many students in class had not encountered autoethnography before, I did not want to present a new concept that might eclipse the key rhetorical concepts (invitational rhetoric and rhetoric as mutual inquiry) crucial to this series. Theoretically, I do not want to be reductive about autoethnography as a research method and genre, as it encompasses much more than this brief prompt could cover.

REFERENCES

Baker, Marsha Lee, Eric Dieter, and Zachary Dobbins. 2014. "The Art of Being Persuaded: Wayne Booth's Mutual Inquiry and the Trust to Listen." *Composition Studies* 42 (1): 13–34.

Bone, Jennifer Emerling, Cindy L Griffin, and T. M. Linda Scholz. 2008. "Beyond Traditional Conceptualizations of Rhetoric: Invitational Rhetoric and a Move Toward Civility." *Western Journal of Communication* 72 (4): 434–62.

Charland, Maurice. "Constitutive Rhetoric: The Case of the Peuple Québécois." 1987. *Quarterly Journal of Speech* 73 (2): 133–50.

Dow, Bonnie J. "Feminism, Difference(s), and Rhetorical Studies." 1995. *Communication Studies* 46 (1–2): 106–17.

Elbow, Peter. 1998. *Writing without Teachers*. 2nd ed. New York: Oxford University Press.

Foss, Sonja K., and Cindy L. Griffin. 1995. "Beyond Persuasion: A Proposal for an Invitational Rhetoric." *Communication Monographs* 62 (1): 2–18.

Fulkerson, Richard. 1996. "Transcending Our Conception of Argument in Light of Feminist Critiques." *Argumentation and Advocacy* 32 (4): 199–217.

Gagarin, Michael. 2001. "Did the Sophists Aim to Persuade?" *Rhetorica: A Journal of the History of Rhetoric* 19 (3): 275–91.

Haidt, Jonathan. 2013. *The Righteous Mind: Why Good People Are Divided by Politics and Religion*. Reprint ed. New York: Vintage.

Hesford, Wendy S. 1998. *Framing Identities*. Minneapolis: University of Minnesota Press,.

Hochschild, Arlie Russell. 2016. *Strangers in Their Own Land: Anger and Mourning on the American Right*. New Press.

Jackson, Michael. 2014. *The Politics of Storytelling: Variations on a Theme by Hannah Arendt*. 2nd ed. Chicago: Museum Tusculanum Press.

Juzwik, Mary, Anne Whitney, April Baker Bell, and Amanda Smith. 2014. "Re-Thinking Personal Narrative in the Pedagogy of Writing Teacher Preparation." *Teaching/Writing: The Journal of Writing Teacher Education* 3 (1): 27–35.

Kirtley, Susan. 2014. "Considering the Alternative in Composition Pedagogy: Teaching Invitational Rhetoric with Lynda Barry's *What It Is*." *Women's Studies in Communication* 37 (3): 339–59.

Knoblauch, Abby. 2012, "Disrupting Disruption: Invitational Pedagogy and Issues of Authority in the College Writing Classroom." In *Disrupting Pedagogies and Teaching the Knowledge Society: Countering Conservative Norms with Creative Approaches*, edited by Julie Falkner, 122–35. Hershey, PA: IGI Global.

Koziak, Barbara. 2000. *Retrieving Political Emotion: "Thumos," Aristotle, and Gender*. University Park: Penn State University Press.

Lozano-Reich, Nina M., and Dana L. Cloud. 2009. "The Uncivil Tongue: Invitational Rhetoric and the Problem of Inequality." *Western Journal of Communication* 73 (2): 220–26.

Lugones, María. 1987. "Playfulness, 'World'-Travelling, and Loving Perception." *Hypatia* 2 (2): 3–19.

Lynch, Dennis A. 1998. "Rhetorics of Proximity: Empathy in Temple Grandin and Cornel West." *Rhetoric Society Quarterly* 28 (1): 5–23.

Lyon, Arabella. 2013. *Deliberative Acts: Democracy, Rhetoric, and Rights*. Penn State University Press.

Martinez, Aja Y. 2014. "A Plea for Critical Race Theory Counterstory: Stock Story versus Counterstory Dialogues Concerning Alejandra's 'Fit' in the Academy." *Composition Studies* 42 (2): 33–55.

Mooney, Chris. 2011. "The Science of Why We Don't Believe Science." *Mother Jones*, May/June. http://www.motherjones.com/politics/2011/04/denial-science-chris-mooney/.

Narayan, Uma. 1988. "Working Together across Difference: Some Considerations on Emotions and Political Practice." *Hypatia* 3 (2): 31–47.

Pollock, Mark A., Lee Artz, Lawrence R. Frey, W. Arnett Pierce, and Bren A. O. Murphy. 1996. "Navigating between Scylla and Charybdis: Continuing the Dialogue on Communication and Social Justice." *Communication Studies* 47 (1–2): 142–51.

Ratcliffe, Krista. 2005. *Rhetorical Listening: Identification, Gender, Whiteness*. Carbondale: Southern Illinois University Press.

Rothfelder, Katy, and Davi Johnson Thornton. "Man Interrupted: Mental Illness Narrative as a Rhetoric of Proximity." *Rhetoric Society Quarterly* 47 (4): 359–82.

Schlib, John. 1996. *Between the Lines: Relating Composition Theory and Literary Theory*. Heinemann.

Shermer, Michael. 2017. "How to Convince Someone When Facts Fail." *Scientific American*, January 1. https://www.scientificamerican.com/article/how-to-convince-someone -when-facts-fail/.

Young, Morris. 2004. *Minor Re/Visions: Asian American Literacy Narratives as a Rhetoric of Citizenship*. Southern Illinois University Press.

Zhang, Sarah. 2016. "The Physical Damage Racism Inflicts on Your Brain and Body." *Wired*, July 16. https://www.wired.com/2016/07/physical-damage-racism-inflicts-brain -body/.

PART III

Institutional, Community, and Public Transformations

9

DESIGNING ACROSS DIFFERENCE
Intersectional, Interdependent Approaches to Sustaining Communities

Laura Gonzales and Ann Shivers-McNair

INTRODUCTION

In this chapter, we argue that researchers, teachers, and practitioners need multiple perspectives in theorizing and intervening across difference (beyond a single axis of identity and beyond a single theoretical framework) because, as legal scholar and critical race theorist Kimberlé Crenshaw (1989) demonstrates in discussing the marginalization of Black women, the explanatory and interventional power of a perspective from a single axis fails to account for the experiences of the intersections of identities—particularly multiply marginalized identities. For us, multiple perspectives come from engaging beyond a single axis of identity, beyond a single theoretical framework, beyond a single institution, and even beyond a single field or discipline. In other words, to work and engage across difference in our classrooms and professional contexts, we must recognize that race and power shape all relations, and we must work and engage across differences in theoretical frameworks, as well as across institutions and communities. To this end, we articulate an intersectional, interdependent, community-sustaining approach to designing rhetorical compositions and technologies that positions difference not as a problem to solve, nor as a possibility for tapping into new markets, but as an opportunity to seek new collaborations, understandings, and innovations by designing with and for culturally and linguistically diverse communities. We frame this approach by way of three conceptual topoi: intersectionality, interdependency, and community sustainment.

In the sections that follow, we discuss and contextualize these topoi, and then we offer examples of the topoi in praxis. Here, we briefly overview the topoi in light of our argument for multiple conceptual topoi for working across difference. Drawing on the work of Crenshaw (1989), we contend intersectionality allows researchers to account for the

https://doi.org/10.7330/9781646421732.c009

intertwining layers of experience, history, power, and positionality that exist as individuals navigate communication and action across contexts. Drawing on the work of Julie Jung (2014), we view interdependency as "an ethic for intellectual work" in which participants, researchers, and other stakeholders involved in a research project (e.g., audiences and community members) take an active role in making learning accessible for all those involved (101). And we define community-sustaining work as relational, centered on mutuality and shared goals, and responsive—a dynamic, flexible practice of listening deeply and actively, setting aside our assumptions, and making space for distributed creation and negotiation of knowledges and designs. By tracing commitments to intersectional, interdependent, community-sustaining work in these examples, we illustrate how rhetoric and composition teachers and researchers can develop methodologies, pedagogies, and practices that position difference as central to our discipline.

Taking up the commitment of this collection to offer both theorizations of and interventions in difference as it pertains to writing in and beyond the university, we begin with a discussion of theory that introduces the frameworks we draw upon and that traces how we bring them together. We then turn to a discussion of interventions that introduces the ways we blend theoretical frameworks with community practices in and beyond universities. This structure separates theory and intervention, as well as the frameworks and examples within each section, in order to introduce and explain each element in relation to other elements. We emphasize that, ultimately, our goal is to highlight and demonstrate the importance of cumulative, coconstituting relations of theoretical frameworks and community practices for engaging across difference in and beyond our classrooms. Therefore, we highlight these cumulative, coconstituting relations in the examples we offer, which include the development of multilingual user experience as an approach that advocates for an asset-based approach to language diversity and the development of culturally sustaining writing pedagogies for Hispanic-serving institutions.

THEORIZING DIFFERENCE

Like the editors of this collection, we are guided by Stephanie Kerschbaum's (2014) articulation of difference as dynamic, relational, and emergent rather than a static property. As Kerschbaum explains, "Attention to marking difference, when performed in conjunction with attention to various identification processes, can help us mediate between broad conceptual tools for talking about difference and the unique qualities of individual moments of interaction" (7). Describing what she refers to as the "contingency of identity" (9), Kerschbaum notes that "our ability to claim particular self-constructions and to have those self-constructions recognized by the others is always mediated by the power dynamics influencing an interaction" (10). Focusing on such interactions, or "specific moments of writing, teaching, and learning," is key to Kerschbaum's "new rhetoric of difference" that brings together "broader identification processes" and "the lived experiences that bring differences alive in the classroom" (15). Kerschbaum's articulation highlights the importance of understanding identity and difference *in relation* to each other and *as relational* phenomena.

Therefore, we are also guided by Raúl Sánchez's (2017) work on identity. In theorizing identity, Sánchez acknowledges that while our field has tended to resist essentializing views of identity in favor of poststructuralist, performative conceptualizations, strictly poststructuralist conceptualizations of identity lack the "material specificity" needed to theorize identity in ways that support the research and teaching of writing (xviii). As a solution, Sánchez proposes theorizing identity "as something that happens detached from human intention yet within the realm of human action," which in turn helps us "conceptualize acts of writing as moments in which a writer's agency is neither sovereign nor constricted but, rather, functional or symptomatic" (54). In other words, by approaching identity as an event, as Sánchez argues, we can dwell in the complex, dynamic relations of lived experiences, concepts, contexts, and interactions involved in specific acts of writing. Indeed, as Sánchez explains,

> Even though we know that writing is complexly ecological, even though we know that signification is not a process with neat or even identifiable beginnings and endings, and even though we know that "it's signifiers all the way down," we also know that individual, empirical acts of writing begin and end. These moments might be mere punctuations, bumps in the otherwise smooth flow of difference, temporary and even illusory. But they seem to occur, just the same. And conceptualizing them is what an event-based theory of identity hopes to do. (21)

If events are acts of writing that punctuate (or mark) differences in identity, then through identity-as-event, we can trace and intervene in how differences are marked in specific acts of writing, as Kerschbaum (2014) argues.

We agree with Sánchez's (2017) and Kerschbaum's (2014) orientations to identity and difference, and we, too, are compelled to approach identity and difference as emergent, relational, dynamic, and contextual (grounded in specific events or interactions). Such approaches high-light the multiplicities and nuances of identity and difference. We add that bringing together multiple theoretical frameworks and traditions of practice for describing and intervening in difference complements an orientation to difference as a relational, contextual phenomenon. Thus, we turn to three conceptual topoi that offer us both vocabularies for theorizing and traditions of practice for intervening in difference. These conceptual topoi—intersectionality, interdependence, and com-munity sustainment—draw across disciplines and fields and across the boundaries of theory and practice. In what follows, we describe each of these topoi and trace the relations among them.

Intersectionality

Crenshaw (1989) argues that in order to understand acts and experi-ences of discrimination that proceed from the marking of difference, we must account not just for a single axis of difference (for example, gender) but for the intersections of different identities (for example, gender, race, class, dis/ability, etc.). Crenshaw's work, centering the experiences and positionalities of Black women, is an important correc-tive to white feminist approaches that describe difference and discrimi-nation by separating gender identity from other identities such as race, class, dis/ability, sexual orientation, faith tradition, and more. Instead, Crenshaw (2017) argues, "Intersectionality is a lens through which you can see where power comes and collides, where it interlocks and inter-sects. It's not simply that there's a race problem here, a gender problem here, and a class or LGBTQ problem there. Many times, that framework erases what happens to people who are subject to all of these things." Thus, intersectionality highlights both the multiplicity of identities and the material consequences of relations among these multiple identities in the lived experiences of bodies and communities.

We recognize that using the concept of intersectionality, particularly as a white woman and a white Latina, can be problematic, especially if intersectionality is applied without attention to race and racial privilege. As Sami Schalk (2018) explains, "Intersectionality is also too often . . . understood in purely additive and ever expanding terms" or applied as a label to signal multiple identities while also ignoring race (8). We also agree with Schalk in recognizing "the potential of intersectionality" as "an important means for untangling the mutual constitution of oppres-sions such as racism, ableism, and sexism and for understanding how systems of power work within and beyond identity claims alone" (8).

Thus, we apply intersectionality to our ongoing work in the theory and practice of writing and technology design in and beyond the classroom by "emphasizing the interconnectedness of technological practices and gender, race, class, and sexuality, as well as their coconstitution and shaping of each other" (Shivers-McNair, Gonzales, and Zhyvotovska 2019, 46) In so doing, our goal is not only to "bring awareness to the interactions that community members (typically referred to as 'users') experience among language use, cultural practices, power positionalities, and technology use" but also to develop technologies and compositions that "actively embrace and shift power relations to center the goals and objectives of linguistically and ethnically diverse communities" (46). In other words, for teachers—as for researchers and practitioners—of writing, it is important both to account for intersectionality through critical, reflexive description and to actively design our pedagogies, compositions, and technologies to be inclusive of the intersectional identities of our students, audiences, and users.

Interdependence

In attending to intersectionality in our work as writing teachers, researchers, and designers, we are also compelled by the complementary relations of intersectionality and the disability studies framework of interdependence. For example, Laura brings together intersectionality and interdependence in her account of creating accessible, multilingual digital content (Gonzales 2018a). Drawing on the work of disability studies scholars Margaret Price and Stephanie Kerschbaum (2016), Gonzales (2018a) explains that interdependent research methodologies "center 'care, commitment, and acting with others in mutually-dependent relationships,' where relying on others to access information is not a matter of choice but an intentional, necessary practice" (35). Gonzales goes on to explain, furthermore, that "the notion of interdependency as central to inclusive research practice also has a long, though differently-named, history in research on language and racial diversity," noting Crenshaw's work on intersectionality and the work of African American language scholars who show "race, power, and language are always inherently tied and intertwined" (36). Through narratives of her experiences with recording, captioning, and publishing video records of translation activities, Gonzales highlights the need for "de-centering the current dichotomy between captions and subtitles, between English and other languages, and between deaf or hard-of-hearing and bi or multilingual audiences" and "acknowledging their collective interdependence and intersectionality" (43). In other words, an intersectional and interdependent approach to technology design moves past thinking about designing *either* for multilingual audiences *or* for deaf or hard-of-hearing audiences and, instead, encourages us to aim for creative, inclusive design for the interdependent intersections of multiple identities. Gonzales also advocates for "practices that not only recognize the additional labor of creating bilingual digital data, but that also prepare students, professionals, and researchers to successfully plan for and complete this work" (43).

In acknowledging and bringing together intersectionality and interdependence, we aim to show how these frameworks complement and therefore can enrich both our analysis and our practice as writers and technology designers. The characteristics of intersectionality and interdependence enrich our understanding of difference as relational and contextual. Intersectionality reminds us our identities are never separate from each other in our own lived experiences and in our interactions with others. Interdependence reminds us that (dis)ability is constructed by the kinds of relationships we create (and specifically, the bodies we assume are "normal" and therefore design for) and that we must recognize and be intentional about the ways our relations (among humans, technologies, bodies, environments) are interdependent.

Community Sustainment

To complement the intersectional and interdependent approaches we draw upon in our teaching and practice of writing across difference, we follow a tradition of community-engaged research in writing studies (and especially in technical and professional communication) that emphasizes coconstructing knowledge with communities (Grabill 2013) through a commitment to flexibility and reflexivity (Agboka 2013) and through a commitment to "pursuing questions of mutual interest and sharing power and decision making" (Rose et al. 2017, 215). For example, in a research and writing partnership, Clarissa San Diego (founder and CEO of Makerologist and a professional practitioner of writing across difference) and Ann (San Diego and Shivers-McNair 2017) describe and advocate for a practice of community strategy that emphasizes relationship and community building not only between designers and users/stakeholders but also among users, stakeholders, and communities. Thus, community strategy starts with relationships and leverages those relationships to identify issues and problems and to create localized, sustainable designs.

This articulation and practice of community strategy informed our approach to collaborative community building in the creation of a multilingual user experience (UX) research center (which we describe further in the next section). We emphasize that "collaborative community building in technology design is *relational* and *responsive*" (Shivers-McNair, Gonzales, and Zhyvotovska 2019, 44). By relational, we mean both that relationships are a given reality of this work and that these relationships must be central and mutual. And by responsive, we mean our relationships "must emphasize a dynamic, flexible practice of listening deeply and actively, setting aside assumptions, and making space for distributed creation and negotiation of knowledges and designs" (44). Thus, in addition to drawing upon community-engaged traditions, we also draw upon traditions of feminist mentoring that emphasize inclusivity, participation, and recursion in the practice of writing and teaching/mentoring across difference (Torrez et al. 2017). Across these specific traditions, practices of deep listening, flexibility, and respect are crucial, and we believe they are also key to the work of theorizing and intervening in difference in the frameworks we describe here.

We add, furthermore, that in addition to community strategy and community building, community sustainment is a vital practice in theorizing and intervening in the work of writing across difference. Our use of the term "community sustainment" is guided by the work of Django Paris (2012), who describes culturally sustaining pedagogy as a practice that "seeks to perpetuate and foster—to sustain—linguistic, literate, and cultural pluralism as part of the democratic project of schooling" (95). This requires moving away from pedagogical practices grounded in the hegemony of "the seemingly panoptic *White gaze* (Morrison 1998)" and instead asking questions like, "What if the goal of teaching and learning with youth of color was not ultimately to see how closely students could perform White middle-class norms, but rather was to explore, honor, extend, and, at times, problematize their cultural practices and investments?" (Alim and Paris 2017, 2–3). In other words, sustaining communities in and beyond our classrooms involves decentering and interrogating white norms and creating space for multiple identities, knowledges, and practices.

Therefore, we are also guided by the work of Chris Dayley and Rebecca Walton (2018), who argue that the field of technical and professional communication (and, we would add, rhetoric and composition as a whole) should work "not only to bring more diverse groups of people into the field but to welcome the range of expertise, experiences, and insights from underrepresented groups in shifting and shaping the identity of the field itself" (10). This happens both in the ways we teach in our classrooms and in how we build the theoretical concepts we teach in our classrooms. After all, following Victor Del Hierro (2018), we seek to build theories, as well as tools and technologies, that are "community-driven, localized, and accessible to a wide range of audiences" (11) because this impacts how we teach and engage with communities in and beyond the university, as scholars like Juan Guerra (2016) have argued. Approaching community sustainment through intersectionality and interdependence, then, allows researchers and teachers to both recognize the interlocking identities present in our classrooms, workplaces, and research sites and understand that supporting and sustaining differences in our identities benefits not only the individuals with whom we build and interact but also the broader context and community in which this work happens.

INTERVENING IN DIFFERENCE

The conceptual topoi of intersectionality, interdependence, and community sustainment guide not only how we understand and theorize the work of writing across difference but also how we intervene in the work of writing across difference, both in and beyond the university. As Keith Gilyard (2016) reminds us, it is not enough to recognize the fluidity and constant presence of difference in identity and language; we must also intricately understand how degrees and ranges in difference impact the material realities of people in their everyday contexts and how race and power intersect with other identity markers and lived experiences that should be acknowledged in working across difference on multiple levels. In the sections that follow, we describe two ongoing initiatives we are building to not only recognize but also intervene in the ways through which the fields of rhetoric and composition and technical communication engage with difference on multiple levels, including technology innovation and pedagogy and curriculum design.

Multilingual User Experience (UX)

The first initiative we describe crosses the boundaries of languages, institutions, professions, and communities in order to address and redress the marking of difference in the design of written communication and communication technologies. In 2017, Laura co-founded the Sites of Translation Multilingual User Experience (UX) Research Center at her university, with Ann as associate director, and we began planning a symposium to bring together academic researchers, students, professional practitioners, and community members. As we explained on the center's website (which is no longer live),

> Developed as a partnership among community organizations, academic researchers, and technology industry professionals, *Sites of Translation User-Experience Research Center* is envisioned as **the place where social-justice oriented organizations come to request help in creating and disseminating their bi- or multilingual content (e.g., websites, web applications, informational tools) aiming to meet the needs and highlight the assets of linguistically diverse users**. (emphasis in original)

For our readers who may not be familiar with user experience, we first describe UX in relation to rhetorical practice, and then we describe our framework of multilingual UX.

The field of UX seeks to directly incorporate humanities research into technology design, working under the assumption that humans' needs and practices should shape how technologies are built and developed. More specifically, UX research uses inquiry-based humanities methods and methodologies to explore questions such as:

- How can technologies be designed or improved to facilitate the daily activities of people?
- How can digital tools, applications, and interfaces be made more accessible to a diverse range of audiences?
- How do users adapt or manipulate existing technologies to accommodate their needs?
- And in turn, what can technology designers learn from users' manipulations and adaptations of technologies?

Working within the understanding that technologies should be adapted to meet the needs of humans (and not vice versa), the field of UX highlights the creativity of people from various backgrounds, focusing on how individuals incorporate technology use in their everyday lives.

In articulating the intersections of UX and technical communication, Claire Lauer and Eva Brumberger (2016) reiterate that UX is a multidisciplinary, applied field about "designing for interconnectedness, where tasks and texts no longer exist individually or in a silo, but instead connect across a broad and complex landscape of interfaces and environments" (249). Such a view resonates with approaches in multimodal composition that acknowledge the ways rhetorical meanings are made in the interactions of multiple modalities. Lauer and Brumberger add, furthermore, that "ideally, UX also strives to accommodate how users appropriate information products and content in unanticipated ways and for their own purposes as well as how those products position users to act in the world by the way they are designed and the options they allow for" (249). In other words, rhetorical meanings and possibilities not only exceed single modalities but also exceed the intentions of individual designers and users. As Lauer and Brumberger point out, understanding and engaging audiences is at the heart of both UX practice and technical communication practice (261).

We add that this audience-centric focus also connects UX to the broader field of rhetoric and composition, particularly as we seek to intervene in practices of writing across technologies, situations, and contexts. After all, Susan Miller-Cochran and Rochelle Rodrigo (2009) made a similar argument about the intersections of composition and usability studies (which is now encompassed in UX) more than a decade ago. Rhetorical skills and responsibility are crucial for just and effective interventions across difference, particularly when these interventions are designed through intersectional, interdependent methodologies. Indeed, scholars working at the intersection of technical communication and UX are bringing an increased focus on human dignity and social justice to the design of communication and technologies. Emma Rose, Robert Racadio, Kalen Wong, Shally Nguyen, Jee Kim, and Abbie Zahler (2018) argue that "when certain types of people are consistently centered [in design], others are intentionally or unintentionally pushed to the margins or left out altogether" and that "centering overlooked, vulnerable, or marginalized audiences leads to different design considerations, methods, practice and resulting designs" (1).

And this brings us to multilingual UX, specifically. Because technologies are now being distributed in more culturally and linguistically diverse environments than ever, UX researchers must work closely with technology designers to develop tools and systems inherently cross-cultural and multilingual. That is, UX researchers now seek to conduct UX research (e.g., interviews, observations of digital interface interaction) with diverse, multilingual users who navigate digital platforms (e.g., social media sites, phone applications) across languages (Rose et al. 2017; Sun 2006, 2012). Within this framework, we argue that the goal of multilingual UX is not only to design technologies that can sell in multilingual, global markets but also "to highlight the value of community-based, multilingual practices and discourses in the design and development of contemporary technologies" specifically designed with a social justice agenda (Shivers-McNair, Gonzales, and Zhyvotovska 2019, 44). We explain that

> although many researchers and practitioners have pointed to the need to make technologies accessible in languages other than English, in proposing Multilingual UX, we move beyond language-only concerns prompted

by capitalist models for designing technologies—models that present linguistic diversity as a design "challenge" to be fixed or overcome or as a feature that should be leveraged to sell products or services. Instead, Multilingual UX focuses on how technologies can be developed with and for culturally and linguistically diverse communities in local contexts, resulting in the design and dissemination of multilingual technologies that incorporate the expertise and goals of community members, professionals, and local users. (44)

In other words, multilingual UX positions language and culture difference not as a problem to solve, nor as a possibility for tapping into new markets, but as an opportunity to seek new collaborations, understandings, and innovations by designing with and for culturally and linguistically diverse communities. Through this perspective, language, race, and power are always connected and centralized in the technology-design process. For example, rather than emphasizing the design of multilingual technologies that adhere to standardized language practices, multilingual UX recognizes language fluidity and variation as a constant part of all communication that should be incorporated into technology design and multilingual writing assessment. Therefore, multilingual UX is about "building reciprocal, ongoing collaborations with linguistically and ethnically diverse communities, blurring the boundaries between the roles and definitions of 'researchers,' 'designers,' and 'users' to develop tools and technologies inherently driven by and for community goals and objectives" (45).

At our Multilingual UX Symposium in the fall of 2017, we brought together academic researchers and students from the fields of rhetoric, composition, and technical communication to learn from and work with practitioners from a range of communities and professions. In assembling the participants, we considered our collective intersectional identities, seeking to amplify the perspectives of marginalized and multiply marginalized communities. In our conversations and activities, we created space for all our expertises, vocabularies, and practices to intersect across institutional and disciplinary boundaries in ways that highlight our interdependence. We discussed projects in classrooms and writing programs and in communities and industries, often blurring the boundaries among these sites in order to imagine interventions that connect students and teachers with community members and practitioners. These conversations and connections were informed both by concepts and practices from rhetoric and composition, like Guerra's (2016) model of writing across difference in classrooms and communities, and by concepts and practices from practitioners, like Clarissa San Diego's (Shivers-McNair and San Diego 2017) model of community strategy (as we describe above). In these conversations, and in the ongoing relation-ships and initiatives that continue from these conversations, we seek out community-building and community-sustaining practices of pluralizing knowledges, expertise, and meanings rather than privileging dominant ways of knowing.

While the research center itself has shifted and changed since its initial design, current projects stemming from the multilingual UX initiative purposely seek to bridge connections between intersectional identities and various disciplinary orientations. These projects include:

1. *Women of Color in Technology Design*: A project funded by the Kapor Center in Oakland and the Coalition for Women of Color in Computing that brings together multilingual women and women of color interested in technology design with other women in the tech industry. Throughout the course of a year, student fellows in this project work on individual projects related to multilingual UX, and they come together with mentors from across the country to get feedback, test prototypes, and innovate solutions to design challenges. Current fellows are working on designing more accessible websites for international students seeking to apply to graduate programs in the United States, developing participatory archiving platforms and practices with commu-nities in Nepal, creating protocols for empathetic usability testing with multilingual users, and collaborating with Indigenous communities on a digital publication related to Indigenous language interpretation.

2. *Participatory Translation of Healthcare Materials on the Mexico/US Border*: A project funded by the Conference on College Composition and Communication in collaboration with Lucía Durá (University of Texas at El Paso), which seeks to design health-related tools that are localized for bilingual, binational communities in El Paso, Texas. In collaboration with community organizations such as the local Diabetes Association, participants in this project are working with bilingual community mem-bers to design health-management systems in variations of Spanishes and Englishes (rather than standardized Castilian Spanish or standard-ized American English).

Throughout these projects, difference is centered as expertise critical to the design and dissemination of tools and technologies for a broad range of communities and stakeholders. In the Women of Color in Technology Design project, our fellows' multilingual expertises are key assets not only in their individual design efforts but also in the project itself. Centering their multilingual and multicultural expertises creates possibilities for multidirectional mentoring among fellows, project leaders, and the pro-fessionals we network with. For example, in a meeting with professionals in a major technology company, our project fellows drew upon their ex-periences and expertise to challenge language and culture biases in that company's technology designs in a productive, generative conversation. Ultimately, successful or effective designs in the context of these projects are those that meet community goals and needs, highlight the expertise of diverse stakeholders and designers, and emphasize the importance of collaboration across difference as central to effective communication.

Culturally Sustaining Pedagogies in Hispanic-Serving Institutions

Our work in multilingual UX has also informed and enriched our work building culturally sustaining writing programs and pedagogies at our institutions. During the 2017–2018 and 2018–2019 academic years, we were both designing and proposing writing majors at our respective institutions, both Hispanic-serving institutions. Hispanic-serving institutions (HSIs) are defined in federal law (HACU 2020) as accredited, degree-granting, public or private nonprofit institutions of higher education with 25 percent or more total undergraduate Hispanic full-time equivalent (FTE) student enrollment. Once an institution is designated an HSI, it is eligible to receive federal grant funding that should be used to improve retention and success of Latinx students because while HSIs represent 17 percent of all higher ed institutions, they serve more than 67 percent of all Hispanic students (HACU 2020). Together with Kendall Leon (California State University, Chico), we proposed and were awarded a grant in 2018 from the Council of Programs in Technical and Scientific Communication (CPTSC)—which is more or less analogous to the Council of Writing Program Administrators in the field of rhetoric and composition—to study and develop technical and professional writing pedagogies and program designs at and across HSIs that, like our multilingual UX initiatives, highlight the assets of culturally and linguistically diverse students and communities. Drawing on ongoing work that advocates for the importance of honoring students' cultural and linguistic practices in writing program administration, this project allowed us to work toward developing more culturally sustaining programs in our local contexts while also connecting with faculty across the country interested in localizing technical and professional writing curricula for and with Latinx students and communities.

Over the last decade, the field of technical communication has encouraged an emphasis on diversity and social justice not only in research and practice but also in programs and pedagogies (Haas 2012; Jones, Savage, and Yu 2014; Matveeva 2015; Williams and Pimentel 2014; Yajima and Toyosaki 2015). While scholarship has focused on overall approaches and methodologies for teaching technical and professional writing (TPW) through social justice perspectives, our goal is to extend this conversation to develop practical activities, syllabi, and course materials for and with the linguistically and ethnically diverse students that increasingly make up the majority in our classrooms and university contexts—both in and beyond HSIs. Our data-collection methods for this project have several stages, including (1) individual program mapping, (2) interviews with faculty teaching TPW at HSIs, (3) student surveys, and (4) a resource prototype, which we envision as a digital space for networking and sharing resources. Through these methods, we continue seeking to answer the following questions:

- How do we make a case for the value of TPW at minority-serving institutions such as HSIs?
- How do we develop TPW curricula tailored specifically for Latinx students at HSIs and for other historically minoritized students? How do we establish professional-development opportunities for faculty who teach or want to teach TPW at HSIs and other minority-serving institutions?
- How do we learn about and from students' perspectives with TPW at HSIs and other minority-serving institutions?
- How do we stay in touch with other TPW faculty at HSIs and other minority-serving institutions, especially given the fact that many of us work at institutions with high teaching loads and service commitments?

To begin to address these questions, we have spent time building relationships with faculty at HSIs and creating spaces for us to come together to work toward answers collectively. During the 2018–2019 academic school year, we interviewed faculty at ten different HSIs, engaging in conversations about the possibilities of designing TPW curricula that leverage the affordances of our Latinx student demographic. While the specific details of these interviews are beyond the scope of this chapter, one of the biggest lessons we learned by connecting with faculty across the country who are interested in designing writing programs grounded in cultural sustainability is that localizing TPW curricula specifically for Latinx students at HSIs requires added attention to difference of various interlocking, interdependent levels.

For example, most of the faculty we interviewed noted that although several technical and professional writing teachers at their institutions are implementing practices on an individual level to support Latinx students, efforts to centralize Latinx students' perspectives, histories, abilities, and interests within these programs are rare at a programmatic or institutional level. Technical and professional writing programs at

HSIs are frequently situated in teaching-focused institutions with higher teaching loads. As such, innovation for Latinx-tailored technical and professional writing curricula within these institutions is often reliant on already over-committed faculty who do not receive compensation or time or have the power to make large curricular shifts in their programs. Further, technical and professional writing programs at HSIs are not always supported with tenure-track hires and institutionalized or mandatory curricular initiatives. In short, while many HSIs acknowledge the value of difference in terms of student demographic, an attunement to differences in faculty demographics, disciplinary orientations, and departmental values will be critical as scholars in technical and professional writing continue pushing for more localized curricula in minority-serving contexts such as HSIs.

As we seek to intervene in technical and professional writing program practices in HSIs, we are guided by the same conceptual topoi that are foundational to our multilingual UX initiatives: intersectionality, interdependence, and community sustainment. Through a lens of intersectionality, we can account for the mismatch in the identities of HSI technical and professional writing faculty and the students and communities they serve. For example, Ann is a white woman directing a program in technical and professional writing at an HSI, and in our conversations with faculty at nine other HSIs, we found most of these other programs are also led by white women. This has led us to advocate—at our own institutions and in our presentations and publications on our research—for the importance of recruiting and retaining Latinx faculty in technical and professional writing programs at HSIs. Furthermore, through a lens of interdependence, we recognize how our programmatic and pedagogical designs, while localized for institutional and geographic contexts, are also interdependent across contexts and interconnected with the multiple different identities encompassed within the Latinx community. A key goal of our research is to respond to our own desire, which has been echoed by participants in our study, for HSI faculty and students to be able to share resources and connect with each other across contexts. Finally, through a lens of community sustainment, we highlight the importance of moving beyond deficit-based models of writing pedagogy that treat bi- and multilingual writers as in need of remediation or enculturation to dominant discourses. Instead, we highlight the assets of multilingual writers by making their rhetorical skills visible in and central to the curricula we design. To illustrate this, in what follows, Laura describes an activity and an assignment she uses in her TPW and rhetoric courses.

ACTIVITY: TRANSLATING ASSIGNMENT SHEETS

Through research I conducted with Rebecca Zantjer and Howard Fooksman in 2015, we learned students often have a difficult time understanding the disciplinary language writing teachers use on assignment sheets. Words like *analyze, synthesize,* and *explain* have various meanings and mean different things to teachers than they might to students. For this reason, drawing on research in translation, I find it useful to ask my students to deconstruct or translate my own assignment sheets into terms that might be more accessible. We first read and watch videos about the untranslatability of language. I especially like the video titled *Untranslatable* by Anne von Petersdorff and Rebecca Zantjer, in which participants describe words and terms in their heritage languages they deem untranslatable into English (see Gonzales and Zantjer 2015).

After discussing the fact that language is fluid and always changing, students are asked to mark up and translate my assignment sheets. To do this, I upload my assignment sheet to a Google doc, give students editing and commenting access, and then ask students to identify specific words that might be confusing or hard to understand. I ask students to provide sample definitions of the terms they identify, and then we have a conversation about how these terms should be understood in our particular class context. For example, students might translate the term *analyze* into something like *read between the lines.* Rather than asking them to analyze in the assignment, I will then revise and ask students to read between the lines as they look at a particular text or artifact. This simple notion of making my assignment sheets editable and leveraging digital technologies to both understand and practice translation helps students and teachers recognize the rhetorical nature of language and work toward common objectives together. Including students' language choices in the assignment sheet can also help teachers to recognize students' linguistic practices as rhetorically effective and valid within the classroom.

ASSIGNMENT: TRACING TRANSLATION MOMENTS

In my book, I introduce the concept of translation moments as an analytical framework that can help researchers trace the rhetorical activities that multilingual communicators engage in as they translate information. For example, during the process of translating information from one named language (e.g., Spanish, English) to another, translators might pause to ask themselves questions such as, How should I translate this word in a way that will be most accessible to audiences who speak a specific variation of Spanish? Is a word most useful in this translation, or would a picture work better? Am I translating for audiences from science backgrounds or from backgrounds in the arts (or both)? In short, translation moments are instances in time when multilingual communicators pause to make a rhetorical decision about how to best translate a specific word or phrase from one language to another (see Gonzales 2018b).

In my writing courses, I share the concept of translation moments as a way to situate conversations about rhetoric in the expertise of multilingual communicators.

I then explain that everyone, regardless and inclusive of their linguistic backgrounds, experiences translation moments. These moments can take place when we communicate with individuals who speak multiple languages that differ from our own or simply when we try to explain to our families what we mean by the word *rhetoric.* Translation moments can also help illustrate how language is always racialized and connected to power and privilege, which explains why white language speakers and white language practices are often considered standard and "appropriate" in classroom and professional contexts (Smitherman and Villanueva 2003). Following these conversations, I ask students to trace their own translation moments throughout the course of a week, logging the translation moments they experience, as well as the strategies they use to navigate these moments. We use these translation moments as opportunities to discuss issues of race and language and as an avenue for students to recognize their own language choices as rhetorical. I then ask students to compile their translation moments and navigation strategies into a multimodal and/ or digital text to share with their classmates; in this text, students must consider issues of accessibility not only in terms of language choices but also in connection to listeners and community members who identify with various disabilities. This allows us to put translation moments in sequenced conversations not only with students' broader communicative and material contexts but also with each other and with a wide range of audiences.

My suggestions for intentionally combining multilingual and digital pedagogies are not necessarily innovative or new, and they draw on long-standing research in cultural and digital rhetorics, as well as disability studies. The overall purpose of this work is to make and sustain spaces for students to employ the communicative practices they are already familiar with in writing classrooms and to continuously (re)assess what we as writing teachers value as effective communication.

CONCLUSION

In this chapter, we provide grounded examples of design across difference as it takes place in research, professional, and community contexts, as well as in pedagogy. Through these examples, we argue that the frameworks of intersectionality, interdependence, and community sustainment can help researchers, teachers, and practitioners design platforms, tools, technologies, and pedagogies through transcultural and transdisciplinary collaboration. In our discussion of these frameworks and projects, we also want to emphasize that the work of designing across difference is complex and rigorous. Rather than sharing standardized protocols for collaborative design, our discussion of multilingual UX and culturally sustaining pedagogies in TPW programs at HSIs seeks to emphasize the fact that designing across difference requires the balancing and (re)orientation of priorities from an individualistic perspective to a community-driven perspective that does not necessarily adhere to traditional disciplinary, cultural, or linguistic standards. In short, designing across difference means working with stakeholders and collaborators from different backgrounds and orientations to develop tools and practices that make our classrooms, professions, and communities collectively more successful.

REFERENCES

Agboka, Godwin. 2013. "Participatory Localization: A Social Justice Approach to Navigating Unenfranchised/Disenfranchised Cultural Sites." *Technical Communication Quarterly* 22 (1): 28–49.

Alim, H. Samy, and Django Paris. 2017. "What Is Culturally Sustaining Pedagogy and Why Does It Matter?" In *Culturally Sustaining Pedagogies: Teaching and Learning for Justice in a Changing World*, edited by H. Samy Alim and Django Paris, 1–17. New York: Teachers College Press.

Crenshaw, Kimberlé. 1989. "Demarginalizing the Intersection of Race and Sex: A Black Feminist Critique of Antidiscrimination Doctrine, Feminist Theory and Antiracist Politics." *University of Chicago Legal Forum* 1989 (1): 139–67.

Crenshaw, Kimberlé. 2017. "Kimberlé Crenshaw on Intersectionality, More Than Two Decades Later." Columbia Law School. https://www.law.columbia.edu/news/archive/kimberle-crenshaw-intersectionality-more-two-decades-later.

Dayley, Chris, and Rebecca Walton. 2018. "Informing Efforts to Increase Diversity: Academic Programs and Student Motivation in Technical and Professional Communication." *Programmatic Perspectives* 10 (2): 5–46.

Del Hierro, Victor. 2018. "DJs, Playlists, and Community: Imagining Communication Design through Hip Hop." *Communication Design Quarterly*, October 6. OnlineFirst. https://dl.acm.org/doi/abs/10.1145/3358931.3358936.

Gilyard, Keith. 2016. "The Rhetoric of Translingualism." *College English* 78 (3): 284–89.

Gonzales, Laura. 2018a. "Designing for Intersectional, Interdependent Accessibility: A Case Study of Multilingual Technical Content." *Communication Design Quarterly* 6 (4): 34–45.

Gonzales, Laura. 2018b. *Sites of Translation: What Multilinguals Can Teach us about Digital Writing and Rhetoric.* Ann Arbor: University of Michigan Press.

Gonzales, Laura, and Rebecca Zantjer. 2015. "Translation as a User-Localization Practice." *Technical Communication* 62 (4): 271–84.

Grabill, Jeffrey T. 2013. "On Being Useful: Rhetoric and the Work of Engagement." In *The Public Work of Rhetoric,* edited by John M. Ackerman and David J. Coogan, 191–203. Columbia: University of South Carolina Press.

Guerra, Juan. 2016. *Language, Culture, Identity, and Citizenship in College Classrooms and Communities.* New York: Routledge.

Haas, Angela. 2012. "Race, Rhetoric, and Technology: A Case Study of Decolonial Technical Communication Theory, Methodology, and Pedagogy." *Journal of Business and Technical Communication* 26 (3): 277–310.

HACU (Hispanic Association of Colleges and Universities). 2020. "Hispanic-Serving Institutions across the Nation Total 539." HACU News, April 16. https://www.hacu.net/NewsBot.asp?MODE=VIEW&ID=3188.

Jones, Natasha, Gerald Savage, and Han Yu. 2016. "Tracking Our Progress: Diversity in Technical and Professional Communication Programs." *Programmatic Perspectives* 6 (1): 132–52.

Jung, Julie. 2014. "Systems Rhetoric: A Dynamic Coupling of Explanation and Description." *Enculturation* 17. http://enculturation.net/systems-rhetoric.

Kerschbaum, Stephanie L. 2014. *Toward a New Rhetoric of Difference.* Urbana: National Council of Teachers of English.

Lauer, Claire, and Eva Brumberger. 2016. "Technical Communication as User Experience in a Broadening Industry Landscape." *Technical Communication* 63 (3): 248–64.

Matveeva, Natalia. 2015. "Teaching Technical, Scientific, or Professional Communication at Hispanic-Serving Institutions." *Programmatic Perspectives* 7 (1): 3–20.

Miller-Cochran, Susan K., and Rochelle L. Rodrigo, eds. 2009. *Rhetorically Rethinking Usability: Theories, Practices, and Methodologies.* New York: Hampton.

Paris, Django. 2012. "Culturally Sustaining Pedagogy: A Needed Change in Stance, Terminology, and Practice." *Educational Researcher* 41 (3): 93–7.

Price, Margaret, and Stephanie L. Kerschbaum. 2016. "Stories of Methodology: Interviewing Sideways, Crooked and Crip." *Canadian Journal of Disability Studies* 5 (3): 18–56.

Rose, Emma J., Robert Racadio, Kalen Wong, Shally Nguyen, Jee Kim, and Abbie Zahler. 2017. "Community-Based User Experience: Evaluating the Usability of Health Insurance Information with Immigrant Patients." *IEEE Transactions on Professional Communication* 60 (2): 214–31.

Sánchez, Raúl. 2017. *Inside the Subject: A Theory of Identity for the Study of Writing.* Urbana: National Council of Teachers of English.

Schalk, Sami. 2018. *Bodyminds Reimagined: (Dis)ability, Race, and Gender in Black Women's Speculative fiction.* Durham, NC: Duke University Press.

Shivers-McNair, Ann, and Clarissa San Diego. 2017. "Localizing Communities, Goals, Communication, and Inclusion: A Collaborative Approach." *Technical Communication* 64 (2): 97–112.

Shivers-McNair, Ann, Laura Gonzales, and Tetyana Zhyvotovska. 2019. "An Intersectional Technofeminist Framework for Community-Driven Technology Innovation." *Computers and Composition* 51: 43–54.

Smitherman, Geneva, and Victor Villanueva. 2003. *Language Diversity in the Classroom: From Intention to Practice.* Urbana: Southern Illinois University Press.

Sun, Huatong. 2006. "The Triumph of Users: Achieving Cultural Usability Goals with User Localization." *Technical Communication Quarterly* 15 (4): 457–81.

Sun, Huatong. 2012. *Cross-Cultural Technology Design: Creating Culture-Sensitive Technology for Local Users.* Oxford: Oxford University Press.

Torrez, J. Estrella, Santos Ramos, Laura Gonzales, Victor Del Hierro, and Everardo Cuevas. 2017. "*Nuestros Cuentos*: Collaborative Storytelling with Latinx and Indigenous Youth." *Bilingual Review/Revista Bilingue* 33 (5): 91–106.

Williams, Miriam. F., and Octavio Pimentel. 2014. *Communicating Race, Ethnicity, and Identity in Technical Communication*. New York: Routledge.

Yajima, Yusaku, and Satoshi Toyosaki. 2015. "Bridging for a Critical Turn in Translation Studies: Power, Hegemony, and Empowerment." *Connexions: International Professional Communication Journal* 3 (2): 91–125.

10

ANTIRACIST TRANSLINGUAL PRAXIS IN WRITING ECOLOGIES[1]

Sumyat Thu, Katie Malcolm, Candice Rai, and Anis Bawarshi

The discourses of diversity, equity, and inclusion have become ubiquitous in universities—evident in the rise of strategic plans, committees, statements, retention plans, and hiring practices. While such work can include the necessary labors of radical transformation, we also hold Sara Ahmed's critique of diversity close to heart. As Ahmed (2012) argues, diversity discourses within universities often pay public lip service to difference without significantly changing structures of discrimination and exclusion (53), which can, in fact, perpetuate violence and inequity by appearing to value difference without addressing foundational and ongoing systemic racism and the logics of White[2] supremacy and settler colonialism embedded in US educational systems. In an effort to resist this "smile of diversity" (72), this chapter brings together conversations in translingual and antiracist scholarship to advocate for long-term structural changes that seek to acknowledge and transform the ways racial capitalism and White supremacy shape the practices and policies within our writing programs, universities, and broader communities.

Particularly in the past decade, translingual approaches in composition studies have advocated for structural changes to our field, institutions, and classrooms by offering a dynamic conception of language that stresses the heterogeneity of all language performances, and language norms as emergent, negotiated, relational, situated within, and translated across fluctuating standards, material conditions, and asymmetrical power relations (Canagarajah 2013; Lu and Horner 2013). One of translingualism's central tenets is that language difference is the norm of all communication, which opposes the monolingual language ideology that pervades our US institutions and dominant culture and that conceives language as static, discrete, and self-contained. Instead of imagining *language* as a monolithic, transparent, standardized tool that writers use more or less effectively depending on the assessment of readers in dominant positions

https://doi.org/10.7330/9781646421732.c010

of power, translingualism conceptualizes language use as an active process of *languaging* in which language by its very nature is always performative, dynamic, emergent, and relational. In this sense, language is not a property one possesses but an ongoing negotiation situated in spatiotemporal and power relations that requires a rhetorical capacity for laboring across difference; rather than something one *has*, languaging is something one *does* with language within and against fluctuating norms and contexts that are also shaping what one can do with language.

By moving towards a conception of language difference as the norm and toward a unilateral critique of monolingualism, translingual scholars (and allied scholars working to develop translanguaging praxis; see García 2009; García and Wei 2014), disrupt the binary between language practices considered "normal" (with respect to dominant, generally White, norms) and those marked (or dismissed) as different (or deviant). Translingual orientations, therefore, can help us transform writing program ecologies—reorienting readers and writers toward linguistic difference that create opportunities for individuals to draw on, develop, and activate their diverse literate repertoires to communicate more strategically, nimbly, and ethically across contexts (Bou Ayash 2019; Guerra 2016; Leonard 2014).

While understanding difference as a vital site of meaning making and agency is necessary for equitable writing ecologies, Keith Gilyard (2016) has argued that consolidating differences risks masking the ways institutions have used difference to denigrate particularly working-class students of color. As Gilyard argues, "Translingualists are clear about the fact that we all differ as language users from each other and in relation to a perceived standard"; however, what is "often elided" is the "recognition that we don't all differ from said standard in the same way" (286). Gilyard's argument highlights the need to resist empty liberal pluralisms that celebrate a pacifying notion of diversity as inclusion but fail to address structures of inequity and violence reinforced across difference. This orientation is particularly important in the teaching of writing given that language users with perceived deviations from dominant English standards have been historically and systemically marginalized within US and global contexts.

Drawing on Juan Guerra's and Gilyard's scholarship, Missy Watson and Rachael Shapiro (2018) further punctuate these arguments by insisting we must center the "political project translingualism offers" within the "material realities of language difference" and by refusing to articulate "translingualism as foremost a process and practice (i.e., translanguaging) rather than as an ideology with material consequences (i.e.,

our cultural attitudes about language and their effects on individuals)."
Building on these critiques, we argue that translingualism's normalization of language difference must be grounded in an antiracist critique of
structural inequity and a decentering and decolonizing of normalized,
White-supremacist, racist institutional structures, practices, and pedagogies. And, beyond critique, we advocate ongoing praxis, grounded
in local contexts and driven by intentional, active efforts to resist and
transform the structures of inequity that promote racism, anti-Blackness,
settler-colonial epistemologies, linguistic discrimination, and other
forms of exclusion embedded within our writing programs, institutions,
and broader communities.

We situate these concerns within stories about ongoing changes
we have made towards an antiracist translingualism in our local context within the Expository Writing Program (EWP)[3] at the University
of Washington–Seattle. The EWP supports seventy-five-plus instructors
(most of whom are graduate students) who teach approximately 240
composition courses to over five thousand undergraduate students each
year. The work we describe here—including shifting our teacher-training
and program practices and vocabularies, interrogating our assessment
practices, and developing program statements—builds on longstanding
commitments in our program to antiracist and equity-oriented writing
practices and language policies[4] and in urgent response to the movement
for Black lives and protests against racial violence and systemic injustice.
In sharing our experiences and attempts at transforming our writing program, we cannot offer a blueprint that can be unrolled in other contexts
or a curriculum that can be implemented wholesale. Rather, we offer
stories about our ongoing work, challenges we have encountered, some
changes we have made, and ways we have fallen short.

Before we turn to a discussion of these stories, we next draw together
conversations on translingual and antiracist approaches to situate our
central argument that translingual approaches to writing praxis must
actively engage the realpolitik of language by making visible and seeking
to resist and transform the structural inequalities that perpetuate social,
racial, and linguistic injustices as they exist within and are perpetuated
by our writing classrooms and programs, colleges and universities, and
broader society.

ON ANTIRACIST TRANSLINGUAL ORIENTATIONS TO WRITING

Social, racial, and linguistic injustices are pervasive and insidious within
our institutions and everyday lives—and they are perpetuated in ways

that are often unconscious and unintentional. Consequently, when integrating antiracist translingual approaches into our writing programs, we argue it is necessary to confront the historical legacies of racism and colonialism in order to reflect on how monolingual and racist ideologies are embedded within local contexts. In this section, we examine the relationship between monolingualism and racism and also explore how they entangle and manifest within our university and writing program, even amid attempts to promote antiracist praxis. Woven throughout this section are stories[5] from our own writing program and university ecology that offer glimpses into ordinary ways monolingualism and racism entwine; they are representative of other such stories we (and likely you) could conjure about how structural racism, linguistic injustice, and other inequities manifest pervasively in everyday institutional life.

Institutional Monolingual Racism

We operate from the evidence-based understanding that English monolingual ideology is thoroughly enmeshed with the historical and global legacies of ongoing racist and colonial epistemologies, which shaped and continue to inform the normative policies, pedagogy, and practices in US dominant culture, educational systems, and writing programs that persist in perpetuating inequitable literacy education and English instruction across the globe. As Frankie Condon and Vershawn Ashanti Young (2017) argue, racism is not simply a "product of individual actions that deviate from the normal, nonracist actions of most of us or from the sensitive practice of suppressing our racism" but also includes broader, institutional effects from social structures that systemically reproduce "long term and cumulative effects of . . . everyday racisms" (6). As the NCTE's "Statement on Anti-Racism to Support Teaching and Learning" suggests, "Racism in America is the systematic mistreatment and disenfranchisement of people of color who currently and historically possess less power and privilege than white Americans" (Moore, Manning, and Villanueva 2018). Through institutional and everyday policies and practices, racism and monolingualism have operated in tandem with one another to subjugate multilingual people of color.

Scholars within writing studies have examined monolingualism's racist underpinnings. Ellen Cushman (2016), for example, argues that "the primacy of English in composition studies and classrooms at its very heart maintains an imperialist legacy that dehumanizes everyone in different and differing ways" (236). Scholars such as Rosina Lippi-Green (2012), Laura Greenfield (2011), Asao Inoue (2015), and Victor

Villanueva (1993) have critiqued how monolingual English as the standard language ideology serves as a proxy for maintaining structural racism in writing and literacy education at large. Kate Mangelsdorf (2010) offers a similar critique: "Because so many people who speak non-standard forms of 'English' or languages other than 'English' are not white, these manifestations of the standard language ideology, for some, serve as coded expressions of racism" (117). Given the extent to which "every aspect of the WPA architecture is prone to influence from monolingualism in ways that inadvertently harm students" (Watson and Shapiro 2018), translingualism's efforts to promote linguistic diversity and writing across difference must exist alongside efforts to make visible and actively resist how racism has been inconspicuously codified in customs, norms, practices, and policies of writing programs and institutions that shape the unequal terrain of educational conditions for students and scholars/teachers of color (Condon and Young 2017; Inoue 2015; Müeller and Ruiz 2017; Tardy 2011).

In order to hold ourselves accountable as we write, work, live on, and benefit from this terrain, we are responsible for continually reflecting on and transforming our local writing program ecologies through an analytical lens of power and equity. In so doing, it is imperative that we recognize literacy education in the United States was built on racist, settler-colonial violence in which the language (and cultural) practices and standards of White colonizers were historically used to shore up power and to exclude, shame, invisibilize, and discriminate against the language practices, cultures, and epistemologies of people of color and other marginal and poor communities. We see this starkly in the forced displacement of Native American children into boarding schools designed to eradicate Indigenous languages and "tribal identity and culture, replacing them with the knowledge and values of white civilization" (Lyons 2000, 449), as well as within the slavery system, which criminalized "teach[ing] enslaved people to read or write" (Prendergast 2003, 16). Further, in postslavery education, Black people continued to overwhelmingly be given a restricted, second-class literacy education controlled by discriminatory literacy tests and other forms of oppression marking their use of English as inferior, incorrect, and lacking value—a legacy that manifests to this day in social controversies and stigma around African American English.

In the post-*Brown v. Board* (1950) education system, despite a social win for desegregating schools, the landmark decision did not spur appropriate structural changes within the educational systems but rather left intact literacy education centered around achieving the discursive and linguistic traits of Whiteness. Learning to speak and write in dominant White language norms opened the doors for Black, Indigenous, and other students of color, but it also required them to abandon their various home dialects and languages in order to assimilate into the invisibilized ideals of "literacy as White property" (Prendergast 2003, 20). With regards to immigrant populations, the US government has historically and continuously created and enforced policies that intertwine immigration, citizenship, and literacy to alleviate national anxieties and xenophobic fears over how diverse languages and cultures of immigrant communities could potentially change the social and political landscape. Literacy education, in this case, has been largely designed to reproduce idealized immigrant citizens who are English speaking, economically productive, and socially compliant (Wan 2014).

In holding together these interconnected historical junctures of literacy, colonial violence, and institutional racism, we argue that a crucial first step in performing antiracist praxis is to recognize we are always already complicit in participating in systems that reproduce racial and other intersectional forms of oppression and inequity, albeit from very different positionalities. As part of antiracist translingual praxis, we must carry such historicized analysis, including of the ways that monolingual ideologies are built on colonial notions of nation-states and their associated boundary marking practices (Anderson 1983; Motha 2014), into our everyday work on theorizing language and into our writing pedagogy and programs.

One high-stakes place where the codification of racism in our writing ecologies exists is in the ways language is assessed. As Inoue (2015) has argued, "If we care about antiracist or social justice projects in the writing classroom, we need to care about and address explicitly the way race functions in our classroom writing assessments" (25). Drawing on translingual orientations, Jerry Won Lee (2016) advocates for "linguistic social justice," which entails "confronting the inequitable discursive economies that afford disproportionate amounts of social capital to certain language practices over others," in part by paying "fuller attention to the question of assignment design, commenting practices, and assessment" (176). The following story from our own institutional context highlights how race and racism can manifest within everyday assessment practices throughout our universities. If we hope to counter monolingual racism, we must pay more attention to such stories and work to shift the ecologies that allow such assessment practices to be perceived as neutral and unbiased.

> One day, an international student came to the writing program office for help choosing the best writing course. They expressed anxiety about an elite program's timed writing test that would determine whether they'd be admitted into their desired major. They pulled up the prompt for the test. Students have ninety minutes to write two essays that test their ability to "think analytically and communicate ideas" in "written English." The exam rubric states that essays demonstrating "a pervasive pattern of errors in written English (grammar, syntax, vocabulary, punctuation, spelling)" that is "so severe that meaning is obscured" will be designated "fundamentally deficient." The student wondered which composition course would prepare them to pass the test.

In this example and others to follow, we are not concerned with critiquing individuals or departments that uphold such policies per se. Instead, we hope to stress the pervasive entanglement of monolingual and racist ideologies that manifest in seemingly neutral and objective practices and highlight the need for ongoing reflexivity on how we participate in and might act against linguistic racisms or other forms of discrimination. The above story is a commonplace instance of inequitable gatekeeping and assessment that disproportionately penalizes language-minoritized students who are often racially minoritized, if not also economically disadvantaged. For these reasons, some of the shifts within our writing program toward antiracist praxis have been to change how we talk about and practice writing assessment within our classrooms and writing programs.

The following story on assessment highlights the emergent and always in-process nature of antiracist translingual work:

> In our practicum course for new writing instructors, a graduate student deeply committed to antiracist pedagogy is struck by the realization that their assessment practices are at odds with their political investments. While their course content centers diverse perspectives and addresses issues of racial and linguistic justice, their assessment practices privilege standardized English in ways they had not recognized and may have been inadvertently penalizing minoritized students. This simply hadn't been visible, and realizing this is a powerful turning point in their praxis.

We share this story, in part, to stress that antiracist translingual praxis requires a disposition of ongoing reflexivity. Because we exist within a broader ecology that reproduces and naturalizes monolingual and racist ideologies, it makes sense that we will see these ideologies slip out and pop up everywhere, including in our own teaching praxis and program policies and ecologies. On a meso level, writing programs play a very critical role in shifting and sustaining an ecology in which more collective reflexivity and action can happen and in which wisdom about how to engage in equitable writing praxes can accumulate over time.

Intersubjective Monolingual Racism

An antiracist translingual orientation also must account for the complex ways racism has been inscribed into our intersubjective and relational ways of being and knowing, which Inoue (2015) refers to as the "white[6] racial habitus." Drawing on Pierre Bourdieu's work, Inoue conceives "white racial habitus," specifically within the contexts of writing programs and classrooms, as perpetuating dominant White discourses, practices, "linguistic codes," and ways of being that exclude the language practices and experiences of "many students of color, working class students, and multilingual students" (17). Conceptions of writing across difference, therefore, must account for the ways "difference" is unevenly and inequitably structured by institutional racism that conditions spaces in which "white listening subjects" (Rosa and Flores 2017) are produced; in which the capacity to perceive difference as a site of learning and meaning making becomes blocked and obscured; and in which some linguistic, cultural, and other differences are privileged and others are penalized and dismissed.

In referencing "white racial habitus" and "white listening subjects," we do not refer only to individuals perceived and socialized as White but rather, in drawing on critical race perspectives, to signal the pervasiveness of racism embedded in everyday interactions, biases, and behaviors. Further, we recognize and stay critically reflexive to the reality that individuals from different races, ethnicities, and positionalities can perpetuate and enact a white racial habitus as a structural iteration of racism, albeit varying in social impact dependent on one's relationship with power within any context. Below we offer two stories from our campus to illustrate the pervasiveness of the intersubjective monolingual racism in university settings and the challenges students, teachers, and administrators face in resisting linguistic racism present in fleeting everyday interactions.

> In a first-year writing class, a student who is a native speaker of English from the United States is grouped with two international students for a peer review. Visibly frustrated, the aforementioned student verbally comments on his peer's paper that they can't read it or give any feedback because the paper is "full of grammatical errors and made-up words."

> A professor teaching an upper-division course in their discipline comes to discuss grading their international students' papers with the writing program director. "I can't read the papers. They are filled with typos. I'm not sure how to help these students. Some of them may not pass the class," they note. "Do you have any tips or pointers?"

In these examples of peer and instructor assessment, the refusal to engage with language difference and the entrenched belief that such difference is substandard, wrong, or unworthy can be read as acting from a positionality of a white listening subject. These instances highlight the power of the white racial habitus to privilege certain discourses and to sanction the disengagement and dismissal of perceived nonstandard language practices as valid forms of meaning making. Racially and linguistically minoritized students are often taught to assimilate or negotiate their own literacy practices, further illustrating that language difference is not evenly distributed.

Focusing on the systemic, embodied racial power differentials and how they shape everyday lived experiences of individuals and communities can help us avoid conceptions of difference that uphold political ideologies running counter to the Left-leaning democratic aims for which translingual scholars generally advocate—for example, boutique, apolitical liberalisms that parallel accusations of "reverse racism" or "oppression" made by conservative white male individuals in public arenas. In classrooms, these understandings of linguistic difference can merely mimic sound bites of translingualism and equity-oriented education without the pointed critique of English monolingualism and discrimination in the context of centuries of colonial violence and racism. For example, the following story is representative of similar others that have been reported by our instructors in our writing program and illustrates how this risk can manifest in the classroom:

> In a first-year writing class, a conflict arises in heated class discussion on a controversial public issue. A white male student offers what is described by the instructor as a position that forwards racist discourses and that alienates several students, including students of color, as well as the teacher. In a follow-up conversation, the teacher talks with the student about why his argument was unacceptable. The student quotes a line from the syllabus where the teacher encourages a linguistically, culturally, racially, and politically diverse classroom space where all could feel safe and voice their ideas. The student asks, "Doesn't this apply to me? I do not feel safe. I do not feel like I can use my language or express my ideas. What about my rights?"

This story highlights the danger of promoting language (or other conceptions of) difference without a critical focus on systemic racism and power. We advocate, therefore, for an actively antiracist translingual approach that resists the structural manifestations of literacy education as White property (Prendergast 2003) in writing pedagogy and program administration.

It is important to also stress that the above story offers a glimpse into the emotional and affective labor involved in *writing across difference.*

Emphases on fluidity, movement, and dynamism in translingualism need also to consider the pain and trauma, and impasse and resistance, that can also come with laboring across difference. The above encounter gestures towards complicated and fraught tensions that antiracist translingualism surfaces. For example, *What does it mean that the students and instructor in the above story are laboring across difference from positionalities that are historically, politically, and ideologically at odds with each other and that have carried uneven burdens within social and educational structures? How might we navigate this encounter in ways that keep open the possibilities to listen and change in formative ways across difference?* There are no easy answers to these questions, but they are challenges we have negotiated in different ways as we lean further into this work. While beyond the scope of this chapter, the tensions implicated in the above questions are explored intellectually in the program through undercurrents of feminist scholarship on ethics, vulnerability, empathy, and listening across radical difference (Blankenship 2019; Ratcliff 2005; Royster and Kirsch 2012). Transforming structures of inequity involves examining and changing worldviews and lifeways, emotional landscapes and embodied experiences—which points to hard personal, interpersonal, and collective work, uncomfortable and painful at times, to missteps and impasses, and to exhausting labors experienced unevenly. We advocate for incisive analysis of and action against legacies of institutional racism and linguistic discrimination—as well as for grace, empathy, hope, joy, and community in this collective work to be fostered as each can risk and bear.

Next, we tell the story of changes we made in our writing program starting with the crafting of our statement on antiracist writing pedagogy and program praxis and a narrative of how we've begun translating this statement into changes in our writing ecology.

TOWARD ANTIRACIST TRANSLINGUAL WORK IN A LARGE WRITING PROGRAM

In taking up Ligia Mihut's (2018) calls for an explicit vision of translingualism as a "concrete form of social justice" rooted in "practical suggestions for its active implementation" (69–70), in this section, we describe some of our attempts to engage in antiracist translingual work. It is important to note that some of our work began in the political aftermath of the 2016 presidential election. Prior to this moment, our program drew on translingual orientations, and many instructors were experimenting with translingual-inspired pedagogy; however, this postelection exigence was a catalyst for deepening our commitments to antiracist praxis and ethical communication. The aftermath quickly transported us to an intensified collective acknowledgment that the United States has never been post-racial. While instructors were eager for antiracist writing curriculum that could be immediately implemented (which we did circulate), we also resisted the rush to ready-made curricula as a starting or ending point. We imagined our work as ideally bringing about long-term, sustainable changes to the broader ecology in our writing program that involved shifting the terrain of what is possible. Rather than simply ask, *What can we do in our classrooms?* or *What kinds of assignments should I develop that enact antiracism?*, as a writing program, we wanted to also foreground meso-level questions aimed at making programmatic changes that could guide microlevel practices long term, such as, *How can we actively change the material conditions and ideological vectors that guide our praxis, practices, and policies to be more equitable on a systemic level? How can we shift our ecology so certain sorts of questions, conversations, habits of mind, policies, curricula, investments, and practices (about racial injustice and linguistic, cultural, and economic differences in our institution) become more possible (or to ensure others are less possible)? How might we nurture individual and collective capacities for ongoing transformation in our program rooted in our various embodied positionalities and experiences?*

We began this transformational work by listening and inviting conversations about our program's values and commitment to equitable and inclusive praxis. Especially in the aftermath of the 2016 election, we asked instructors, both in an open forum and on an anonymous survey, what kinds of support they felt they needed from our program. We facilitated graduate student-led teacher-development workshops[7] on antiracist praxis and that also responded to the urgent sociopolitical exigencies surfacing in our first-year writing classrooms. These discussions led to an early drafting of a syllabus blurb, some of which was eventually incorporated into the English Department's statement on diversity and equity. This broader departmental statement highlights the relationships between language and power and provided a basis for our subsequent development of an antiracist writing praxis statement.

In spring 2018, our writing program formed a subcommittee[8] to draft an antiracist writing praxis document to articulate our values, guide teaching practices, and serve as a dynamic, living touchstone for ongoing conversations and transformation in our program that could be discussed, interrogated, and continually revised. After drafting the document, we shared it with our writing program staff and graduate students who served as assistant directors, and we collectively discussed the key ideas and approaches on antiracist pedagogy that we wanted to include in the document as well as how the statement would function as a living document in our program ecology and inform our pedagogical practices and praxis. The full statement (most recently revised in spring 2021) is included in appendix 10.A, but we discuss some relevant aspects of the statement below that seek to actively meld antiracist and translingual frameworks. The statement begins with a conception of writing as "social action" tied to different communities' asymmetrical relationships to power. Because we recognize language use has no inherent moral value or meaning apart from its performance in specific contexts, we state that it is imperative that we practice and teach writing as "ethical communication" accountable to the consequences of language use for diverse communities. Building on these ideas, the statement seeks to ground some translingual conceptions of language within an explicit acknowledgment of and commitment to work against the historical and systemic devaluing of language practices from historically minoritized peoples.

> We acknowledge that literacy education and language policies in the U.S. are built on a foundation of racial capitalism, White supremacy, and settler colonialism that persists and has delegitimized and often penalized the language practices, experiences, and knowledges of minoritized and historically underrepresented peoples. We therefore reject Eurocentric assumptions about the written word as a superior form of literacy and define composition and literacy in our program ecology as multi- or trans-modal, translingual, anti-colonial, and culturally affirming communication practices. We also reject the binary formations of standard/non-standard Englishes and native/non-native English speakers that racial capitalism has exploited at the expense of multilingual communities of color. We seek to transform this ongoing systemic inequity and discrimination by developing writing curriculum, assessment practices, teacher development programs, and language policies that recognize linguistic and other differences as the norm of communication and that stress rhetorical effectiveness and ethical language use across different lived experiences, contexts, genres, purposes, audiences, and writing occasions within and beyond the academy. ("EWP Statement" 2021)

This statement was crafted for a broad set of audiences, public and internal, but primarily for students, instructors, program directors, and other campus stakeholders. The document articulates our political investments as they intersect with composition theories—including translingual, feminist, intersectional, anticolonial, and antiracist perspectives—that inform our work. We hoped this statement would serve as a starting point for ongoing reflexivity and change.

In the statement, we intentionally articulated language difference as the always already norm of languaging practices but also stressed language difference must be addressed in relation to structural and material constructs of power, informed by antiracist pedagogy. We tried to balance abstract theoretical underpinnings with examples of writing praxis (without foreclosing possibilities for what antiracist praxis might look like). For example, the statement encourages the crafting of "writing assessment criteria for grading, peer-reviews, and students' self-assessment that emphasizes writers' development and their language choices and rhetorical effectiveness based on the writing occasion, genre, purpose, and audience rather than strictly on monolingual and dominant academic English norms and standards of correctness" ("EWP Statement" 2021).

The statement offers concrete ideas to help teachers and students see language difference as the always already norm of reality, albeit not the status quo of power. For example, by encouraging instructors to "resist Eurocentric and White US-centric curricula and engage in curating reading and writing curricula that centers voices, knowledges, and experiences from marginalized authors and discourse traditions" and to teach students to "practice their multilingual, translingual, and multimodal language and literacy repertoires for different audiences, contexts, media, and situations with varying stakes" in their writing ("EWP Statement" 2021), we hoped to cultivate in students rhetorical curiosity and flexibility in reading authors who write in different language and literacy repertoires and discourse traditions, as well as expand students' imagination for how their academic and public writings can take shape when they question the construct of monolingual "standard English" and draw on fluid and permeable languages, registers, and discourses students already practice in their everyday life. Such articulation of antiracist translingual writing pedagogy, we hope, addresses translingualism's unintentional bind of flattening language difference Gilyard and others have critiqued.

In translating our program values and stance of antiracist writing praxis into teacher orientation and practicum training, we aimed to create the groundwork for antiracist pedagogical principles first and then situate translingual dispositions and practices into those principles. For example, following our call to "nurture classroom learning environments in which students and teachers are committed to engaging in critical and productive dialogue on issues of equity, justice, difference, and power as they manifest in class readings, writing, discussion, and more broadly" ("EWP Statement" 2021), in our one-week intensive teacher orientation in 2017, we[9] began day one with an identity-mapping activity that asked new instructors to draw on their holistic, intersectional identities to formulate how their teacher positionality in the classroom would take shape and to think about what antiracist pedagogy might mean, given their own positionality. We began with teacher positionality as the seedling of developing praxis because as scholars of antiracist pedagogy argue, antiracist praxis is not a set of decontextualizable practices ready to be adopted but rather an orientation and "process that begins with faculty as individuals, and continues as they apply the antiracist analysis into the course content, pedagogy, and their activities and interactions beyond the classroom" (Kishimoto 2018, 543).

Connecting teacher positionality to antiracist pedagogy, we framed the next activity through a discussion of the myth of a colorblind or politically neutral writing classroom. In the form of a gallery-walk exercise, people rotated around multiple blank posters and wrote their ideas on some overarching aspects of antiracist pedagogy: for example, what our own versions of antiracist pedagogy mean in relating to teacher positionality, developing course rationale and content, navigating day-to-day classroom dynamics, and assessing students' writing. Since this was an opening activity paving the way for developing more concrete teaching materials, we concluded the session with mapping and translating the elements of antiracist pedagogy into the first-year writing course outcomes that inform our program's curriculum. Our hope was that instructors would explore their teacher identity and positionality in tandem with giving critical attention to developing their own antiracist teaching practices.

Another activity from the orientation to highlight is a workshop designed by Sumyat Thu on feedback practices informed by antiracist and translingual perspectives. As we describe in the previous section, institutionalized assessment practices are arguably the most visible space to examine how literacy as White property becomes codified and reinforced in writing pedagogy behind seemingly neutral and objective language standards. We wanted to help instructors take up translingualism and develop assessment practices that evaluate language from the standpoint of rhetorical effects rather than monolithic standards. We first offered a presentation and discussion on intertwined ideologies of language and race in literacy education and how translingualism attempts to counter them. We encouraged instructors to prioritize student incomes and agency and to be reflexive on the culture in which students have been conditioned to put aside their fluid literacy repertoires and instead pursue the myth of Standard English in their academic and professional writing. In discussing how instructors might assess student writing, we emphasized the importance of translingualism's push for retraining ourselves to read texts seemingly written in monolingual English to discern the intertextuality of registers, conventions, and discourses at work. We also encouraged instructors to give attention to and address languaging politics in class discussion of students' work and peer reviews often structured by default to give unfair capital and authority to students perceived as monolingual white speakers (Mangelsdorf 2010).

While it is beyond our scope to detail other shifts made in our writing program, we want to end this section by describing how we built on activities mentioned above by creating opportunities for teachers to reflect on their assessment praxes in the hopes of creating conditions for larger-scale programmatic changes. In our composition pedagogy seminar, which is required for new graduate instructors,[10] one assignment, *"Antiracist Student Assessment and Response Praxis,"* asks instructors to articulate an assessment philosophy and praxis in light of the scholarly conversations they read in class on antiracist writing praxis, translingualism, and assessment from scholars such as Asao Inoue, Jerry Won Lee, Mya Poe, and others. For this essay, instructors articulate their philosophy and approach to student feedback and assessment by engaging with the following questions: *What are the theories, philosophies, and assumptions (about language, writing, student learning, the purpose of assessment/feedback, etc.) that underscore your response practices? How do you understand and enact equitable, antiracist writing assessment and feedback practices in your teaching?* In developing their essays, instructors are encouraged to reflect on their teaching philosophy; situate their conversation within the scholarship on assessment, writing across difference, translingualism, and antiracist praxis; and ground their discussion in concrete feedback strategies and sample comments from student papers that illustrate their praxis in action, reveal moments when their practice contradicts their philosophy, and/or highlight challenges and tensions they are negotiating.

New instructors also attend a three-hour portfolio-assessment session before they assess their first student portfolios. This session has historically been called the "portfolio norming session," but we renamed this session "portfolio assessment praxis session" and revised the structure to better align with our evolving program values. The portfolio session already supported a robust understanding of collective norming that we built on: for example, our norming sessions were not centered on decontextualized grade calibration but on developing evidence-based narratives of how and why various instructors were assessing student learning based on their philosophies, classroom contexts, and teaching practices (as well as on students' demonstration of course learning outcomes, which are informed by CWPA writing outcomes).

Our program redesigned the session around questions such as, *How might we negotiate the complex programmatic and institutional demands for communal grade standards while also helping instructors develop flexible and responsive assessment practices that help support, make more visible, and value students' diverse literate and meaning-making practices?* For example, we held conversations that leaned into differences and disagreements among small groups of instructors who read each other's students' sample portfolios, not to calibrate but to open a space for instructors to deepen and productively challenge each other's assessment philosophies, praxis, processes, and rationales, with particular emphasis on how their practices were actively antiracist, equitable, and inclusive of diverse literate practices, tethered to the learning outcomes, and rooted in their own classroom contexts. We also asked instructors to consider how they were assessing student learning and development that might not be visible on the page and how they might redesign their curriculum to provide more opportunities for activating, making visible, and assessing a broader range of student learning and literate practices and for involving students in the process (such as through self-assessment and co-crafting criteria).

Program changes such as these continually remind us that an antiracist translingual praxis is an ecological phenomenon. It does not exist in a single policy, philosophy, pedagogy, or document; rather, it emerges from constant and ongoing intra-actions, internalizations and externalizations, embodiments, responsiveness, and transformations.

CONCLUSION

We see antiracist translingual praxis as part of a politics for which Ahmed (2012) advocates—a pragmatic and local politics committed to "generat[ing] knowledge *of* institutions *in the process of* attempting to transform" the sedimented and sedimenting terrains that continue to participate in the culture of institutional racism (173; emphasis added). We argue that writing scholar-teachers and program administrators should have an accountable analysis of the historical and ongoing ways monolingualism is enmeshed in racism and has shaped the normative policies, pedagogy, and interpersonal practices in writing programs, making writing education inequitable and exclusionary for students of marginalized identities. In order to help shift educational contexts, and society more broadly, toward accepting language difference as the norm without obscuring the inequities built into ways we differ, we need writing programs that invest in and co-construct knowledge of both antiracist pedagogy and translingualism, which can inform changes toward more equitable and inclusive praxis. We caution that translingual practices not situated in antiracist principles could be subsumed under diversity, equity, and inclusion efforts institutions and corporations tend to favor, ones that may do more violence and harm by signaling progressive sentiments without actually addressing the equity issues in material conditions nor the unequal and inequitable labor and penalties language-minoritized students bear. In looking at how each of us might transform our writing program ecologies long term, we must ask ourselves, *What is our antiracist and translingual agenda for our own institutional and classroom contexts?* We argue that our collective, ongoing project should be one of making writing education socially equitable by changing the status quo conditions of teaching and learning that ask for language-minoritized students' assimilation. Instead, we call us all to work toward more liberatory pedagogy and praxis rooted in countering and dismantling ongoing legacies of White supremacy and its organizing epistemologies so Black, Indigenous, and other students of color, multilingual students, and other minoritized students also have access to power and agency in their different language and literacy practices. In advocating for long-term structural changes that invite more equitable and inclusive language practices and policies, we seek to understand the myriad ways that writing can be sociopolitical and to promote social justice within writing programs, universities, and broader communities.

APPENDIX 10.A

STATEMENT ON ANTIRACIST WRITING PEDAGOGY AND PROGRAM PRAXIS

OUR COMMITMENTS AND VISION

We in the Expository Writing Program—program directors, instructors, and staff—approach the teaching of writing as consequential social action and ethical communication and we understand language as political and tied to identity, culture, and power. In our role as educators, we commit to reflect on the communities to which we are accountable and the language practices we are sustaining. We further commit to work against the various forms of systemic oppression emanating from racial capitalism and White supremacy that shape the social conditions of teaching, learning, and living in the university, in our social institutions, and in our everyday lives.

Rather than being simply a matter of individual biases or prejudices, we understand that various forms of oppression are pervasive, intersectional, and built into our educational, economic, and political systems. Racism, sexism, oppression of gender nonbinary and queer people, ableism, and oppression on the basis of language and citizenship all work in intertwined ways to reproduce the conditions of racial capitalism and colonialism.

These systemic oppressions are ongoing problems that concern all of us, that we all participate in perpetuating even unconsciously and unintentionally, and that require us to understand the important differences between intent and impact. We commit to working together, with compassion and critical intention, to resist and transform normative systems within our university and program and to rebuild our teaching and learning communities to be more socially equitable, culturally sustaining, and just.

We acknowledge that literacy education and language policies in the U.S. are built on a foundation of racial capitalism, White supremacy, and settler colonialism that persists and has delegitimized and often penalized the language practices, experiences, and knowledges of minoritized and historically underrepresented peoples. We therefore reject Eurocentric assumptions about the written word as a superior form of literacy and define composition and literacy in our program ecology as multi- or trans-modal, translingual, anti-colonial, and culturally affirming communication practices. We also reject the binary formations of standard/non-standard Englishes and native/non-native English speakers that racial capitalism has exploited at the expense of multilingual communities of color. We seek to transform this ongoing systemic inequity and discrimination by developing writing curriculum, assessment practices, teacher development programs, and language policies that recognize linguistic and other differences as the norm of communication and that stress rhetorical effectiveness and ethical language use across different lived experiences, contexts, genres, purposes, audiences, and writing occasions within and beyond the academy (see links at end of this document for more information).

OUR PRAXIS

In teaching writing as social and ethical literacy, we are committed to developing antiracist and equitable pedagogical frameworks in our writing program and policies, in our teaching preparation and mentoring efforts, and in our curriculum and classroom practices. Antiracist pedagogical frameworks, as we understand them, are intersectional, which means that they center different forms of intersecting marginalizations as well as the power relations among race, class, gender, and other social, political, and cultural identities and experiences that may manifest in texts that we read and write, in students' and teachers' experiences, and in classrooms as well as broader social dynamics. While this statement and the below examples only signal the start to ongoing work, we seek to support our students and instructors through active antiracist and equity-focused pedagogies and program praxis that:

- contextualize writing as a socio-political practice that helps students and instructors examine how writing might be practiced as personally and socially impactful, ethical, and empowering forms of literacy;
- practice ongoing metacognition and self-reflexivity with regards to our own teaching philosophies, classroom practices, power, policies, and positionality to help create more equitable classrooms and curricula;
- create a culture of unlearning the norms and characteristics of systems of White supremacy and continually build a more actively antiracist writing program and praxis;
- make instituted and sustained efforts on recruiting and retaining instructors and administrators of color and of historically marginalized identities through equitable hiring practices and antiracist forms of support for teacher development;
- integrate language justice work as part of writing courses in which we examine how systemic racism is often encoded in practices that uphold "academic language" or "Standard English";
- encourage and support all instructors to practice antiracist pedagogy that is critically responsive to the contexts of their social identities, positionalities, teaching philosophies, and disciplinary and course objectives;
- nurture classroom learning environments in which students and teachers are committed to engaging in critical and productive dialogue on issues of equity, justice, difference, and power as they manifest in class readings, writing, discussion, and more broadly;
- conceptualize and practice teaching and learning with accessibility and Universal Design principles within the context of antiracism and anti-oppression;
- resist Eurocentric and White U.S.-centric curricula and engage in curating reading and writing curricula that centers voices, knowledges, and experiences from marginalized authors and discourse traditions;
- help students engage with course curricula in reflexive and compassionate ways that do not ask students of marginalized identities to relive trauma, but that ask all students to engage in social issues and how they relate to composing with criticality;

- explore the relationships among writing, language, power, and social identities such as race, class, gender, sexuality, disability, mobility, faith/religion, and citizenship;
- encourage students to make connections between their lived experiences and academic research and inquiries that complicate the notions of objectivity and neutrality in writing and academic learning;
- encourage students to think about the social impact of their writing and the social groups and communities they are accountable to as part of audience awareness;
- create composing occasions through assignment design that invite students to practice their multilingual, translingual, and multimodal language and literacy repertoires for different audiences, contexts, media, and situations with varying stakes;
- develop writing assessment criteria for grading, peer-reviews, and students' self-assessment that emphasizes writers' development and their language choices and rhetorical effectiveness based on the writing occasion, genre, purpose, and audience rather than strictly on monolingual and dominant academic English norms and standards of correctness.

Please view a few samples of the EWP course syllabi located on the EWP website that demonstrate the above teaching practices. These samples are not meant to be perfect or exhaustive examples, but rather to serve as a concrete basis for thinking together how we can put a teaching idea into practice and how we can continually revise teaching materials and necessarily evolve in the way we practice antiracist writing pedagogy.

This statement on antiracist writing pedagogy and program praxis has been informed and inspired by the following publications and documents:

1. This Ain't Another Statement! This Is a DEMAND for Black Linguistic Justice! By April Baker-Bell, Bonnie J. Williams-Farrier, Davena Jackson, Lamar Johnson, Carmen Kynard, Teaira McMurtry
2. CCCC Position Statement on White Language Supremacy
3. CCCC Statement on Students' Right to Their Own Language
4. CCCC Statement on National Language Policy
5. UW Tacoma Writing Center's Statement on antiracist & social justice
6. UW Public Health Program's Commitment to Anti-Racism

NOTES

1. Sumyat Thu planted the seeds of bringing antiracist and translingual orientations together, which she has further developed in her dissertation work (see Thu 2020) at the University of Washington.

2. The choice to capitalize White emerged from a discussion and colearning process, including multiple viewpoints among the authors. While we share the concerns of those who use the lowercase to resist White supremacist/nationalist organizations that capitalize the *W* to signal their power, we decided to use *W* when referring to such groups to make visible the prevalence of institutional racism and complicity and to ask ourselves and readers to engage with accountability. Our choice here resonates with the Center for the Study of Social Policy (Nguyễn and Pendleton 2020): "While we condemn those who capitalize 'W' for the sake of evoking violence, we intentionally capitalize 'White' in part to invite people, and ourselves, to think deeply about the ways Whiteness survives—and is supported both explicitly and implicitly." We especially debated the use of lowercase when referring to individuals or general groups of people (e.g., white people, white student). Kwame Anthony Appiah (2020) makes a compelling case for capitalizing all instances of White, but, ultimately, we decided to use lowercase to distinguish between White supremacy/institutions/logics versus white people/teachers/students in order to emphasize our understanding that we are working against institutional racism and not individuals.

3. While Candice Rai and Sumyat Thu, among the coauthors, served as EWP director and assistant director of the program during this time, these were collaborative changes including other directors, faculty, instructors, and staff. We acknowledge those who contributed most centrally to this chapter.

4. In particular, we acknowledge our colleagues who have served as EWP directors/associate directors, Anis Bawarshi, Kimberlee Gillis-Bridges, Juan Guerra, Michelle Liu, Elizabeth Simmons-O'Neill, Gail Stygall, and John Webster, who have made significant contributions to establish a writing culture committed to issues of social justice. Without their investments, all we describe would not be possible.

5. These stories occurred within our writing program and university. To protect anonymity, we selected stories that have occurred multiple times with similar patterns over the years. Our aim in sharing them is to illuminate the pervasive and ordinary tethering of linguistic racism and monolingualism that circulate broadly and can easily go unnoticed within the institutional ecology, not to emphasize individuals per se.

6. While we made the choice to capitalize White in instances that refer to White supremacy and institutionalized logics, as we describe in note 2, we have decided not to alter the usage within others' quotations.

7. The workshops were co-led by Denise Grollmus and Belle Kim, who served as EWP assistant directors at the time, alongside UW graduate students and other EWP staff.

8. This subcommittee began work in 2018 and included Sumyat Thu, Emily George, and Candice Rai.

9. This 2017 teacher orientation was co-led by EWP Assistant Directors (ADs) Belle Kim, Sumyat Thu, and T. J. Walker, along with former director Candice Rai; this work also builds on contributions made by ADs Denise Grollmus and Holly Shelton during the 2016 orientation.

10. This course has evolved over decades with significant contributions from Anis Bawarshi, Nancy Bou Ayash, Juan Guerra, Candice Rai, and Gail Stygall, who have co-taught the course on a rotating basis.

REFERENCES

Ahmed, Sara. 2012. *On Being Included: Racism and Diversity in Institutional Life.* Durham, NC: Duke University Press.

Appiah, Kwame Anthony. 2020. "The Case for Capitalizing B in Black." *Atlantic*, June 18.

Anderson, Benedict. 1983. *Imagined Communities: Reflections on the Spread and Origin of Nationalism.* New York: Verso.

Blankenship, Lisa. 2019. *Changing the Subject: A Theory of Rhetorical Empathy.* Logan: Utah State University Press.

Bou Ayash, Nancy. 2019. *Toward Translingual Realities in Composition: (Re)Working Local Language Representations and Practices.* Logan: Utah State University Press.

Canagarajah, A. Suresh. 2013. *Literacy as Translingual Practice: Between Communities and Classrooms.* New York: Routledge.

Condon, Frankie, and Vershawn Ashanti Young. 2017. Introduction to *Performing Antiracist Pedagogy in Rhetoric, Writing, and Communication,* edited by Frankie Condon and Vershawn Ashanti Young, 3–16. Fort Collins, CO: WAC Clearinghouse.

Cushman, Ellen. 2016. "Translingual and Decolonial Approaches to Meaning Making." *College English* 78 (3): 234–42.

"EWP Statement on Antiracist Writing Pedagogy and Program Praxis." 2021. Expository Writing Program, University of Washington. https://english.washington.edu/diversity-equity-and-justice.

García, Ofelia. 2009. "Education, Multilingualism and Translanguaging in the Twenty-First Century." In *Social Justice through Multilingual Education,* edited by Tove Skutnabb-Kangas, Robert Phillipson, and Ajit K. Mohanty, 140–58. Clevedon: Multilingual Matters.

García, Ofelia, and Wei Li. 2014. *Translanguaging: Language, Bilingualism and Education.* Basingstoke: Palgrave Macmillan.

Gilyard, Keith. 2016. "The Rhetoric of Translingualism." *College English* 78 (3): 284–89.

Greenfield, Laura. 2011. "The 'Standard English' Fairy Tale: A Rhetorical Analysis of Racist Pedagogies and Commonplace Assumptions about Language Diversity." In *Writing Centers and the New Racism,* edited by Laura Greenfield and Karen Rowan, 33–60. Logan: Utah State University Press.

Guerra, Juan. 2016. "Cultivating a Rhetorical Sensibility in the Translingual Writing Classroom." *College English* 78 (3): 228–33.

Inoue, Asao B. 2015. *Antiracist Writing Assessment Ecologies: Teaching and Assessing Writing for a Socially Just Future.* Fort Collins, CO: WAC Clearinghouse.

Kishimoto, Kyoko. 2018. "Anti-Racist Pedagogy: From Faculty's Self-Reflection to Organizing within and beyond the Classroom." *Race, Ethnicity and Education* 21 (4): 540–54.

Lee, Jerry Won. 2016. "Beyond Translingual Writing." *College English* 79 (2): 174–95.

Leonard, Rebecca Lorimer. 2014. "Multilingual Writing as Rhetorical Attunement." *College English* 76 (3): 227–47.

Lippi-Green, Rosina. 2012. *English with an Accent: Language, Ideology and Discrimination in the United States.* New York: Routledge.

Lu, Min-Zhan, and Bruce Horner. 2013. "Translingual Literacy, Language Difference, and Matters of Agency." *College English* 75 (6): 582–607.

Lyons, Scott Richard. 2000. "Rhetorical Sovereignty: What Do American Indians Want from Writing?" *College Composition and Communication* 51 (3): 447–68.

Mangelsdorf, Kate. 2010. "Spanglish as Alternative Discourse: Working against Language Demarcation." In *Cross-Language Relations in Composition,* edited by Min-Zhan Lu and Pau Kei Matsuda, 113–26. Carbondale: Southern Illinois University Press.

Mihut, Ligia. 2019. "Linguistic Pluralism: A Statement and a Call to Advocacy." *Reflections* 18 (2): 66–86.

Moore, Jazmen, Logan Manning, and Victor Villanueva. 2018. "Statement on Anti-Racism to Support Teaching and Learning." Urbana, IL: NCTE. https://ncte.org/statement/antiracisminteaching/.

Motha, Suhanthie. 2014. *Race, Empire, and English Language Teaching: Creating Responsible and Ethical Anti-Racist Practice.* New York: Teachers College Press.

Müeller, Genevieve Garcia de, and Iris Ruiz. 2017. "Race, Silence, and Writing Program Administration: A Qualitative Study of US College Writing Programs." *WPA: Writing Program Administration* 40 (2): 19–39.

Nguyễn, Ann Thúy, and Maya Pendleton. 2020. "Recognizing Race in Language: Why We Capitalize 'Black' and 'White.'" Center for the Study of Social Policy. https://cssp.org/2020/03/recognizing-race-in-language-why-we-capitalize-black-and-white/.

Prendergast, Catherine. 2003. *Literacy and Racial Justice: The Politics of Learning after Brown v. Board of Education.* Carbondale: Southern Illinois University Press.

Ratcliffe, Krista. 2005. *Rhetorical Listening: Identification, Gender, Whiteness.* Carbondale: Southern Illinois University Press.

Rosa, Jonathan, and Nelson Flores. 2017. "Unsettling Race and Language: Toward a Raciolinguistic Perspective." *Language in Society* 46 (5): 621–47.

Royster, Jacqueline Jones, and Gesa Kirsch. 2012. *Feminist Rhetorical Practices: New Horizons for Rhetoric, Composition, and Literacy Studies.* Carbondale: Southern Illinois University Press.

Tardy, Christine M. 2011. "Enacting and Transforming Local Language Policies." *College Composition and Communication* 62 (4): 634–61.

Thu, Sumyat. 2020. "Navigating and Responding to Raciolinguistic Ideologies: Refugee and Immigrant Students' Literacy Practices across Contexts." PhD diss., University of Washington.

Villanueva, Victor. 1993. *Bootstraps: From an American Academic of Color.* Urbana, IL: NCTE.

Wan, Amy J. 2014. *Producing Good Citizens: Literacy Training in Anxious Times.* Pittsburgh: University of Pittsburgh Press.

Watson, Missy, and Rachael Shapiro. 2018. "Clarifying the Multiple Dimensions of Monolingualism: Keeping Our Sights on Language Politics." *Composition Forum* 38. http://www.compositionforum.com/issue/38/monolingualism.php.

11
CONFRONTING SUPERDIVERSITY AGAIN
A Multidimensional Approach to Teaching and Researching Writing at a Global University

Jonathan Benda, Cherice Escobar Jones,
Mya Poe, and Alison Y. L. Stephens

The translingual turn in US composition studies has brought increased attention to linguistic diversity in writing classrooms and writing centers (Horner and Trimbur 2002; Matsuda 2006; Young and Martínez 2011). Local studies of linguistic diversity have demonstrated how linguistic identity is tied to mobility and globalization (Fraiberg, Wang, and You 2017; Gonzales 2018). At our own institution, the concept of superdiversity has been useful to think about linguistic diversity, globalization, and mobility. Coined by Steven Vertovec (2007) to describe the increasingly complex forms of migration patterns in Europe, the concept of superdiversity grew out of two post-Cold War trends: "new and more complex forms of migration, and new and more complex forms of communication and knowledge circulation" (5). In Vertovec's formulation, the contexts in which people live, work, and socialize today are shaped by global migration flows, resulting in layered literacy and languaging practices. As a conceptual framework for the study of languaging, superdiversity illuminates how multiple stratifications of standard and nonstandard languages either destabilize formerly hegemonic sociolinguistic economies or are constrained by those hegemonic forces (Blommaert and Rampton 2016, 39).

To study the geography of superdiverse spaces, many researchers have studied the linguistic landscapes of cities due to their typically heterogeneous linguistic and sociocultural compositions (Cadier and Mar-Molinero 2012; Davydova 2013; Peukert 2013). Within writing studies, researchers have turned to global sites of college writing, like English-medium higher education schools in Qatar and Lebanon, to understand how their linguistically superdiverse characteristics can inform postmonolingual approaches to writing studies in the United

https://doi.org/10.7330/9781646421732.c011

States (Nebel 2017) and to assess current writing-pedagogy practices at English-medium institutions (Annous, Nicolas, and Townsend 2017). Superdiversity thus offers writing researchers a conceptual framework to move beyond old frameworks that cast linguistic diversity as a subordinate identity; it also helps, as we see it, to correct a tendency in some translingual work to flatten linguistic identities against the triad of race-class-gender.[1]

At Northeastern University (NU), the concept of superdiversity is useful to describe the complex interplay of migration, mobility, and multilingualism that shapes the contexts in which we teach and tutor. In a previous study of NU's writing program, Jonathan Benda, Michael Dedek, Chris Gallagher, Kristi Girdharry, Neal Lerner, and Matt Noonan (2018) showed how superdiversity provided the writing program with an alternative concept to conventional administrative categories (e.g., nationality, visa status, and ethnicity) to spur curricular change and new types of program research. Insights drawn from our previous studies informed our move away from traditional placement testing to guided self-placement, in which students decide for themselves what kind of community of writers they want to join in first-year writing. Superdiversity also informed the design and analysis of a Multilingual Writers' Survey that was given in 2014 (Benda et al. 2018).

Today, we find that the work of remaking the NU writing program requires confronting superdiversity repeatedly in different contexts within the writing program and even the English department. Take the case of the Multilingual Writers' Survey: while Benda et al. (2018) reported that the survey revealed surprising aspects of our student population—out of the 1,210 multilingual undergraduate students surveyed, 46 percent identified two languages other than English and 13 percent identified three additional languages as either spoken in the home or important to their cultural identity—it also revealed the limits of our survey methodology in capturing mobility and students' relationships to their linguistic identities. Moreover, while the survey results showed students came from "layered origins"—that is, multiple cities and nations—it could not tell us about their linguistic identities across these geographies. Take the case of one student who had lived in "Mexico City, Caracas (Venezuela), Kenya" before coming to Boston (Benda et al. 2018, 93): to merely note and celebrate these rich experiences overlooks other factors at work in terms of race, capital, and mobility. In other words, we repeatedly find ourselves needing to resist the temptation to simply equate superdiversity with "very much diversity" (Vertovec 2017, 3).

In this chapter, we take lessons from our previous study to demonstrate how we have returned to superdiversity to rethink writing instruction and tutoring at three Northeastern sites: the writing program (Jonathan), the writing center (Alison and Cherice), and the writing minor (Mya). Each site illustrates how teachers and tutors have adapted to the superdiverse context of our university. We also demonstrate institutional barriers to such work.

SUPERDIVERSITY AT THREE WRITING SITES

Northeastern University is a private four-year university in Boston, Massachusetts. In fall 2019, NU enrolled more than 20,400 degree-seeking undergraduates, 17 percent of whom were international. Those international undergraduates came from 141 countries, representing (unequally) all regions of the world (Northeastern University 2019). Of the remaining 83 percent of undergraduate domestic students, the population is 44.8 percent White, 13.6 percent Asian, 8.4 percent Hispanic or Latinx, and 4.7 percent Black or African American. The remaining students are American Indian or Alaskan Native (<1%) and Native Hawaiian or Pacific Islander (<1%). Yearly tuition and fees are currently $52,420 (Northeastern University 2019). NU also enrolled more than 17,370 graduate students, over 53 percent of whom were international.

Northeastern University's development from a school that served mostly working-class White American males into a "global" university with a large international student population happened over the last forty years and has accelerated in the last ten to fifteen years. Since 2006, the percentage of full-time international undergraduates at Northeastern has steadily climbed. In the last ten years, the university has reshaped its international identity once again to one enmeshed in the mobile global economy. To do this, NU expanded internationally focused programs such as study abroad, international co-ops (in which undergrads work abroad), and bridge programs that bring international students to Northeastern. Given NU's history, it is clear the university has viewed international students as a source of revenue and, more recently, a source of prestige; the *global* label Northeastern has cultivated over the last fifteen years is one that merges well with its experiential focus. It's no surprise this combination has helped the university's meteoric rise in university rankings. The school's emphasis on global experiential education ties student mobility and academic achievement to preparation for participation in the global economy. It is safe to predict NU's global expansions will continue with the implementation of the Northeastern

2025 Academic Plan, an institution-wide strategy that emphasizes "flexible," "mobile," "agile," "intercultural," and "immersive" learning with "no boundaries" (Northeastern University 2016).

Superdiversity in the Writing Program: Pedagogy and Placement

Within this rapidly globalizing context, the writing program currently offers two types of courses—First-Year Writing (FYW) and Advanced Writing in the Disciplines (AWD). Although about 40 percent of entering students are exempt from FYW because of IB or AP credit, all students are required to take AWD. AWD is currently offered in eleven disciplinary versions aimed at students in various colleges, such as the technical professions, the business administration professions, the sciences, and the social sciences, as well as one interdisciplinary version.

This section focuses mainly on one teacher's (Jonathan Benda's) experiences and observations teaching FYW and AWD for multilingual students. As discussed in Benda et al. (2018), the complexity of the student population entering Northeastern previously strained not only resources but also the very ability of the writing program to meaningfully describe or define the "international" students we were attempting to teach. Here, Benda approaches the superdiverse context of the writing program in terms of how it has manifested itself in the classroom. While not necessarily "representative" of what occurs in all multilingual writing classes in our program, the following anecdotes point to some ways our pedagogy might be taken up by students to reveal both the challenges and benefits of "the diversification of diversity" (Hollinger 2000, 12), which can move us beyond seeing diversity as categorical, with students embodying markers of difference, and toward viewing identity as an ever-fluid and changing relational process (Kerschbaum 2012, 2014).

First-Year Writing

Since I arrived at Northeastern in 2011, the writing program has relied on a version of directed self-placement called *guided self-placement* that allows students to select what kind of first-year writing course best suits them—most recently, First-Year Writing (ENGW 1111) or First-Year Writing For Multilingual Students (ENGW 1102) (for discussion of guided self-placement at NU, see Gallagher and Noonan 2017). Despite this placement choice, the first-year writing program previously used a common text, David Bartholomae and Anthony Petrosky's (2011) *Ways of Reading*, in both multilingual and traditional sections. Since I was hired primarily to teach multilingual sections of mostly international students, I chose readings about language, ethnicity, and education I thought would interest these students, such as Gloria Anzaldúa's "How to Tame a Wild Tongue." However, over time I came to notice complex relationships (or barriers) between the international students and the authors of these readings. Asking students to write autoethnographies after reading Mary Louise Pratt's "Arts of the Contact Zone" and Anzaldúa was, for some, asking them to take on an uncomfortable role in those "highly asymmetrical relations of power" (Pratt 1991, 34) from which the oppressed subaltern writes in response to the conqueror's representations of them. However, the discomfort students felt—the lack of identification with writers in positions like Anzaldúa's—provided me with an opportunity to view the effects of my pedagogical choices in light of the more privileged perspectives of some in the class. For instance, for some students who had studied English from a young age and for whom English was deeply tied to their educational experience, as they graduated from English-medium international high schools and/or international baccalaureate programs, the connection between a personal "mother tongue" and identity was tenuous. At least that's what one international student implied as she explained to me that, for her friends and her, using different languages in different contexts had nothing to do with their sense of who they were—she felt there was no issue of one language being of higher or lower status than another or no language to which they felt closer. For students like her, that is, "students of the new global elite (SONGE)," the "incorporation of various cultures and languages does not happen at as deep a level as one might imagine, considering their life circumstances; these students still have a firm sense of their privileged identity that is rooted in their countries of origin" (Vandrick 2011, 162). One can dispute that student's conclusions or dismiss her view as being one of privilege, but that's exactly the point: students in her position might not have reason to view their relationship to language in the same light as Anzaldúa might. As Andrew Anastasia (2015) has argued, one cannot assume that discomfort as a pedagogical strategy (or, in this case, a pedagogical accident) will result in students' changing their minds or will act as "an effective means to inaugurate reflective, critical change of deeply held beliefs and assumptions about the world" (47).

If some students exhibited a sense of privileged identity and disinterest in issues such as language and power (or languages of power) in relation to their own lived experiences, other students raised points that demonstrated heterogeneity in a group that looks homogenous at first blush. In their texts, these students reflected on the various ways their identities as "international students" in the United States interacted with other identities ascribed to them or claimed by them. For an assignment in which I asked students to write a "Mary Louise Prattian" autoethnography that would speak back to "metropolitan" representations of them, a Chinese student wrote powerfully of the representation in China and abroad of people who study abroad as 富二代 (*fu er dai*, "second-generation rich"—see Fraiberg, Wang, and You [2017] for discussion of this term). This student said she even told some classmates in China she was studying at Northeastern University (东北大学) in Shenyang, China, rather than admitting he was studying in the United States. Another student described how different levels of familiarity with English and with Western-style educational practices created contact zones among international students—specifically, between students who went to international schools in their home countries (or abroad) versus students who did not. At the same time, however, she pointed out how Americans see those international students as being a homogeneous community, ignoring the fact that students who went to international schools abroad might feel they have more in common with students from different countries who also went to international schools than with their own compatriots who went through the local educational system.

Stephanie Kerschbaum (2014) emphasizes the need for theories that can "account for rhetorical agency and the ways that people make choices as they interact with others and animate categorical identifications" (81). While the stories of these particular first-year writing students may not be distinct from those of students at other institutions, in the context of a writing classroom where such layered identities are the norm, superdiversity becomes a way to put identities into relation, not in silos. As the examples above demonstrate, in contexts of superdiverse first-year writing, student identities are often the products of rhetorical choices, choices that often confound conventional texts and assignments. However, understanding superdiverse first-year-classroom contexts requires recognizing students' (and teachers') differing capacities or power to exercise rhetorical agency regarding the ways they can align themselves with (or distance themselves from) how they are represented.

Advanced Writing in the Disciplines

As the name Advanced Writing in the Disciplines (AWD) might suggest, the second required writing course for Northeastern students is closely connected to their academic and professional trajectories. Typically, students take AWD after they have had at least one co-op experience, which can provide a resource and a point of reflection for their work in the class. Co-ops, along with career paths, which have been characterized by increasing mobility across international borders and languages, have helped amplify the superdiversity of the student body. This, combined with the rise in international and multilingual students at NU, presents for our consideration productive complications of our understanding about whom we serve and what we teach in AWD for multilingual students.

In the earliest manifestation of multilingual AWD, an AWD SOL (speakers of other languages) version was developed around 2007 for multilingual students who wanted extra support. In spring 2012, there was only one section of AWD SOL, a course populated by students from a variety of majors, including business, international affairs, biology, and industrial engineering. In the 2018–2019 academic year, the writing program offered eleven sections of AWD SOL, including sections specifically for students in business professions and technical professions.

As in the FYW multilingual courses, the students who enroll in AWD SOL sections have complicated the ways we teach writing. Traditional conceptions of international students have depicted them as sojourners from the periphery who most likely would try to stay in the United States after graduation, thus contributing to "brain drains" in their countries of origin. More recent studies have theorized concepts such as talent flow and brain circulation to account for the more complex migration patterns that characterize international student and career trajectories (Saxenian 2005; Tung 2008). In AWD, which primarily focuses on professional and academic writing in English, the assumption has been that wherever students might go after graduation, writing in English will be an important part of their postgraduate studies or careers. However, that assumption and corresponding anxieties about language proficiency are sometimes called into question, as when one Chinese finance major expressed concern that in her future work in China, she would be at a disadvantage compared to her colleagues because she was not used to writing professionally in Chinese. Even more dramatically, for a project in which I asked students to interview a professional in their future career path about the writing done in their job, a Chinese accounting major interviewed the director of a local tax bureau in China. The director told the student that his writing "must walk on the road of socialism with Chinese characteristics." This clearly was not anything my class would prepare that student for, at least not explicitly. I have thus experimented with giving students the option of writing some assignments in other languages while providing translations for my evaluation. While most students don't take me up on this offer, I leave it there, along with the option of using sources not written in English, to signify to students an understanding that not all of them will be working and writing in monolingual English-speaking environments in the future. These examples suggest that the more complex mobility patterns that characterize superdiversity are accompanied by less predictable academic and professional trajectories for students, which complicates our efforts as instructors to serve those students' needs as developing writers. AWD is founded on exposing students to writing as a mode of professionalization and discourse-community acclimation, but the lens of superdiversity helps us recognize the US-centric assumptions we have about professional and disciplinary identities and illuminates the need for instructors—and programs—to attend more closely to how the work of the class is framed.

Superdiversity in the Writing Center: Research and Training

Whereas Jonathan has illuminated how a superdiverse approach can expose the dynamics of discomfort, collusion, and resistance in the writing classroom, we, Alison (who joined the writing program in 2017 as a multilingual specialist) and Cherice (who entered the English graduate program in 2018), explore how the framework helps interpret challenges within writing centers. Specifically, a superdiversity lens begets dissatisfaction with conventional descriptors of who comes to the center and how often; instead, it drives us to understand dynamics in the writing center through alternative research methods and to consider the impact of geography, class, and mobility on tutors and clients.

The Northeastern Writing Center is a branch of the writing program and serves students, alumni, faculty, and staff with approximately four thousand appointments per year at two physical locations in Boston. Through virtual appointments, our tutors also consult with students studying abroad and on co-op and with graduate students at NU's satellite campuses in Seattle, Charlotte, and Silicon Valley. The center employs undergraduate and master's tutors from across Northeastern's nine colleges, as well as doctoral students from English.

In this section, we present three observations derived from a superdiverse approach. First, in order to begin describing the clientele of the writing center, we consider the multiplicity of categories and silos of information administrators must cross. Second, we explore the importance of researching what remains invisible beyond identity categories. For this, we are inspired by Kerschbaum's (2012) concept of

"difference-as-relation": Kerschbaum reconstitutes the concept of difference as a lived experience that perpetually changes from one interaction to another based on situational and emerging disparities in power
and agency. This "difference as relation" approach provides a complementary framework to the superdiversity lens by attending to local
moments while retaining perspective on the overarching global factors
that shape identity formation, interactions, and dynamics of the writing
center. Finally, we consider the role of mobility and economic privilege
in constructing the climate of the writing center.

Institutional Categories of Difference

Writing centers can be particularly susceptible to using basic demographic categories to create narratives about their functions in institutions. NU has been no exception to this phenomenon, though over time
we have tried to collect demographic data with a wider sense of our clients' linguistic identities. For instance, to understand whether the writing center population was representative of the larger global institution,
we compared data from the internal registration system and students'
self-reported first/home language. We observed that 61 percent of writing center clients in 2017–2018 identified a language other than English
as their first/home language.

To further understand whether writing center clients were representative of the wider NU population, we collaborated with the registrar to
receive anonymized data of country of citizenship and visa status about
writing center clients and compared this information to institutional
data about the Northeastern student population. As table 11.1 shows,
55 percent of writing center clients in 2017–2018 were international
compared to 32 percent of the overall student body, which confirmed
for us that the writing center was seeing a higher proportion of international students compared to the percentage of that population in the
student body at-large.

Yet, these broad data—despite their value in making a case for the
writing center to senior administrators—obscure some of the patterns
that shape our everyday interactions in the writing center, as they do not
reveal the shifting layered complexities of identity that superdiversity
highlights. We realized, for example, through an attempt to gather institutional data on language proficiency (by way of requesting anonymized
TOEFL and IELTS scores on record for our clients), that first-language
data are heavily siloed across various admissions units and difficult to
compile. At the undergraduate level, admissions units in colleges determine and hold proficiency scores; at the graduate level, the data are

Table 11.1. Percentage of international clients in the Northeastern Writing Center compared to the overall student population (2017–2018)

	Writing Center Clients		Northeastern University Students	
	Total clients	International clients (%)	Total students (degree- + non-degree-seeking)	International students (%)
All clients/students	1,553	852 (55%)	37,800	12,136 (32%)
Undergraduate students	819	369 (45%)	22,038	4,706 (21%)
Graduate students	661	416 (63%)	16,730	7,403 (44%)
Non-degree-seeking students	73	67 (93%)		

even more fragmented, as individual departments and programs make decisions based on test scores. Even though the data we gathered from writing center clients and the registrar were illuminating, the results offered only a limited understanding of who visited the writing center and how they handled language and authority with our tutors. More important, the data we acquired on clients' country of nationality and visa status did not tell us how tutors and clients were negotiating the challenging realities of being in a "globally minded" university.

Investigating Relational Differences

To illuminate superdiversity within writing center tutoring practices, we developed research projects that have clarified and added nuance to the writing center and registrar data. These studies helped us observe power relations in the writing center through other sources of data. In one study (Stephens et al. 2019), we examined a semester's worth of appointment forms on which clients had requested grammar help. For some years, our staff and research team had been discussing the implications of a translingual approach to the writing center, the "recognition that we are all . . . constantly negotiating multiple languages, conventions of writing, and linguistic loyalties" (Trimbur 2016, 226), which prompted us to wonder how tutors were reacting to requests for grammar help. We discovered that in over 75 percent of 452 cases, tutors indeed worked on standard-English conventions with tutees when asked—a surprising finding given historical training priorities to focus on higher-order concerns over lower-order concerns. Yet the results helped us grapple with the realities of responding to students within a superdiverse university that still establishes hierarchies along the lines of linguistic privilege. When we presented the results of the study to tutors, many felt validated—some even relieved—that they weren't breaking writing center best practices by working on lower-order concerns. As Lori Salem (2016) has argued, writing center administrators should challenge one another "to abandon policy-as-pedagogy—to reject the idea that the writing center director's role is to define a set of practices that are to be used in all tutoring sessions" (164). Instead, our practices must begin from the ground up, dynamically responding to the diversities present among tutors and clients.

Mobility and the Writing Center

Beyond pushing us to rethink our research practices, a superdiversity framework to writing center administration has compelled us to interrogate not just salient categories of race, language, visa status, and so forth but also the roles of class, capital, and mobility in constructing our climate. While many writing centers position themselves as egalitarian spaces, offering free support to any campus member, writing centers can also reinscribe social hierarchies (Denny 2005; Grimm 2011; Villanueva 2006). Indeed, it can be difficult in isolated, one-to-one sessions to capture how the privilege of mobility affects the sessions. Yet, class and mobility are noticeable undercurrents that shape our staffing.

Perhaps in contrast to many undergraduate institutions, Northeastern students frequently participate in co-ops and study-abroad opportunities, leading to significant turnover in the writing center. In 2017–2018, undergraduate students took part in 8,253 co-ops in forty states and seventy-eight countries (Northeastern University, University Decision Support). As a result, half to three-quarters of our staff leave every four months due to these opportunities.

Despite, or perhaps *because of*, these recurring changes in the center, our training curriculum has remained relatively consistent, with an emphasis on attentive reading (Gillespie and Lerner 2008; Matsuda and Cox 2011) and rhetorical listening (Jordan 2011; Ratcliffe 2005) while also raising awareness of the power structures embedded within both language and tutoring (Canagarajah 2013; Carino 2003). While the act of rhetorical listening helps tutors identify the client's priorities for a given session, it does not explicitly equip tutors with the tools they need to address the growing requests from clients to focus on grammar. To meet this need, we spend at least one training session per semester on support for multilingual writers, exposing tutors to a variety of resources and concerns (e.g., Ferris 2002; Phillips, Ryerson, and Stewart 2017). Still, because of the regular turnover of our tutors, we risk missing important areas of training. In one attempt to mitigate these gaps, we conducted a survey to pinpoint areas where our tutors feel least equipped in the teaching of grammar. We then created self-paced, modular tool kits that focused on specific components of grammar conventions, grammar resources, and inclusive language practices. Although in the past we had glossed over this need, we found through reassessment that such materials were necessary given our highly mobile student population. Our writing center's deployment of these self-paced resources takes place within a staff-wide reflection on power, authority, and "the uneven distribution of language resources" (Blommaert 2010, 11)—a necessary ongoing conversation as our consultants explore what it means to be a "peer" tutor in a rapidly globalizing university.

In sum, the superdiversity framework for writing center administration compels us to move beyond the fixed categories of national origin, first language, and visa status, as explored in this section. While markers such as these, typically gathered from institutional demographic data, can be useful to understand pieces of a population, a superdiverse framework encourages an analysis of alternative factors such as the roles of class, capital, and mobility. Since Northeastern University views itself as a global institution, we then must account for the proliferation of identities that have come as a result of a globalizing world. Moreover, the exigence for a framework such as this becomes more pertinent as our writing center reflects higher proportions of international students when compared to the university at large. Writing centers, in this sense, function as egalitarian spaces for a multitude of identities to explore their relationships with language. It then becomes imperative for administrators to make visible the various intersections of identities that comprise writing centers in order to facilitate a more sustainable and responsive approach to tutor training.

Superdiversity in the Writing Minor: Modest Beginnings

If superdiversity as a conceptual framework is a useful approach to rethinking writing instruction and tutoring practices, we have also found it useful as a way to reimagine the minor in writing. I, Mya, have been teaching at Northeastern since 2013 and have been part of the redesign of the writing minor, which traditionally had a creative writing focus. One course I proposed was Writing in Global Contexts, a writing course that would have linguistic diversity—and superdiversity—at its core. Writing in Global Contexts explores the various ways linguistic diversity shapes our everyday, academic, and professional lives. Students learn about the changing place of World Englishes in globalization, what contemporary theories of linguistic diversity mean for writing, and how multilingual identities can be included in writing research. The course also invites students to research their own multilingual communities and histories.

In many ways, the course is not unlike other writing and rhetoric courses today that place multilingualism at their core. What is different, though, is that in attending to the local context of multilingualism at NU, Writing in Global Contexts does not just attend to the linguistic identities of students who identify as multilingual but invites all students in the course to draw on their multilingual identities and put those in relation to the linguistic landscape of the university and city. To accomplish this goal, the readings from the class interrogate the history and status of Englishes (e.g., Fishman 2004; Kachru 1997), linguistic and sociolinguistic research (e.g., Blommaert 2010; Lippi-Green 1997; Pennycook and Otsuji 2015), and research on multilingual writing (e.g., Leki 2001; Lillis and Curry 2006; Matsuda 2006).

Superdiversity is a key theme in the course, and the assignments ask students to trace various linguistic landscapes against a trajectory of personal linguistic histories, institutional linguistic landscapes, and metrolingualism. The course assignments encourage students to build on what they know, then expand outward to study the university and city. For example, the linguistic-history assignment does not ask students to write solely from an individual identity. Instead, students are asked to weave together the story of their linguistic identity with the story of their family's linguistic identity and the sociocultural and historical forces that have shaped that identity. In this way, linguistic identity is layered, it's historical, and it's relational. For students who identify as multilingual, the assignment is generally accessible. Some students can draw on their multilocal experiences, such as Megan (pseudonym), who contrasted the pressures of standardized Mandarin in China with the coexistence of multiple main languages in Malaysia, including Bahasa Melayu, English, Mandarin, and Hokkien.

For students who do not have such immediate histories, the linguistic-history project is harder but also can prompt rich discussions of linguistic histories, if only through linguistic fragments. For example, Brad wrote about his family's history as Polish speakers in Buffalo, New York. Large numbers of Polish immigrants came to the city in the mid-1800s and established a community they called Polonia. While Polish immigrants felt pressure to learn English, especially after the assassination of President McKinley by a Polish American in Buffalo in 1901, they clung to Polish, largely because of the influence of the Catholic Church. The

Catholic Church did not merely offer masses or religious instruction in Polish. Father Pitass, a local priest, also controlled *Polak w Ameryce, The Pole in America*, which was one of the largest Polish-language newspapers in the United States at the time. Later, as the church began to decline and Polish immigrants began moving to the suburbs, use of the Polish language became more fragmented. Today, these linguistic fragments are important remnants of linguistic histories and provide important lessons to students like Brad that linguistic identity has always been a relational process in the United States. While Brad may not initially see the history of Buffalo as one about superdiversity, tracing the histories of linguistic fragments reminds us that "the current globalization processes are best seen as part of longer and wider and deeper globalization processes, in which they represent a particular stage of development" (Blommaert 2010, 6).

If the linguistic-history assignment gets students thinking about their linguistic identities as a relational process, then the next two assignments use that standpoint to study the linguistic landscape of the university and city. For example, the assignment "Multilingual Northeastern" is framed around institutional discourses about globalization. Such institutional discourses at NU clearly invoke globalization, but they only hint at (or completely elide) multilingualism. In fact, almost all official documents currently produced by the university are in Standard Edited English (previously, the university website included some pages in other languages). Moreover, although the university president is a multilingual speaker, he uses English almost exclusively in official university communication. The question, then, for students in Writing in Global Contexts is what NU's global identity means in terms of linguistic diversity.

In researching Multilingual Northeastern, students go to unexpected sites. For example, Odelia looked at institutional policy surrounding the language requirement. Specifically, she studied how the apparent benefits of multilingualism can break down for students who have limited negotiation strategies—that is, they have learning disabilities that make language learning especially difficult. The premise of the language requirement at NU is to foster multilingualism in support of the university's global identity, but as Odelia's case demonstrates, mandated multilingualism can penalize some students. Odelia observed how university communication surrounding disability elided the global (and multilingual) identity it promotes publicly on its website: on one hand, the university touts a "transformative experience" that invites students to be "engaged citizens of the world" and "address problems across the world." Yet, its Disability Resource Center has a more parochial vision to "foster a welcoming and supportive environment." Globalization is notably lacking in the description. To be exempt from the language requirement, students must provide results from neuropsychological testing and diagnoses. The requirement of testing and diagnosis thus is targeted at students who have the financial means to provide such evidence. And as Odelia notes, the university offers only limited exceptions, preferring instead that students be provided accommodations for language learning, including more time for tests and software assistance from programs like Text to Speech. In the end, Odelia's study reveals how superdiversity as an ongoing process reveals the limitations of institutional requirements, such as mandated language learning. Simply taking an additive approach to identity in which disability was "added" to race, class, and gender would not have revealed such distinctions.

In the end, the Writing in Global Contexts course has provided a way to bring multilingualism into the writing minor, a minor that could easily be an English-only space. It has allowed students to reflect on their own linguistic histories, the superdiversity that informs their NU experience and their living in Boston. By drawing on readings that connect language and literacy learning to superdiversity, students can go beyond seeing that language practices emanate out of their individual bodies, that the goal of language practices is fluency, and that language practices are static as well as hierarchical. Instead, they see that language is deeply tied to our identity and that our linguistic identities are about the historical, social, and cultural conditions that have formed our selves in our communities. Language practice is not about fluency but about collaborative work. And finally, they come to see that language resources are stratified (Blommaert 2010).

IMPLICATIONS AND CONCLUSION

The translingual turn in US composition studies has brought increased attention to linguistic diversity in writing classrooms, as well as increased attention to the ways we construct multilingual writers. At Northeastern, the rapidly shifting demographics of our student population have pushed us to confront—and reconfront—how we teach, how we research, and how we think about the landscape of our institutional context. As a conceptual lens, superdiversity has helped us rethink our teaching and research in the writing program, the writing center, and now the writing minor.

First, superdiversity has given us purchase on changing how we ask questions of our students—whether it be writing center research on tutoring practices or the kinds of questions we ask students to engage with in our classes. In doing so, our goal has been to neither exoticize linguistic diversity nor imply a subordinate status.

Second, superdiversity as a conceptual framework has given us language to break from the conventional race-class-gender triad (or, now, the race-class-gender-ability tetrad). Ana Deumert (2014) argues for superdiversity "as a theoretical and epistemological perspective [that] . . . draws our attention to pluralities of meaning which underpin—even if only momentarily—what may look like a stable dichotomy on the surface" (119). As we have found in our use of superdiversity as a lens for observing the teaching and learning of writing at Northeastern, mobility, complexity and unpredictability (three key terms associated with superdiversity) challenge the measurement or placement of multilingual students into categories or classes. They also challenge our understandings of who (we think) students are. Superdiversity as a theoretical perspective allows us to focus on the choices we have to position ourselves in relation to one another, including how we represent ourselves and each other in everyday classroom interactions or tutoring sessions. And it has given our students a language to describe their experiences at Northeastern. "Difference-as relation," in all its messy, shifting, layered forms, underwrites the world in which we teach and tutor (Kerschbaum 2012, 2014).

Third, superdiversity as a perspective on difference has implications for pedagogy. For instance, while the possible assumptions behind using texts like Anzaldúa's in class might have made some students uncomfortable, that very discomfort helped foreground their privilege and mobility and the associated assumptions they had about language and identity. This suggests writing instructors might work to make the implications of superdiversity part of the work of the class. For instance, in FYW for multilingual students, Jonathan has asked students to write about "international students" in ways that speak back to popular or academic representations of international students (such as the "second-generation rich," the "immigrant," and other images that circulate in the United States and/or abroad). Results of such student writing can be revealing both to students themselves and their instructors. One student, for instance, surprised us with the revelation that although he was a US citizen, the university considered him an international student because he had been educated abroad up through high school. Such assignments can exercise students' critical reading and writing practices while giving them opportunities to consider and respond to how they are represented by and "placed" in the university.

Finally, superdiversity helps us look for friction points that stem from students' exposure to the global export of English education in primary and secondary schools. Increasingly, Western-style educational practices create alliances among international students. The shared experience of secondary school curricula like the International Baccalaureate or the International General Certificate of Education, for example, creates commonalities among some "international" students while potentially marginalizing those who go through local school systems. Put another way, the complex layering of identities increasingly typical of NU undergraduate students stems from the university's ability to build an elite, global undergraduate brand. Yet students who are "only" bilingual in English and one other language, who didn't have the mobility of their peers, or who didn't have access to the privileged spaces of international schools, are marked as "accented"—more likely to be flagged by advisors as needing multilingual writing sections or less able to gain a US co-op placement on their first try. If we as a writing program adopted reductive interpretations of nationality, or visa status, or first language, we would overlook these contact zones experienced by our students every day. If superdiversity is constituted relationally across numerous categories, so too are its marginalizing effects. According to Umut Erel (2011), "'super-diversity' requires an analysis of racism not in a dichotomous or top-down frame but as differentially positioning and constituting different groups and individuals" (705).

This is not to say superdiversity as a conceptual framework is not without its difficulties. For example, as Vertovec (2017) has noted, superdiversity "is not a theory (which . . . would need to entail an explanation of how and why these changing patterns arose, how they are interlinked, and what their combined effects causally or necessarily lead to)" (2). Furthermore, superdiversity does not rely on a set of agreed-upon methods, which means sussing out how to study superdiversity is an ongoing project. While ethnographic studies of cityscapes or even institutional spaces may lend themselves to the layered realities of superdiversity, large dataset analysis is more tricky; our writing center surveys show how institutional data-gathering norms lag behind the realities of the student population and our desire to use superdiversity as a guiding framework for data gathering. Deumert (2014) has even called the use of superdiversity to measure levels of diversity "a theoretical *cul-de-sac*" (117) because of the impossibility of quantifying the difference between a very diverse context and a superdiverse context.

Despite these limitations, the layered, ever-shifting demographics of higher education communities today mean researchers need more dynamic ways of understanding how to recognize and respond to the needs of student writers. Superdiversity is a powerful conceptual framework to help us respond to and reimagine our programs and classrooms. Like translingualism, superdiversity is "an orientation to . . . difference and the reading, writing, and teaching practices that emerge from that orientation" that can help us account for the rapidly shifting contexts we teach in today and the students we teach in those contexts (Gallagher and Noonan 2017, 175–76). At Northeastern that orientation has informed our teaching, research, and curricular change, as we have come to realize the diversity we see today is itself constantly in flux.

NOTE

1. This is not to say superdiversity is oblivious to considerations of race, gender, or class. In fact, these are part of the multiple interacting identity markers taken up in superdiversity (along with markers such as mobility, languaging, and geography).

REFERENCES

Anastasia, Andrew G. 2015. "Teaching Discomfort: Students' and Teachers' Descriptions of Discomfort in First-year Writing Classes." PhD diss., University of Wisconsin. https://dc.uwm.edu/etd/853/.

Annous, Samer A., Maureen O'Day Nicolas, and Martha A. Townsend. 2017. "Territorial Borders and the Teaching of Writing in English: Lessons from Research at the University of Balamand." In *Emerging Writing Research from the Middle East-North Africa Region*, edited by Lisa R. Arnold, Anne Nebel, and Lynne Ronesi, 85–115. Fort Collins, CO: WAC Clearinghouse.

Bartholomae, David, and Anthony Petrosky, eds. 2011. *Ways of Reading: An Anthology for Writers*. 9th ed. Boston: Bedford/St. Martin's.

Benda, Jonathan, Michael Dedek, Chris Gallagher, Kristi Girdharry, Neal Lerner, and Matt Noonan. 2018. "Confronting Superdiversity in U.S. Writing Programs." In *The Internationalization of U.S. Writing Programs*, edited by Shirley K. Rose and Irwin Weiser, 79–96. Logan: Utah State University Press.

Blommaert, Jan. 2010. *The Sociolinguistics of Globalization*. Cambridge: Cambridge University Press.

Blommaert, Jan, and Ben Rampton. 2016. "Language and Superdiversity." In *Language and Superdiversity*, edited by Karel Arnaut, Jan Blommaert, Ben Rampton, and Massimiliano Spotti, 21–48. New York: Routledge.

Cadier, Linda, and Clare Mar-Molinero. 2012. "Language Policies and Linguistic Super-Diversity in Contemporary Urban Societies: The Case of the City of Southampton, UK." *Current Issues in Language and Planning* 13 (3): 149–65. doi:10.1080/14664208.2012.722376.

Canagarajah, A. Suresh, ed. 2013. *Literacy as Translingual Practice: Between Communities and Classrooms*. New York: Routledge.

Carino, Peter. 2003. "Power and Authority in Peer Tutoring." In *The Center Will Hold: Critical Perspectives on Writing Center Scholarship*, edited by Michael Pemberton and Joyce Kinkead, 96–113. Logan: Utah State University Press.

Davydova, Julia. 2013. "Detecting Historical Continuity in a Linguistically Diverse Urban Area." In *Linguistic Superdiversity in Urban Areas: Research Approaches,* edited by Joana Duarte and Ingrid Gogolin, 193–225. Philadelphia: John Benjamins.

Denny, Harry. 2005. "Queering the Writing Center." *Writing Center Journal* 30 (2): 95–124. www.jstor.org/stable/43442222.

Deumert, Ana. 2014. "Digital Superdiversity: A Commentary." *Discourse, Context and Media* 4–5: 116–20. https://doi.org/10.1016/j.dcm.2014.08.003.

Erel, Umut. 2011. "Reframing Migrant Mothers as Citizens." *Citizenship Studies* 15 (6–7): 695–709.

Ferris, Dana. 2002. *The Treatment of Error.* Ann Arbor: University of Michigan Press.

Fishman, Joshua A. 2004. "Multilingualism and Non-English Mother Tongues." In *Language in the USA: Themes for the Twenty-First Century,* edited by Edward Finegan and John R. Rickford, 115–32. Cambridge: Cambridge University Press. doi:10.1017/CBO 9780511809880.009.

Fraiberg, Steven, Xiqiao Wang, and Xiaoye You. 2017. *Inventing the World Grant University: Chinese International Students' Mobilities, Literacies, and Identities.* Logan: Utah State University Press.

Gallagher, Chris, and Matt Noonan. 2017. "Becoming Global: Learning to 'Do' Translingualism." In *Crossing Divides: Exploring Translingual Pedagogies and Programs,* edited by Bruce Horner and Laura Tetreault, 161–77. Logan: Utah State University Press.

Gillespie, Paula, and Neal Lerner. 2008. *The Longman Guide to Peer Tutoring.* 2nd ed. New York: Pearson Longman.

Gonzales, Laura. 2018. *Sites of Translation: What Multilinguals Can Tell Us about Digital Writing and Rhetoric.* Ann Arbor: University of Michigan Press.

Grimm, Nancy M. 2011. "Retheorizing Writing Center Work to Transform a System of Advantage Based on Race." In *Writing Centers and the New Racism: A Call for Sustainable Dialogue and Change,* edited by Laura Greenfield and Karen Rowan, 75–100. Logan: Utah State University Press.

Hollinger, David A. 2000. *Postethnic America: Beyond Multiculturalism.* Rev. ed. New York: Basic Books.

Horner, Bruce, and John Trimbur. 2002. "English Only and U.S. College Composition." *College Composition and Communication* 53 (4): 594–630. doi:10.2307/1512118.

Jordan, Jay. 2011. "Revaluing Silence and Listening with Second-Language English Users." In *Silence and Listening as Rhetorical Acts,* edited by Cheryl Glenn and Krista Ratcliffe, 278–92. Carbondale: Southern Illinois University Press.

Kachru, Braj. 1997. "World Englishes and English-Using Communities." *Annual Review of Applied Linguistics* 17: 66–87. https://doi.org/10.1017/S0267190500003287.

Kerschbaum, Stephanie L. 2012. "Avoiding the Difference Fixation: Identity Categories, Markers of Difference, and the Teaching of Writing." *College Composition and Communication* 63 (4): 616–44. https://www.jstor.org/stable/23264231.

Kerschbaum, Stephanie L. 2014. *Toward a New Rhetoric of Difference.* Urbana, IL: NCTE.

Leki, Ilona. 2001. "Hearing Voices: L2 Students' Experiences in L2 Writing Courses." In *On Second Language Writing,* edited by Tony Silva and Paul Kei Matsuda, 17–28. Mahwah, NJ: Lawrence Erlbaum.

Lillis, Theresa, and Mary J. Curry. 2006. "Professional Academic Writing by Multilingual Scholars: Interactions with Literacy Brokers in the Production of English-Medium Texts." *Written Communication* 23 (1): 3–35. https://doi.org/10.1177/07410 88305283754.

Lippi-Green, Rosina. 1997. *English with an Accent: Language, Ideology, and Discrimination in the United States.* New York: Routledge.

Matsuda, Paul Kei. 2006. "The Myth of Linguistic Homogeneity in U.S. College Composition." *College English* 68 (6): 637–51. doi:10.2307/25472180.

Matsuda, Paul Kei, and Michelle Cox. 2011. "Reading an ESL Writer's Text." *Studies in Self-Access Learning Journal* 2 (1): 4–14. https://sisaljournal.org/archives/mar11/matsuda_cox/.

Nebel, Anne. 2017. "Linguistic Superdiversity and English-Medium Higher Education in Qatar." In *Emerging Writing Research from the Middle East-North Africa Region*, edited by Lisa R. Arnold, Anne Nebel, and Lynne Ronesi, 27–41. Fort Collins, CO: WAC Clearinghouse.

Northeastern University. 2016. "Northeastern 2025: Academic Plan." https://www.northeastern.edu/2025/wp-content/uploads/2016/10/07.16.01_AcademicPlan_LR.pdf.

Northeastern University. 2019. "Facts and Figures." https://facts.northeastern.edu/#enrollment.

Northeastern University, University Decision Support. n.d. *Facts: Our Community by the Numbers.* Accessed May 24, 2020. https://provost.northeastern.edu/uds/facts/fact-book/.

Pennycook, Alastair, and Emi Otsuji. 2015. *Metrolingualism: Language in the City.* New York: Routledge.

Peukert, Hagen. 2013. "Measuring Language Diversity in Urban Ecosystems." In *Linguistic Superdiversity in Urban Areas: Research Approaches*, edited by Joana Duarte and Ingrid Gogolin, 75–96. Philadelphia: John Benjamins.

Phillips, Talinn, Candace Stewart, and Rachael Ryerson. 2017. *Becoming an Ally: Tutoring Multilingual Writers.* Athens: The Ohio University Graduate Writing & Research Center. https://vimeo.com/gwrc.

Pratt, Mary L. 1991. "Arts of the Contact Zone." *Profession* 33–40. https://www.jstor.org/stable/25595469.

Ratcliffe, Krista. 2005. *Rhetorical Listening: Identification, Gender, Whiteness.* Carbondale: Southern Illinois University Press.

Salem, Lori. 2016. "Decisions . . . Decisions: Who Chooses to Use the Writing Center?" *Writing Center Journal* 35 (2): 147–71. https://www.jstor.org/stable/43824060.

Saxenian, AnnaLee. 2005. "From Brain Drain to Brain Circulation: Transnational Communities and Regional Upgrading in India and China." *Studies in Comparative International Development* 40: 35–61. https://doi.org/10.1007/BF02686293.

Stephens, Alison, Abbie Levesque, Cara Messina, Quisqueya Witbeck, and Belinda Walzer. 2019. "Aligning Expectations: A Quantitative Study Investigating Tutor Responses to Requests for Grammar Help." Unpublished manuscript.

Trimbur, J. 2016. "Translingualism and Close Reading." *College English* 78 (3): 219–27. https://www.jstor.org/stable/44075111.

Tung, Rosalie L. 2008. "Brain Circulation, Diaspora, and International Competitiveness." *European Management Journal* 26 (5): 298–304. doi:10.1016/j.emj.2008.03.005.

Vandrick, Stephanie. 2011. "Students of the New Global Elite." *TESOL Quarterly* 45 (1): 160–69. https://www.jstor.org/stable/41307620.

Vertovec, Steven. 2007. "Super-Diversity and its Implications." *Ethnic and Racial Studies* 30 (6): 1024–54. doi:10.1080/01419870701599465.

Vertovec, Steven. 2017. "Talking around Super-Diversity." *Ethnic and Racial Studies* 42 (1): 125–39. doi: 10.1080/01419870.2017.1406128.

Villanueva, Victor. 2006. "Blind: Talking about the New Racism." *Writing Center Journal* 26 (1): 3–19. https://www.jstor.org/stable/43442234.

Young, Vershawn Ashanti, and Aja Y. Martinez. 2011. *Code-Meshing as World English: Pedagogy, Policy, Performance.* Urbana, IL: NCTE.

INDEX

ableism, 77–78, 81–84, 178. *See also* anti-ableism

academic discourse. *See* discourse

academic writing, 56, 58, 62, 104, 105, 110, 224

access, 7, 11, 151; accessibility, 176, 179, 190, 191; accessible digital content, 179; accessible technology, 182–84; accessible websites, 186; disability access, 151; inaccessibility, 89; and institutional accommodations, 90, 137, 142, 147–48; to literacy education, 40; to power and agency, 211; practices of, 137, 150, 151; to social mobility, 44; Universal Design, 213. *See also* accommodations; disability

accommodations, 136–37, 138, 142, 146–51, 232. *See also* access; disability

activism, 5, 12, 22, 53n2, 83, 119, 139

affect, 13, 77, 126, 153–56, 166, 171, 203; schizoaffective, 144–45. *See also* embodiment; emotion

agency, 48, 52, 70, 196, 223–26; disability and, 136; student, 33, 208, 211; of writers, 33, 177

Agboka, Godwin, 180

Alim, H. Samy, 37, 181

Ahmed, Sara, 21–22, 137, 195, 210

Anastasia, Andrew, 222

anthropocene, 4

anti-ableism, 77–78, 81

anti-Blackness. *See* Blackness

antiracism, anti-ableism, 77–78; communities, 12; disciplinary perspectives on, 3–4, 8, 9, 13; intersectional values of, 14; methodologies, 40; pedagogy, 10, 77–78, 205, 213; translingual praxis, 12, 14, 197–98, 200–214

Anzaldúa, Gloria, 10, 33, 58, 60–61, 222, 233

Appiah, Kwame Anthony, 215n2

assessment. *See* writing assessment

asset-based approaches, 176, 183, 186–87, 189

assignments, 29, 49–50, 113, 140, 150, 155, 159, 162, 171n1, 205, 209, 224, 233; antiracism, 205, 209; genre-switching, 112; and linguistic identity, 230–31;

narrative-based, 11; public, 160; science writing, 127–29; and translation, 190; translingual, 29, 33–35, 214

attentive reading, 228

Aztecs, 61, 65–67

Baca, Damián, 59–61

The Baffler, 39

Baker, Marsha Lee, 154, 156, 159

Bartholomae, David, 43, 221

Bawarshi, Anis, 215n4, 215n10

Beech, Jennifer, 45

Benda, Jonathan, 219–21, 225, 233

"Beyond Persuasion: A Proposal for Invitational Rhetoric" (Foss and Griffin), 108

Bilingualism, 29–30, 34, 59, 180, 186, 234

Bizzell, Patricia, 72

Black Lives Matter (BLM), vii, 5, 169

Blackness, 81, 83, 118, 220; anti-Blackness, 78, 197; Black communities and people, 4, 48, 78, 83, 118, 163, 175, 197, 199–200, 211; Black feminism, 6, 175, 178; language, 53, 214; social movements, vii, 5, 169, 49

Bloom, Lynn Z., 40, 44

bodies. *See* embodiment

Bollig, Chase, 53n1

Bone, Jennifer Emerling, 158

Booth, Wayne C., 154, 160

Borkowski, David, 43

Bou Ayash, Nancy, 22–23, 215n4, 215n10

Bowker, George, 119

Bourdieu, Pierre, 85, 202

Bousquet, Marc, 45

Brickhouse, Nancy, 129

Brodkey, Linda, 62, 72

Brown v. Board of Education, 22, 199

Brumberger, Eva, 183–84

Burke, Kenneth, 115n2

Butler, Johnnella, 31

Calmecacs, 65–67

Canagarajah, A. Suresh, 33–34, 195

capitalism, 50; neoliberalism, 10, 40, 48; racial, 3, 78, 197, 206, 211–12; relation to debility, 139

Carroll, Lee Ann, 139

ABOUT THE AUTHORS

James Rushing Daniel is an associate teaching professor at the University of Washington and the author of *Toward an Anti-Capitalist Composition* (2022).

Katie Malcolm (she/her) is the associate director of the Center for Teaching and Learning and an affiliate assistant professor of English at the University of Washington.

Candice Rai is an associate professor of English at the University of Washington. She recently coedited *Field Rhetoric: Ethnography, Ecology, and Engagement in the Places of Persuasion* (with Caroline Gottschalk Druschke) and is the author of *Democracy's Lot: Rhetoric, Publics, and the Places of Invention*. Her work engages in place-based inquiry to study public rhetoric and writing, political discourse and action, and argumentation.

Anis Bawarshi, professor of English at the University of Washington, specializes in the study and teaching of writing, rhetorical genre studies, knowledge transfer, and writing program administration. He is coeditor of the series *Reference Guides to Rhetoric and Composition* and recently coedited *Genre and the Performance of Publics* (with Mary Jo Reiff).

Jonathan Benda is a teaching professor of English at Northeastern University, where he teaches first-year writing for multilingual students, interdisciplinary advanced writing, and travel writing.

Megan Callow is an associate teaching professor in the Department of English at the University of Washington. She currently directs the Interdisciplinary Writing Program, where she teaches writing in science and other disciplines as well as courses on writing pedagogy.

Laura Gonzales is assistant professor of digital writing and cultural rhetorics in the Department of English at the University of Florida. She is the author of *Sites of Translation: What Multilinguals Can Teach Us About Digital Writing and Rhetoric* (University of Michigan Press, 2018).

Juan C. Guerra, professor emeritus of English at the University of Washington, is coeditor of *Writing in Multicultural Settings* (1997), as well as author of *Close to Home: Oral and Literate Practices in a Transnational Mexicano Community* (1998) and *Language, Culture, Identity and Citizenship in College Classrooms and Communities* (2016).

Cherice Escobar Jones is a third-year PhD student at Northeastern University in the department of writing and rhetoric. She previously served as assistant director of the writing center and writing program.

Stephanie L. Kerschbaum is associate professor of English at the University of Washington. Her book *Toward a New Rhetoric of Difference* won the 2015 Advancement of Knowledge Award from CCCC, and with Laura T. Eisenman and James M. Jones, she coedited *Negotiating Disability: Disclosure and Higher Education*. (Preferred pronouns: she/her/hers).

Nadya Pittendrigh is director of composition at the University of Houston–Victoria. Her research focuses on restorative justice, the criminal justice system, and their relevance to rhetoric and teaching.

Mya Poe is an associate professor of English and director of the Writing Program at Northeastern University. Her books include *Learning to Communicate in Science and Engineering* (CCCC 2012 Advancement of Knowledge Award), *Race and Writing Assessment* (CCCC 2014 Outstanding Book of the Year), and *Writing, Assessment, Social Justice, and Opportunity to Learn.*

Iris D. Ruiz is a continuing lecturer for the UC Merced Merritt Writing Program and a lecturer with the Sonoma State University Chicano/Latino studies program. She is the author of *Reclaiming Composition for Chicano/as and Other Ethnic Minorities: A Critical History and Pedagogy* and the coeditor of *Decolonizing Rhetoric and Composition Studies: New Latinx Keywords for Theory and Pedagogy.*

Neil F. Simpkins (he/him/his) is an assistant professor at the University of Washington–Bothell in the School of Interdisciplinary Arts and Sciences, where he teaches first-year writing. His current research examines how disabled students experience writing across their academic careers, with an emphasis on the rhetorical work they do to navigate disability accommodations.

Ann Shivers-McNair is an assistant professor of English at the University of Arizona. She is the author of *Beyond the Makerspace: Making and Relational Rhetorics* (University of Michigan Press, 2021).

Alison Y. L. Stephens is a lecturer in the writing program at Northeastern University specializing in sections for multilingual writers. She formerly served as multilingual writing support specialist for the program and as interim director of the Northeastern Writing Center.

Sumyat Thu (she/her) is an acting assistant professor at the University of Washington–Seattle in the Expository and Interdisciplinary Writing Programs. During graduate school, she worked as an assistant director of the UW Expository Writing Program. In her current position, she continues to work with the program team in mentoring new instructors and teaches a variety of writing courses.

Katherine Xue is a postdoctoral fellow studying microbial evolution at Stanford University. She received her PhD in genome sciences from the University of Washington, where she also completed a certificate in science, technology, and society studies. She has written about science for *Harvard Magazine, The Conversation,* and *The New Yorker.*

Shui-yin Sharon Yam (she/her) is associate professor of writing, rhetoric, and digital studies at the University of Kentucky and a faculty affiliate in the Gender and Women's Studies Department and at the Center for Equality and Social Justice. Her research focuses on questions of identity, citizenship, affect, and race. She teaches courses on transnational rhetoric, digital composing, and political emotion. She is the author of *Inconvenient Strangers: Transnational Subjects and the Politics of Citizenship* (2019, The Ohio State University Press). She is currently researching and teaching on topics related to reproductive justice, particularly childbirth, doulas, and advocacy.